For More Than 25 Years, *IBD* Has Been Helping Investors

2009 Anniversary Issue

I dedicated the 2004 *Stock Trader's Almanac* to Bill O'Neil: "His foresight, innovation and disciplined approach to stock market investing will influence investors and traders for generations to come." I would also add that the inspiring daily column, IBD's *10 Secrets to Success*, by itself, is worth much more that the subscription price.

> YALE HIRSCH, PUBLISHER, EDITOR OF *STOCK TRADER'S ALMANAC*,
> AUTHOR OF *LET'S CHANGE THE WORLD INC.*

I think the consistency of *IBD* and the interesting and informative news on a range of topics that is highly relevant for investors is impressive. The Monday newspaper also adds some interesting variables. I think the item that strikes me as very useful, and well edited day-in, day-out is trends and innovation on the always interesting page 2. Those nuggets just don't turn up anywhere else. Keep up the good work.

> JOHN CURLEY, FORMER CEO OF GANNETT INC.
> AND FOUNDING EDITOR OF *USA TODAY*

The *IBD* editorial pages are a pure, insightful, and factual expression of free market capitalism. A wonder and a marvel to read every day. For me, these pages are a must read.

> LARRY KUDLOW, HOST, CNBC'S *THE KUDLOW REPORT*

History has and will continue to hold a distinct credit of honor to the contributions *Investor's Business Daily* has made on numerous individual and institutional investors over the past 25 years. No other information source can match the fact-based historical research that *IBD* delivers and teaches.

> JOHN BOIK, AUTHOR OF *LESSONS FROM THE*
> *GREATEST STOCK TRADERS OF ALL TIME* AND *MONSTER STOCKS*

Congratulations to *Investor's Business Da*
individual as well as the professional inve
of pertinent information to bisect and dis
> TOM O'BRIEN , CEO

Congratulations to *Investor's Business Daily* on a quarter century of great financial journalism and investing strategies. I'm proud to have played a small role by writing for it as a stringer in the early years and I'm still an avid reader to this day. What a wild ride the last 25 years have been. Here's to 25 more!

DAVID CALLAWAY, EDITOR-IN-CHIEF *USA TODAY*

Congratulations on a Blazin' 25 years in print! Your focus on top-performing companies and successful leaders has continually been educational and enjoyable.

SALLY SMITH, CEO, BUFFALO WILD WINGS

For the past 25 years, *Investor's Business Daily* has been instrumental in providing self directed investors with useful, timely information. Congratulations on your anniversary, *IBD*!

SCOTTRADE

Congratulations to *IBD* for 25 amazing years of success! I would be lost without my *Investor's Business Daily* and Investors.com. There is no better source, I have found, for the clear direction and insights we all need in the financial markets. It is my number one favorite source for finding the right stocks at the right time. It's the very best arrow to have in your investing quiver!

STEVE CROWLEY, HOST OF *AMERICAN SCENE RADIO*

Computer Programs and System, Inc. is pleased to congratulate *Investor's Business Daily* on its 25th anniversary. Achieving such a milestone is a testament to the quality of the publication and the value of the information it provides. In today's difficult economic times, *Investor's Business Daily* is a beacon of common sense, good information and sound counsel.

BOYD DOUGLAS, CEO, CPSI

For 25 years, *Investor's Business Daily* has helped thousands of readers become better investors. Few publications have assisted investors like *IBD* has. Congratulations to Bill O'Neil and his stellar crew!

GABE WISDOM, HOST OF BUSINESS TALK RADIO'S
GABRIEL WISDOM SHOW

In 1984 I bought my first copy of *Investor's Daily* and I was hooked. The charts! The data! The ratings! The advance-decline line! Finally, a financial newspaper with truly useful information. Little did I know that I was also starting on a path of investment enlightenment led by Bill O'Neil.
DAVE WHITMORE, PRESIDENT, SOGOTRADE.COM

Congratulations to *Investor's Business Daily* on a quarter century of service to Americans. I confess that I mutter the phrase, "I wish I had written that!" more often reading IBDeditorials.com than at any other publication.
THOMAS LIFSON, PHD, EDITOR, AMERICANTHINKER.COM

Congratulations on your first 25 years of helping customers to efficiently and effectively monitor their valuable assets. From a security perspective, we share a similar value proposition with our clients so we are delighted to recognize your success and wish you many more years of continued growth.
TOM REILLY, CEO, ARCSIGHT

IBD consistently provides informative financial news for investors. The analysis of various entrepreneurial growth companies is especially valuable. Congratulations on your 25th anniversary.
TOM W. OLOFSON, CHAIRMAN AND CHIEF EXECUTIVE OFFICER,
EPIQ SYSTEMS, INC.

The American Association of Individual Investors congratulates *Investor's Business Daily* on 25 years of providing timely financial data, as well as unique and insightful investment articles, which has served to inform individual investors nationwide.
JOHN MARKESE, PRESIDENT, AAII

IBD has always done a great job providing investors information about companies that are most relevant to current opportunities. We're very pleased to have been one of those companies. Congratulations on 25 years!
GREG HENSLEE, CEO, O'REILLY AUTO PARTS

Investor's Business Daily has had a huge impact on Wall Street and in Washington. My hat is off to *IBD* and publisher William O'Neil for their valuable contribution to America's free press.
CHRISTOPHER RUDDY, CEO AND EDITOR, NEWSMAX MEDIA, INC.

A tip of the hat to *IBD* on 25 years! You're one of the few publications that places a high value on investor education, we commend your dedication to helping investors to make informed decisions.

CORY WAGNER, CO-FOUNDER, INVESTOPEDIA.COM

Congratulations of your 25th Silver Anniversary! Thank you, for these many years of financial education and insights! Looking forward to the next 25 years and your 50th Golden Anniversary!

GINNY W., CALIFORNIA, INDIVIDUAL INVESTOR

Congratulations on your longevity achievement. Truly outstanding. To an investment adviser, news is stock in trade. I can always count on your concise summaries to convey the business day's chief events, and your graphics supplement this in a fine manner. Keep up the good work.

FRANK J., OHIO, INVESTING MANAGER

I have been an *IBD* reader since the beginning. After a lot of mistakes I eventually became a believer in the IBD – CAN SLIM method of investing. The best part is having a lot of cash at the bottom of a bear market. If that doesn't make one a believer, nothing will. Congratulations and keep up the great work!

RON E., NEW YORK, INDIVIDUAL INVESTOR

I have been reading, studying, and implementing the IBD methodology of stock analysis and selection since 1988 and have been a subscriber for much of that time. The IBD team has continued to provide a service to investors small and large with tools to beat the market across a broad spectrum of investment opportunities. Thank you for a quarter century of service.

MICHAEL G., ILLINOIS, INDIVIDUAL INVESTOR

How to Make
Money in Stocks
Success Stories

How to Make Money in Stocks Success Stories

New and Advanced Investors Share Their Winning Secrets

Amy Smith

New York Chicago San Francisco
Lisbon London Madrid Mexico City Milan
New Delhi San Juan Seoul Singapore
Sydney Toronto

The *McGraw-Hill* Companies

2 3 4 5 6 7 8 9 10   DOC/DOC 1 8 7 6 5 4 3

ISBN: 978-0-07-180944-3
MHID: 0-07-180944-9

e-ISBN: 978-0-07-180945-0
e-MHID: 0-07-180945-7

This publication is designed to provide accurate and authoritative information in regard to the subject matter covered. It is sold with the understanding that neither the author nor the publisher is engaged in rendering legal, accounting, or other professional service. If legal advice or other expert assistance is required, the services of a competent professional person should be sought.

—From a Declaration of Principles jointly adopted
by a Committee of the American Bar

McGraw-Hill books are available at special quantity discounts to use as premiums and sales promotions, or for use in corporate training programs. To contact a representative please e-mail us at bulksales@mcgraw-hill.com.

This text contains the following, which are trademarks, service marks, or registered trademarks of Investor's Business Daily, Inc., William O'Neil + Co., Inc. or their affiliated entities in the United States and/or other countries: *Investor's Business Daily*®, IBD®, CAN SLIM®, Stock Checkup®, and *e*IBD™.

This book is printed on acid-free paper.

• CONTENTS •

Foreword   vii

Preface   ix

CHAPTER 1   Entering The Dojo: The Decision to Start Investing or to Achieve Greater Results   1

CHAPTER 2   White Belt: Understanding the Trend and Market Timing   5

CHAPTER 3   Dojo Training: Following a Proven Strategy to Find Winning Stocks   11

CHAPTER 4   Belt Promotion: One Stock Victory at a Time   23

CHAPTER 5   Kicking the Bag: Learning to Take Losses and Sell Rules   33

CHAPTER 6   Sparring with the Opponent: Arguments with the Ego   37

CHAPTER 7   Breaking Boards: Successful Trades and Lessons Learned   45

CHAPTER 8   Black Belt Testing: Life-Changing Moments in Investing   107

CHAPTER 9   Becoming a Master: Continually Studying the Market   129

CHAPTER 10   Black Belt Trading: Investing Like a Pro   137

CHAPTER 11   Grandmaster: Legendary Investor Bill O'Neil   185

APPENDIX A   The Method of Our Success by W. Scott O'Neil   195

APPENDIX B   Chris Gessel   201

APPENDIX C   Matthew Galgani   205

APPENDIX D   IBD Workshops   209

APPENDIX E   Helpful Information   213

Acknowledgments   223

Index   225

How to Make Money in Stocks Success Stories is treasure trove of success stories you should *read carefully*. Author Amy Smith has been investing for many years, saying that her discovery of *Investor's Business Daily* and the CAN SLIM Investing Strategy are what helped her learn how to invest so well.

I first met Amy many years ago at a large, local IBD Meetup event where I spoke. She was a member, and I recall after my presentation, she and others stayed behind to talk. I could tell Amy had figured out how the market works, and other members in this group were also very sharp.

The next time I met Amy was when an associate wanted to hire her and asked if I'd like to meet her. In the interview, she answered questions skillfully and was emphatic about how IBD and CAN SLIM were the keys to good investing. We hired her on the spot as Director of IBD Meetup Development. Years later, she's created a considerable number of new clubs and spoken to thousands of investors who shared their own experiences with Amy.

This book was a logical follow-up to my earlier book, *How to Make Money in Stocks*. In Amy's collection of Success Stories, she catalogs the investing journeys of everyday people as well as a few pros, all of whom achieved a great deal. And she likens the journey of an investor to that of a martial arts student learning the discipline and steps to the Black Belt, which is the highest honor. I found the book full of insights and ideas about what made investing work well for these individuals. Each person shared clues about getting started, developing winning routines, and how they learned to recognize their strengths and weaknesses. These are powerful insights, and most of these investors told Amy they felt investing was worth the time and effort—and that it had changed their lives.

I've no doubt if you read this book and scrutinize their approaches, you can benefit too. Amy and these individuals are living examples of what you can accomplish if you want it badly enough. And I'm convinced that you can do this. The information is ready for you to study and absorb, but getting started is up to you.

Remember, investing is not easy, but if you're determined to learn to make money in the market, then that determination and focus will be your winning edge. *But* if you've decided in the past, or even as you read this now, that it sounds like a lot of work and you're not sure? Then I think both Amy and I have earned the right to tell you: *You are missing out on one of the greatest chances to change the course of your life!* Sounds pretty dramatic, yes? Yet, if hundreds of thousands of individuals have made this system work, there's nothing holding you back but your own doubts or unwillingness to even try.

Maybe this book will lend the encouragement you need, as you read about a woman whose husband died and, shortly after, she lost her job. She is now independently wealthy. She had no background in investing at the start but took up the challenge and made it work. What Amy's interviews will show you is that many good investors started without experience—and not much money. Even some of the pros she talked to knew very little at first. You'll learn their approaches and how they overcame their mistakes and hesitations. You may recognize yourself among some of these people and realize that investing is worth pursuing.

I don't want you to feel that because I've invested for years that it sets me apart from you. I had virtually no experience when I began learning to invest—nor did Amy or many others. Investing is *not* an elite club, or something you cannot do. If you think that way, I believe you are dead wrong. Your biggest challenge will be your own doubts or hesitations. I hope you take up this challenge, promise yourself to stick with it through thick and thin, and remain determined and positive. Then it can work. After you read this book, see if you don't feel encouraged. I read it and felt hopeful for each one of you who wants to succeed. You can do this!

We're here to help you on your investing journey.

Wishing you the very best.

Sincerely,

William J. O'Neil
Chairman and Founder
Investor's Business Daily

· PREFACE ·

"Do not let circumstances control you.
You change your circumstances."

—JACKIE CHAN

Every story in this book proves Jackie Chan's quote. You can control your circumstances in great ways and gain control of your life and your future. My own journey with investing has been amazing, and I'm glad every day that I stepped into a world that was entirely foreign to me.

I was a theater major in college and was a successful private fitness trainer for many years with no background in the stock market at all. One day, a client asked me about a supposedly hot new nutritional beverage. The client was also excited about the company as a possible stock investment. Not knowing anything about stocks or the market, I bought *Investor's Business Daily* (IBD) to do a little research on the company.

When I was checking out this "hot stock tip," I noticed an ad in the paper for a free workshop with IBD Chairman and Founder William J. O'Neil, so I decided to attend. Bill spoke about stocks and the market in a way that made sense to me. He talked about innovative companies that were producing new products or services that were in great demand and, as a result, had soaring earnings and sales. The information seemed logical and didn't sound like a bunch of hype, so I began subscribing to the paper. I quickly realized how well the CAN SLIM Investing System worked (which you will learn about in the book) and what an incredible newspaper IBD was for finding winning stocks!

At that time, the newspaper was delivered in the evening to my home. I would look out the window every five minutes until I saw the delivery guy drop it on my driveway. I'd run out as soon as it was delivered and sit in bed circling stock candidates the way Bill taught us to in the free workshop that I had attended. It was almost unbelievable to me how good the newspaper was for finding winner after winner.

Investing can be a somewhat isolating endeavor however, so wanting to connect with other people that shared the same investing passion that I did, I joined Santa Monica IBD Meetup. I enjoyed the group so much that I wish I had joined years earlier. I met fellow investors who will be lifelong friends. We trade e-mails all the time regarding the market or leading stocks. Eventually, I began volunteering and helping at the meetings and became co-organizer of the group.

One night, to my great surprise, Bill O'Neil showed up. It was very exciting for me to meet one of my heroes in person. I got to know other people at IBD, and eventually Bill offered me a job. It has been a pleasure and a privilege working with Bill and my other terrific colleagues at IBD, all of whom do an outstanding job of bringing the top investing insights and stories to subscribers.

Part of my work at IBD includes heading up the Meetup Development Department. Along with another Meetup director, Tim Reazor, we have expanded the program across the United States as investors flock to the meetings. It has been extremely rewarding to see investors learn and profit as a result of the IBD Meetup program.

In coming across so many successful investors, it became clear that their stories needed to be shared. No matter what your background, education, job experience, or age, you can learn to invest successfully. I hope these stories will encourage, inspire, and motivate you.

Both of my children are black belts in Taekwondo, and I have taken many self-defense classes myself. Needless to say, I've spent countless hours in the dojo (martial arts training facility).

The tenets of martial arts training bear remarkable similarities to those of becoming a successful investor, so I have chosen to use analogies from the martial arts world to discuss investing.

I would like to thank everyone who contributed to this book for their time and willingness to share their stories about investing. Listening to their success stories was energizing and motivating. It is my hope that by reading this book, you will become excited about investing.

Whether you are just starting out or are a more seasoned investor, I believe these success stories will help you become a better investor.

My best wishes for stock market success,

Amy Smith

For more information and
further details about Amy's book:

www.investors.com/stocksuccessbook

Entering The Dojo: The Decision to Start Investing or to Achieve Greater Results

"Teachers open the door, but you must enter by yourself."

—CHINESE PROVERB

The beginning martial artist enters the dojo with some trepidation and hesitancy, wondering what will be expected during the training. The black belt instructor enters the room preparing to teach and yells "Charyot!" (Attention!).

A new investor feels the same uncertainty. What will be required? Can I really learn to be a successful investor? And investors with more experience might wonder if they can improve their results. The answer is yes; absolutely: virtually everyone can learn to invest successfully as long as they are willing to follow a proven system and keep a simple set of rules.

"Nothing is impossible to a willing mind."

—THE BOOKS OF HAN DYNASTY

You have a desire to improve your life and your financial situation. Congratulate yourself for taking the chance.

Whether your motivating factor is to take a vacation, to buy a home, to generate retirement income, to build a college fund for children or grand-children, to do more with your own money, or a wish for complete financial independence, you can learn to invest successfully if you're willing to follow a proven investment strategy and keep some simple rules.

Mike Scott was laid off when defense industry cuts hit California and he needed to replace his income.

Calvin Shih got motivated to learn more about investing after watching his dad's stock account dwindle after the dot-com crash.

Carole Shontere wanted to stop the bleeding in her husband's 401(k).

At the age of 50, **Jerry Powell** was faced with a tough job reassignment and would be on the road 60% of the time.

"Aloha Mike" was disillusioned with the corporate grind.

Jim Taub was looking for retirement income.

Townsend Baldwin was wiped out financially in the dot-com crash while he was on a humanitarian mission in Argentina.

Kathleen Phillips needed to work from home when diagnosed with multi-ple sclerosis.

Gay Walsh's IRA accounts were losing money.

Anindo Majumdar wanted to quit his corporate job and spend more time with his family.

Katrina Guensch lost a significant amount of money that had been left to her by her father during the 2008 bear market.

Bharani was working as an IT professional and wanted to increase his income.

Brian Gonzales wanted to pay off his student loans.

Jeannie McGrew was frustrated watching an investment advisor lose money year after year with her husband's 401(k) and figured she could do a better job.

Ken Chin wanted to be financially independent.

Barbara James' husband died, she lost her job, and she needed an income.

"We are only bound by our limitations to believe."

—MARK BISHOP, OKINAWAN KARATE INSTRUCTOR

Most people lose money in the market, but it definitely doesn't have to be that way.

Contrary to popular belief, you can time the market, or at least you can put the odds in your favor if you follow a few basic rules, the most important one being to follow the market's overall trend.

"Buy and hold" is an investing approach that historically has not worked very well. As a result of that type of investing strategy, many investors lost money in the bear market of 2007–2008, not only in their personal accounts but also in their IRAs. All too many baby boomers are sitting on investments that are simply underperforming their needs for retirement.

The gift that you have as an individual investor is that you can get in and out of the market with greater ease than the professional investor who may take months to fill a huge position in a single stock.

Investor's Business Daily® (IBD®) has research going back to 1880 to help guide investors through every type of market, whether bull or bear. There has also been an in-depth study of the market's biggest winners and the characteristics they had in common prior to making their big runs.

Don't be intimidated by a lack of knowledge or past failure with investing. Everyone starts somewhere, and even if you haven't succeeded in the past, it doesn't mean you can't succeed in the future. The truth is, most people lose money in the stock market because they have no strategy or system that they follow. Many investors buy stocks because they like the company, or someone gave them a hot tip, or the stock seems like a bargain because it has pulled back a lot in price.

It is the institutional investors that drive the money in the market. They are looking for companies that are making products that are in big demand.

We all know the story of Apple, one of the best examples of a company that has been completely innovative and created products that were in big demand from 2004 to 2012. Apple's innovations have produced skyrocketing earnings and sales that captured the attention of the institutional investors—the mutual funds, banks, pension funds, and hedge funds.

Finding these big stock market winners is not as hard as you might think. They appear in every bull market, cycle after cycle. You only need to look at history as your guide. You don't need insider information or a relative who works on Wall Street, and you don't have to take tips that you might hear on TV.

What if you could buy the highest quality merchandise that you can find, the true market winners that are the best the market has to offer? These are stocks that vastly outperform the major moving averages.

Get ready for an exciting and profitable journey in the stock market. The only requirements are the following:

- Set aside sufficient time to analyze the charts.
- Develop discipline.
- Follow a set of time-tested rules.
- Be willing to look at your mistakes and correct them.

Let's get started!

White Belt: Understanding the Trend and Market Timing

"He who knows when he can fight and when he cannot, will be victorious."

—SUN TZU

For a martial artist, bowing is a display of respect. An investor must bow to the market and respect the overall trend. Contrary to popular belief, you *can* time the stock market.

Every investor would like it if the stock market went up all the time, but that's not the way market cycles work. There are times to be in the market to maximize your gains, and there are times when you should step to the sidelines to avoid losses.

Understanding the Trend

It's important to understand whether the stock market is in an uptrend or a downtrend. Investing in an uptrending market is the most important factor for achieving gains.

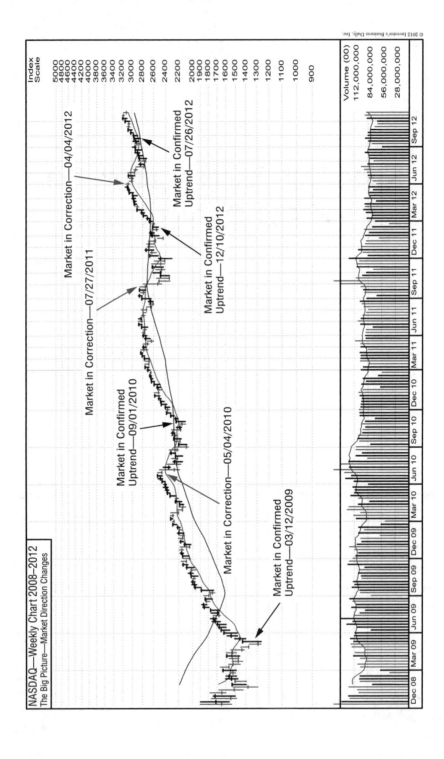

NASDAQ—Weekly Chart 2008–2012
The Big Picture—Market Direction Changes

Index Scale

Market in Correction—04/04/2012

Market in Confirmed Uptrend—07/26/2012

Market in Correction—07/27/2011

Market in Confirmed Uptrend—12/10/2012

Market in Confirmed Uptrend—09/01/2010

Market in Correction—05/04/2010

Market in Confirmed Uptrend—03/12/2009

What Starts a New Uptrend

A follow-through day signals an important change in the general market direction from a downtrend to a new uptrend.

As an index rallies a few days off its lows, one of the major indexes will close the day higher 1.5% or more on bigger volume than the previous day. This signals that professional money is coming into the market, causing the indexes and leading stocks to rise.

While not all follow-through days work, no new uptrend has started without one. Stronger follow-through days will be accompanied by leading stocks breaking out of areas of price consolidations. That is why it is a good idea to always keep a watch list of stocks up to date during any correction and start a position in one of the stocks that is breaking out on the follow-through day.

How to Tell Whether a New Uptrend Has Begun

The *Big Picture* column in *Investor's Business Daily* (IBD) has a *Market Pulse* section that shows one of three stages:

1. Market in confirmed uptrend (it's a good time to be buying stocks)
2. Uptrend under pressure (time for caution, avoid new buys)
3. Market in correction (market is under selling pressure; consider locking in some gains on stocks that you own and avoid new buys)

MARKET PULSE

Tuesday's action:
Market follows through

Current outlook:
In confirmed uptrend

Leaders up in volume:
Celgene^{CELG}
MasterCard^{MA} Visa^{V}

Leaders down in volume:
Red Hat^{RHT}

MARKET PULSE

Wednesday's action:
Down in higher volume

Current outlook:
Uptrend under pressure

Distribution days:
7 on NYSE composite,
5 on S&P 500, 3 on Nasdaq

Leaders up in volume:
Dollar General^{DG}

Leaders down in volume:
Alexion^{ALXN}
Allot Communications^{ALLT}
InvenSense^{INVN}
Michael Kors^{KORS}
SolarWinds^{SWI}

MARKET PULSE

Wednesday's action:
Broad losses in higher trade

Current outlook:
Market in correction

Distribution days:
8 on NYSE composite,
6 on S&P 500, 4 on Nasdaq

Leaders down in volume:
Celgene^{CELG} Polaris^{PII}
Chipotle Mexican Grill^{CMG}
InvenSense^{INVN}
SolarWinds^{SWI}

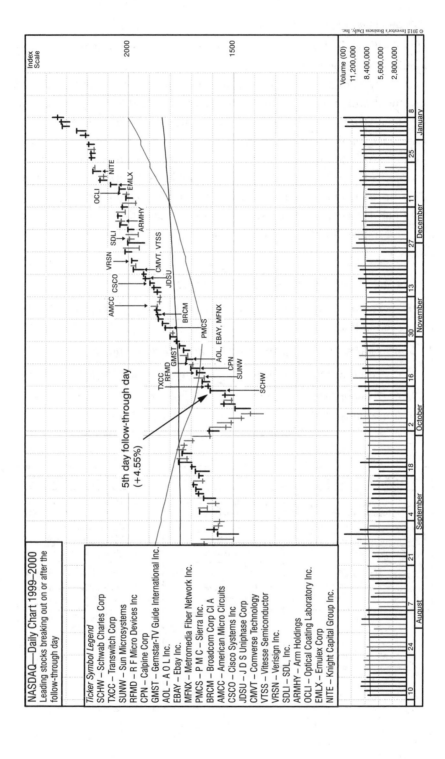

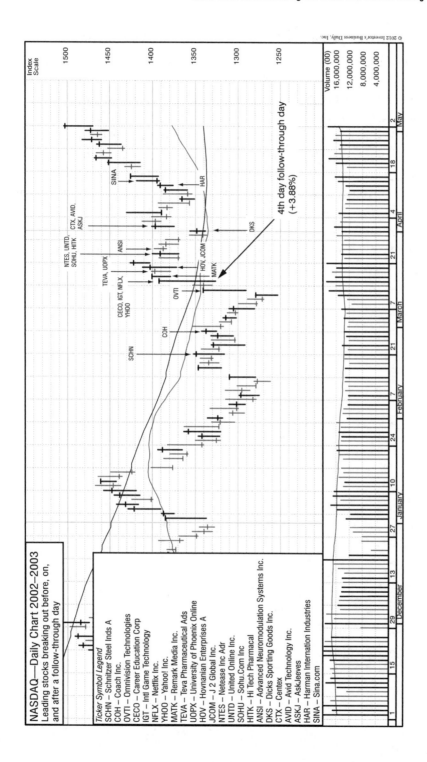

NASDAQ—Daily Chart 2002–2003
Leading stocks breaking out before, on,
and after a follow-through day

4th day follow-through day
(+3.88%)

Ticker Symbol Legend
SCHN – Schnitzer Steel Inds A
COH – Coach Inc.
OVTI – Omnivision Technologies
CECO – Career Education Corp
IGT – Intl Game Technology
NFLX – Netflix Inc.
YHOO – Yahoo! Inc.
MATK – Remark Media Inc.
TEVA – Teva Pharmaceutical Ads
UOPX – University of Phoenix Online
HOV – Hovnanian Enterprises A
JCOM – J 2 Global Inc.
NTES – Netease Inc Adr
UNTD – United Online Inc.
SOHU – Sohu.Com Inc
HITK – Hi Tech Pharmacal
ANSI – Advanced Neuromodulation Systems Inc.
DKS – Dicks Sporting Goods Inc.
CTX – Centex
AVID – Avid Technology Inc.
ASKJ – AskJeeves
HAR – Harman Internation Industries
SINA – Sina.com

Index Scale

1500
1450
1400
1350
1300
1250

Volume (00)
16,000,000
12,000,000
8,000,000
4,000,000

© 2012 Investor's Business Daily, Inc.

What Ends an Uptrend and Puts the Market into a Correction

A distribution day is a heavy day of selling on one of the major indexes. This heavy selling causes one of the indexes to close 0.2% lower on volume higher than that of the previous day. The CAN SLIM System focuses mainly on the S&P and the Nasdaq when counting distribution days.

IBD studies have shown that 5 or 6 days of distribution over a 4- to 5-week period are enough to turn a previously advancing market into decline, especially if distribution days start piling up quickly over a short period.

The increase in heavy selling is a signal to the individual investor that professionals are heading for the exits.

Since three out of four stocks follow the general market trend, it's best not to try and swim against the tide if the market is in a downtrend.

• CHAPTER • 3

Dojo Training: Following a Proven Strategy to Find Winning Stocks

"When the student is ready, the master will appear."

—BUDDHIST PROVERB

The CAN SLIM® Investing System helps you find the market's biggest winners by looking for the traits that they have in common prior to making their big moves.

What Do the Market's Biggest Winners Have in Common?

In the 1960s, IBD Chairman and Founder William J. O'Neil asked this question as a young stock broker and studied all of the market's biggest winners going back to 1950 (IBD's ongoing study of the market's best performing stocks now goes back to 1880). He also did not want to leave any performance details out, so even though computers were in their infancy, he hired programmers and statisticians to catalog stock data so he could see if it somehow made more sense. And it did. His visionary approach to applying computers to his research paid off big. He found seven traits that winning stocks had in common prior to making their big price moves. This became the basis for the CAN SLIM Investing System, which has helped both professional and individual investors for decades.

Each of the letters in CAN SLIM stands for a different trait that winning stocks have in common.

C **Current quarterly earnings.** Minimum of 25% increase in the most recent quarter. Many of the market's biggest leaders will have earnings increases in the triple digits.

A **Annual earnings.** Rate of increase at least 25%, the higher the better.

N **New (new products or services, new management, new highs).** Innovative companies making new price highs indicating institutional buying.

S **Supply and demand.** A product or service that is in big demand by the public.

L **Leadership.** Stocks at the top in their industry group with earnings, sales, return on equity, and price action.

I **Institutional support.** Mutual funds, hedge funds, pension funds, banks. The professional money is what will drive a stock's price higher.

M **Market direction.** Buying leading stocks with top fundamentals in an uptrending market and selling stocks when the market goes into a correction.

• KEY POINTS •

- The biggest winners will have the seven CAN SLIM traits.
- Buy stocks in an uptrending market.

When Is the Right Time to Buy Stocks?

Stocks form chart bases or areas of price consolidation. When they come out of these consolidations on trading volume that is 40% higher than average, we refer to it as a breakout, and this is when a stock should be bought. Buying a stock as it is breaking out of a base pattern puts the odds in your favor. Market history shows that stocks vault out of these areas of consolidation before moving even higher. But buying a stock that is extended in price from a proper base makes the trade more risky since the stock may pull back and can shake you out of a position.

There are three main base patterns that we look for in CAN SLIM Investing.

1. The most common base is the **cup-with-handle** pattern. It looks like a tea cup with a handle.

2. The **double bottom base** looks like a W with the exception that the right part of the W undercuts, or drifts down below, the left side of the W.

3. The **flat base** moves sideways in a tight range as the stock digests a previous move up.

Buying stocks just as they come out of bases or areas of consolidation increases your odds of success. Look for volume that is 40% above average on the breakout.

Some secondary buy points include: (1) A three-weeks-tight pattern (where a stock closes three weeks in a tight range with less than a 1% difference in closing price during that time). (2) A stock may be bought or added to the first or second pullback to the 10-week moving average line on low volume. The low volume shows that institutions are holding onto their positions and not selling heavily.

Base Stages

As a stock is being bought and advances, it forms a series of bases, or areas of price consolidations along the way. Very few stocks move straight up from their first breakout. Most stocks stop and take a breather before moving higher.

We count these bases as first stage, second stage, third stage, and so on. The reason we count base stages is because IBD market studies have shown that earlier stage bases tend to be more successful than later stage bases. By the time a stock has made a big move and is in a third, fourth, or even fifth stage base, it's too obvious, most institutions have made big money in the stock and are ready to lock in profits and sell.

There are exceptions to the rule, and some stocks do continue to move higher in later stage bases, but you want to put the odds in your favor.

Netflix is an example of a stock that formed a series of bases along its move upward.

Look for stocks that are in earlier stage bases.

A Simple Routine for Putting It All Together

To Determine the Market Trend:

1. Check the *Market Pulse* found in *The Big Picture* column of IBD to find the current market trend.

2. Watch the *Market Wrap* video every day to stay in touch with what happened in the market as well as the action of leading stocks at http://investors.com/IBDTV.

MARKET PULSE

Thursday's action:
Down in lower volume

Current outlook:
Confirmed uptrend

Distribution days:
2 for Nasdaq and S&P 500,
1 for NYSE composite

Leaders up in volume:
Questcor[QCOR]
Sociedad Quimica[SQM]

Leaders down in volume:
Union Pacific[UNP]
Canadian Nat'l Railway[CNI]
Kansas City Southern[KSU]
IPG Photonics[IPGP]

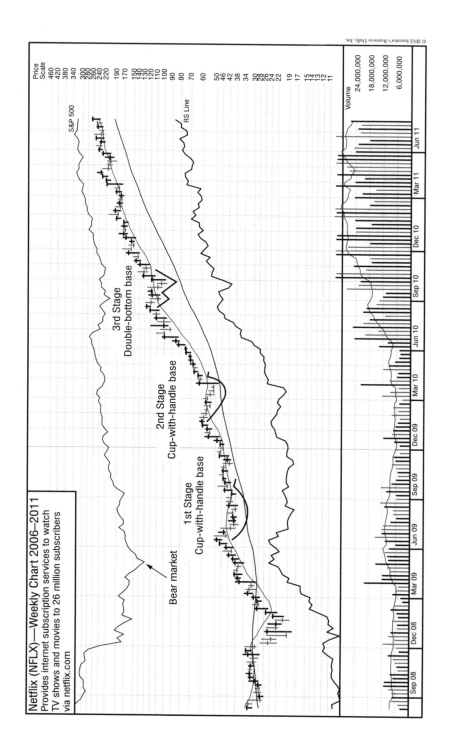

Netflix (NFLX)—Weekly Chart 2006–2011
Provides internet subscription services to watch
TV shows and movies to 26 million subscribers
via netflix.com

Bear market

1st Stage
Cup-with-handle base

2nd Stage
Cup-with-handle base

3rd Stage
Double-bottom base

S&P 500

RS Line

Price
Scale
460
420
380
340
300
280
260
240
220
190
170
150
140
130
120
110
100
90
80
70
60
50
46
42
38
34
30
28
26
24
22
19
17
15
14
13
12
11

Volume
24,000,000
18,000,000
12,000,000
6,000,000

Sep 08
Dec 08
Mar 09
Jun 09
Sep 09
Dec 09
Mar 10
Jun 10
Sep 10
Dec 10
Mar 11
Jun 11

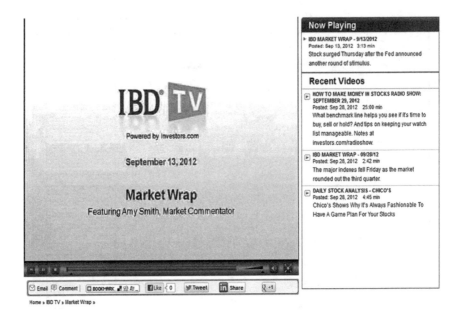

To Find Leading Stocks:

1. Look at the *IBD 50* in the Monday and Wednesday editions of the paper.
2. Read underneath the mini charts to identify a proper buy point in a stock's base pattern.

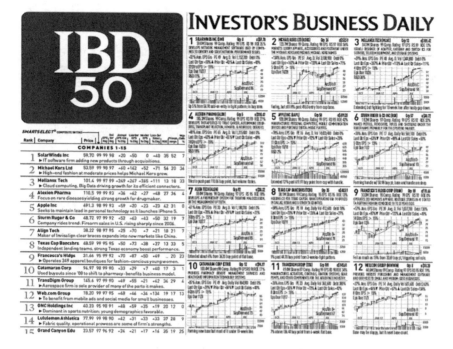

How To Read IBD Stock Charts
A brief explanation of what the numbers mean

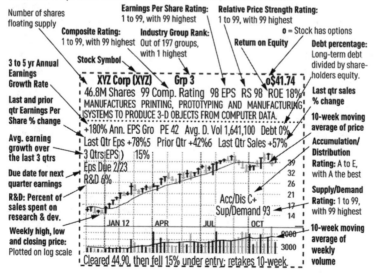

Particular Things to Look for in the Chart

Earnings. Ideally double or triple digit numbers, the higher the better.

Sales. Minimum of 25% increase in the most recent quarter vs. the same quarter last year.

Return on Equity. Minimum of 17%, but many market leaders will have ROEs much higher. This shows how efficient a company is with its money.

See which stocks are rising on unusual volume (meaning institutional buying is coming into the stock) with *Stocks on the Move* at Investors.com (http://www.investors.com) throughout the trading day.

Stay in step with the current market trend. Look at the *IBD 50* and Stocks on the Move to find leading stocks.

Stocks on the Move @ investors.com

IBD Stock Research Tool

MARKET DIRECTION   FIND STOCKS   EVALUATE STOCKS   TRACK STOCKS

Stocks on the Move   ↑ ↓   Add to My Routine **Watch Video »**

Stocks being BOUGHT heavily by institutional investors.
Click icons for analysis. Learn More

Stocks On The Move

Symbol	Company	Price	Price Chg.	Price % Chg.	Volume % Chg.	IBD Tools
TWTC	T W Telecom Inc	27.36	1.27 ↑	4.87% ↑	427%	✔ Ⓜ ⊕
PATK	Patrick Industries Inc	18.28	2.81 ↑	18.16% ↑	427%	✔ Ⓜ ⊕
NSM	Nationstar Mtg Hldgs Inc	34.45	1.27 ↑	3.83% ↑	229%	✔ Ⓜ ⊕
HCSG	Healthcare Svcs Group	23.76	0.90 ↑	3.94% ↑	145%	✔ Ⓜ ⊕
WST	West Pharmaceutical Svcs	53.91	0.84 ↑	1.58% ↑	128%	✔ Ⓜ ⊕

Expand
View All »

Real time prices by BATS. Volume delayed. Last Update: 10/01/2012 03:30 PM EST

Continue Your Education: Join a Free IBD Meetup Group

IBD Meetups are the fastest growing financial clubs in the United States. The reason for this is the success many members have had as a result of joining these groups, which meet once a month to discuss the CAN SLIM Investing System.

At a typical meeting, groups will discuss the current market trend, leading stocks, and how to build a watch list. They also go over a lesson designed by IBD Chairman and Founder Bill O'Neil, and ask questions. More seasoned investors help newer investors learn the system and how to succeed.

Katrina Guensch lives in an area that doesn't have an IBD Meetup Group, so she participates in one that has online monthly webinars: the Chicago/Naperville IBD Meetup. She says, "The group has detailed meetings that have really helped me learn." Through the webinars, she has met other investors to e-mail and discuss the current market and leading stocks.

Gay Walsh is a TV writer and had a desire to do more with her money, so she joined several IBD Meetup Groups in the Southern California area and found that attending so many increased her learning curve. She said, "Watching other people read charts was really helpful. A writer's life can be up and down; I wanted to establish security for retirement. IBD Meetups have been a great resource for me."

Carol Shontere says, "I have attended every single Thousand Oaks Meetup since June 2010. I have been blessed to find the best of the best with this group, including leadership from Mike Scott and Jerry Samet, and I have learned so much."

Prabin Bishoyi is a senior software engineer who works for IBD. He sends out a newsletter to his group after each meeting, summarizing what was discussed as well as what stocks were analyzed from the group's watch list.

As a leader, he engages the group with quizzes to cement key learning points in between meetings. He also has his group participate in creating a mock portfolio to see what kind of gains the group could generate from stocks that were discussed at the monthly meetings. Prabin says, "I am a continual student of the market and work hard so I can help my Meetup group members find success with IBD."

Dennis Wilburn is an IBD Meetup leader from the Bay Area Money Makers, or BAMM for short. The group is "dedicated to technical analysis and, as a group working together, to achieve financial freedom by following CAN SLIM trading techniques." The group first discusses the current trend, builds a watch list of superior growth stocks, and goes over proper entry points and position size as well as exit points, primarily using the *IBD 50*. One of Dennis' most quotable statements is to "clarify and simplify so you multiply." Having studied many different investing methodologies, he has "found the *IBD 50* to be a treasure trove of the market's best performing stocks. This is where the big fish hang out. If you apply strict trading strategies and follow the overall market trend, you can do exceptionally well. That's because the *IBD 50* stocks have to pass stringent criteria before making the list."

Norm Langout is 80 years young and the IBD Meetup leader from Santa Monica, California. This was one of the first IBD Meetup Groups in the country, which Norm started at a Starbucks before moving to a Coco's in 2003. Norm believes strongly in volunteering and doing community work to help other people. He also thought that by starting an IBD Meetup Group, he would find other investors with whom he could discuss the market and stocks and thought "we could learn from each other." Norm has been a good mentor and has spawned several IBD Meetup leaders that originally started with Santa Monica IBD Meetup, including Mike Scott, the Thousand Oaks IBD Meetup leader; John Mackel, the Pasadena IBD Meetup leader; Sherman Neff and Louis Gabriel, the leaders from the Sherman Oaks IBD Meetup Group; and Jerry Samet, who helps teach at several IBD Meetup Groups.

Ted Leplat has taught over 250 IBD Meetup Groups across the country as an IBD national speaker and educator. He says, "Investing is the greatest opportunity, and everyone can learn to profit from the market." From his vast teaching experience, Ted realizes that most people are short on time, so Ted has a simple routine that he teaches to the Meetup groups:

1. First, Ted goes to *The Big Picture* column to determine the overall trend. He makes note of stocks that are up on volume from the *Market Pulse* and starts a watch list.

2. Next, Ted takes the stocks that he found up on volume from the *Market Pulse* and looks for the stock that is highest ranked in the *Timesaver Table*. This provides one new stock to add to a watch list every day.

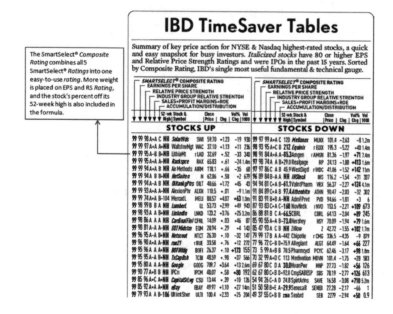

3. Then Ted takes investors to Stock Checkup® on Investors.com as a quick way to check a stock's strength in its industry group, earnings, sales, and other key fundamental data.

Michael Kors Hldgs Ltd (KORS) NYSE

October 22, 2012 (20 min. Delay)

IBD Stock Checkup for KORS:

COMPOSITE RATING
99

About KORS: MARKETS LUXURY APPAREL, ACCESSORIES AND FOOTWEAR UNDER THE MICHAEL KORS AND MICHAEL MICHAEL KORS NAMES

☑ General Market ☑ Fundamental Checklist ☑ Technical Checklist ☑ View Chart

Rate A Stock: [Enter Symbol] ▶

Copyright 2012 Investor's Business Daily, Inc

⚙ PERFORMANCE WITHIN GROUP (KORS)

MICHAEL KORS HLDGS LTD RANK WITHIN THE APPAREL-CLOTHING MFG GROUP (31 STOCKS)

Composite Rating 99 Rank within Group: 1st		**Composite - Group Leaders**
Best in Group 100%		➊KORS
EPS Rating 98 Rank within Group: 2nd		MICHAEL KORS HLDGS LTD
96%		➋UA
Relative Strength Rating 97 Rank within Group: 1st		UNDER ARMOUR INC CL A
Best in Group 100%		➌VFC
SMR Rating A Rank within Group: 1st		V F CORP
Best in Group 100%		➍GIII
Acc/Dist. Rating B Rank within Group: 11th		G III APPAREL GROUP INC
67%		➎PVH
		P V H CORP

4. Finally, Ted consults a chart to see if the stock is setting up in a base pattern.

On the weekend, investors can read other IBD features to validate their picks during the week.

"The person with more time can do this routine with as many of the stocks in the *Market Pulse* as they want to," says Ted.

Rao N. says, "I have learned a lot about CAN SLIM and the importance of a routine from Ted Leplat and the IBD Meetups."

Join a free IBD Meetup Group at http://www.investors.com/Meetup.

Belt Promotion:
One Stock Victory at a Time

"The time to strike is when the opportunity presents itself."

—SIXTH CODE OF ISSHIN-RYU KARATE

The various martial arts forms use belt colors as a way of showing a student's progression. Skills and knowledge are tested along with focus and concentration before a higher level can be achieved. Each promotion leads the martial artist to a deeper level of competency and understanding of the art form.

Investors sharpen their skills with each successful stock trade that they make, while staying steadfast to their rules.

Using IBD Features to Find Winning Stocks

IBD 50

The *IBD 50* is a proprietary list of the 50 top-ranked companies, published every Monday and Wednesday in *Investor's Business Daily*. Companies are

23

ranked based on superior earnings, strong price performance, and leadership within their respective industries.

Stephen Cole

Stephen is a busy lawyer and an IBD Meetup leader in Sacramento, California. His weekend routine includes going through the *IBD 50*. He looks for stocks that are in first or second stage bases, with accelerating earnings 25% or greater, and a return on equity of at least 17%. (Return on equity measures how efficient a company is with its money.) Stephen builds a watch list by looking at the mini chart and the description below each one that describes a potential buy point. He sets an alert in his brokerage account that lets him know if a stock is nearing that price.

Stephen bought Transdigm Group in April and had gains of 14% through the end of September 2012.

• KEY POINTS •

- Look for stocks in the *IBD 50* that are in first or second stage bases.
- Stocks should have quarterly earnings of 25% or greater.
- Return on equity should be at least 17%.
- The description below the *IBD 50* mini chart will help identify a potential buy point.

Stuart Auvian

Stuart is the Meetup leader for the Marin County IBD group located in Northern California. He emphasizes to his group the importance of buying at least one stock when the market issues a follow-through day. "This puts you in the right place psychologically because you're in the game, rather than trying to play catch-up if you get into the market late after a follow-through day," he says. To build his watch list, Stuart pulls four or five stocks from the *IBD 50* that have top fundamentals. Stuart was successful with Alexion Pharmaceuticals, which had earnings growth of 48% and sales growth of 44%. Stuart bought the stock in December 2011 and sold on March 12 for a 20% gain.

<hr>

• KEY POINTS •

- Buy at least one stock if there is a follow-through day.
- Build a watch list from stocks in the *IBD 50* that have top fundamentals.

<hr>

Ted Staub

Ted is a retired executive from the pharmaceutical industry who lives in Florida. He had traveled the world for work and had little time to trade but always had an interest in the market. Before he started reading IBD and following the CAN SLIM principles, he thought that stocks that were going down in price might be a bargain. Through reading IBD, he learned that cheap stocks are cheap for a reason and began to look for stocks with great earnings that were basing or pulling back to the 10-week line when looking for entry points. His first winner was Web.com Group. The stock started moving up on heavier volume in June and Ted bought it. In July, Ted sold Web.com and locked in a gain of 25%, his first winner. He said that he was a little hesitant in the beginning, but "this first victory gave me faith in the CAN SLIM System."

<hr>

• KEY POINT •

- Look for stocks in the *IBD 50* that have big earnings that are basing or pulling back to the 10-week line in low volume, showing that institutions are still holding onto shares.

<hr>

Ashish Dave

Ashish got started in investing in 1996. At that time, he was a young engineer and noticed his boss would put IBD in the recycling bin after he finished reading it. Ashish was interested in the market, so he pulled the paper out of the bin. He found that IBD was an "easy way to find great stocks." His interest led him to read *How to Make Money in Stocks* and to attend several IBD educational workshops. Ashish doesn't buy a stock unless it shows up on the *IBD 50* because he has found that a stock has a greater probability of succeeding if it shows up on this list. Ashish focuses mainly on the top 25 names. He prefers stocks that have low debt, a return on equity above 35%, and a relative strength line that is making new highs. (A relative strength line compares a stock's performance to that of the S&P.) A stock that Ashish found using these strong fundamentals was SolarWinds in October 2011. Through mid-September 2012, he had gains of 122%.

• KEY POINTS •

- Concentrate on the top 25 names in the *IBD 50*.
- Look for low debt, a high return on equity, and a relative strength line making new highs.

Stocks on the Move

Bharani Ramamoothi

Bharani is an IT professional with little time during the trading day. When he has a quick coffee break, he checks *Stocks on the Move* at Investors.com for stocks that are moving up or down on heavier than average volume signaling institutional buying or selling. (Seen in IBD's unique Volume % Change.) This often alerts him to stocks that he puts on his watch list. Bharani bought Tractor Supply out of a 3-weeks-tight pattern in March 2012 for a 20% return.

• KEY POINT •

- Check *Stocks on the Move* at Investors.com for stocks moving up on above average volume.

IBD's Videos and Weekly Radio Show

Brian Gonzales

Brian works in the IBD Meetup Development Department. When he was first learning the CAN SLIM Investing System, he says, "The most helpful tool I found was to watch the *Market Wrap* video on Investors.com/IBDTV because it helped me stay in touch with what the market was doing on a daily basis as well as how leading stocks were performing."

He also watched the *Daily Stock Analysis* video to help learn how to analyze a stock's chart pattern and which fundamental elements he should be paying attention to the most.

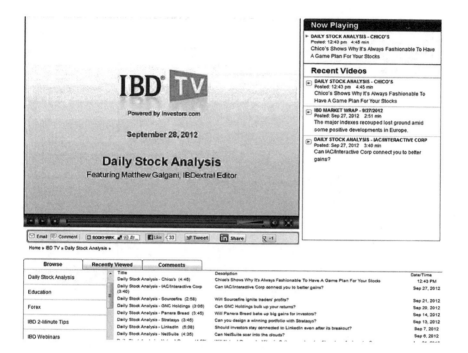

From watching the videos, Brian learned more about Dollar Tree's chart action. He was familiar with the store because his sister shopped there frequently for school supplies, decorations, and party favors for her children's birthday parties.

Brian decided to go into one of the stores to investigate. He thought Dollar Tree reminded him a lot of Target stores, only on a smaller scale, and he observed that the stores were inviting and had several products that seemed to appeal to a large number of people both young and old. There were floral supplies, cleaning products, kitchen and hardware goods, health and personal care items, as well as food items, all at very reasonable prices.

After studying the chart and fundamentals further, he bought the stock March 1, 2011, as it bounced off the 10-day moving average and held the stock till May 8, when the market went into a correction, for a gain of 12%.

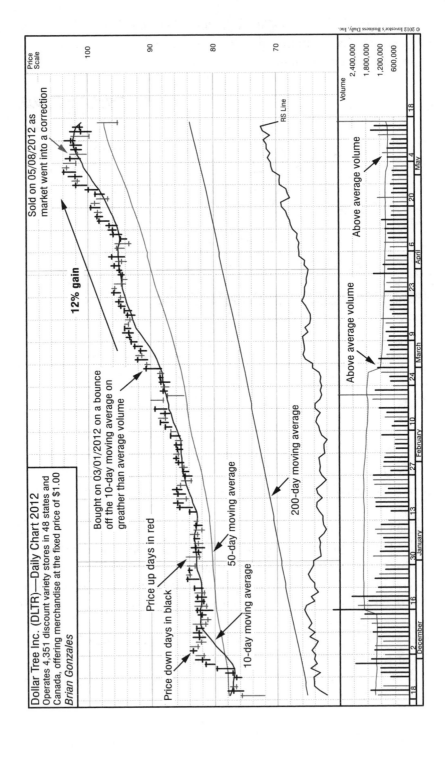

© 2012 Investor's Business Daily, Inc.

Price
Scale

100

90

80

70

RS Line

Sold on 05/08/2012 as
market went into a correction

12% gain

Bought on 03/01/2012 on a bounce
off the 10-day moving average on
greather than average volume

Price up days in red

50-day moving average

Price down days in black

10-day moving average

200-day moving average

Dollar Tree Inc. (DLTR)—Daily Chart 2012
Operates 4,351 discount variety stores in 48 states and
Canada, offering merchandise at the fixed price of $1.00
Brian Gonzales

Volume

2,400,000
1,800,000
1,200,000
600,000

Above average volume

Above average volume

18 4 May 20 6 April 23 9 March 24 10 February 27 13 January 30 16 2 December 18

• KEY POINTS •

- Watch the *Market Wrap* and *Daily Stock Analysis* videos to find winning stocks and to improve chart reading skills.

- Market corrections sometimes cause stock gains to be smaller if the trade was made shortly before the correction.

Jason D'Amore

Jason works in the Meetup Development Department after first working in customer service. He says that listening to the weekly IBD radio show helped cement a lot of the CAN SLIM principles, particularly when he was first learning the system.

Besides working with IBD Meetup Groups, Jason helped on the weekends at several of IBD 's educational workshops. "This gave me the opportunity to listen to some of IBD 's best speakers, such as Justin Nielsen and Scott O'Neil," he says. "Both of these speakers have worked very closely with William O'Neil, so listening to their insights on his investing successes was extremely exciting and helped me understand CAN SLIM on a deeper level.

"Lululemon was my first successful stock trade," Jason says. "It had formed a three-weeks-tight pattern (which is when a stock closes three weeks in a row with less than a 1% closing price change on each of those weeks). I first became aware of Lululemon from listening to the IBD radio show and bought the stock as it came out of an area of consolidation. I had conviction in the stock because I had visited one of their stores and was impressed with the quality of the merchandise."

• KEY POINTS •

- Attend IBD's educational workshops.

- Listen to IBD's *How to Make Money in Stocks* weekly radio show at Investors.com/radioshow.

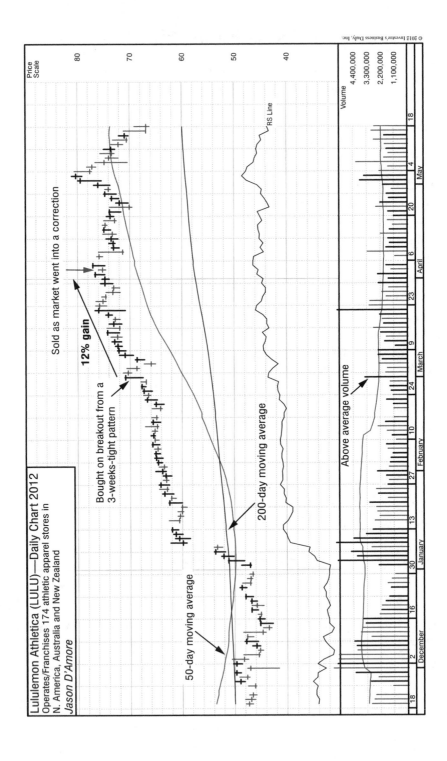

Lululemon Athletica (LULU)—Daily Chart 2012
Operates/Franchises 174 athletic apparel stores in
N. America, Australia and New Zealand
Jason D'Amore

Sold as market went into a correction

12% gain

Bought on breakout from a
3-weeks-tight pattern

200-day moving average

50-day moving average

Above average volume

RS Line

Price Scale

Volume

© 2012 Investor's Business Daily, Inc.

Kevin Dai

Kevin became an IBD subscriber in 2004 but said his learning curve took a big jump when he joined the San Jose IBD Meetup Group. "I started to really learn how to use the paper more effectively to find great stocks," he says. "I also began to understand the importance of follow-through days and paid attention to stocks that broke out of base patterns soon afterward since they often go on to become the big leaders in a rally."

He reads several features in the paper to find stocks but particularly likes the *Industry Themes* article to help him find winning stocks from the top performing industry groups. Kevin has been to IBD's advanced workshops several times and shares his thoughts on what he has learned.

Kevin's five-year cumulative return is 580%.

• KEY POINTS •

- Keep your ego out of trading. Psychology is very important; you must remain unbiased and flexible.

- Respect what the market is doing.

- Establish a regular routine; this will keep you from getting sloppy.

Google Heads Top Stocks In Online Content

IBD INDUSTRY THEMES

BY ALAN R. ELLIOTT
INVESTOR'S BUSINESS DAILY

All in all, it wasn't a great week for industry groups. Just over a third of the 197 groups tracked by IBD gained ground in the five days through Friday. More than half of those rose less than 1%.

The Internet content providers group managed a gain of better than 3%. It edged up to a No. 30 ranking Friday, from No. 54 at the start of August. The industry is home to familiar online names, including Google^{GOOG}, Facebook^{FB} and Yahoo^{YHOO}.

A number of stocks in the group are sketching interesting chart patterns and hold improving fundamentals. Google jumped 3% for the week, ending just 2% below its all-time high, set in 2007. Its vitals earn it a best-possible Composite Rating of 99. Anyone who reads IBD's mini-chart analysis knows the stock is 7% past a three-weeks-

Kicking the Bag: Learning to Take Losses and Sell Rules

"Pain is the best instructor, but no one wants to go to his class."

—TAEKWONDO MASTER HONG HI CHOI

The repetition of kicking the bag in martial arts equals the true birth of skill. The most important thing every investor must learn is to keep all losses small and move on to the next trade. As legendary trader Jesse Livermore put it, "Take your losses and don't brood about them."

No one is right 100% of the time in the stock market. Famous Wall Street investor and political consultant to U.S. presidents Bernard Baruch said it best: "If a speculator is correct half of the time, he is hitting a good average. Even being right three or four times out of 10 can yield a person a fortune if they have the good sense to cut their losses quickly on the ventures where they have been wrong."

The secret to winning big in the stock market is not to be right all the time but to lose the smallest amount of money when you're wrong.

In *How to Make Money in Stocks*, Bill O'Neil says, "You have to realize when you may be wrong and sell a stock without hesitation. How do you know if you're wrong? The price of the stock will drop below what you paid for it!"

The cardinal rule in CAN SLIM Investing is to cut all losses at no more than 7 to 8% below the price you paid for a stock. Preservation of capital is the most critical part of investing.

That means if you paid $30 for a stock, you would sell if the stock dropped to $27.60, 8% below your purchase price. But you don't have to wait till a stock is down 8% from where you bought it. A trade that is going against you can be sold with a smaller loss, say, 4 to 5% below what you paid for it. The point is to keep your losses as small as possible.

Steep losses require big gains just to break even.

- A 25% loss requires 33% gain to break even.
- A 33% loss requires 50% gain to break even.
- A 50% loss requires 100% gain to break even.

"He who hesitates, meditates in a horizontal position."

—SENSEI ED PARKER

Selling a losing position must become automatic. You cannot hesitate. Consider trade triggers through your brokerage account if you have trouble with selling. That way, you've put in a predetermined sell price. This will help keep your emotions under control and keep you from freezing at a critical moment.

Simple Sell Rules

Take most profits at 20 to 25% unless a stock runs up 20% in 2 to 3 weeks, and then it must be held after its breakout for eight weeks. IBD studies show that some of the market's biggest leaders will have a sharp advance before heading even higher, so holding onto these potential big winners is important.

The reason most stocks are sold at 20 to 25% gains is because many stocks will slow down, consolidate their gains, and build another base at that point.

A stock may be topping if it has:

1. **Greatest weekly price spread.** On a weekly chart of a stock with a big weekly gain, consider selling if the spread from the absolute low to the absolute high of the week is wider than any price spread in any week so far.

2. **High volume break of the 50-day moving average.** Consider selling a stock if it clearly drops below the 50-day moving average line and closes the week on heavy volume. It may mean institutions have stopped supporting the stock.

3. **Largest daily price run-up.** If a stock closes for the day with a larger price increase than on any previous up day since the beginning of the whole move up, watch out! This usually occurs very close to a stock's peak.

4. **Heaviest daily volume.** The ultimate top might occur on the heaviest volume day since the beginning of the advance, especially on a high volume reversal day.

5. **Signs of distribution.** Repeated high-volume selling days or heavy daily volume without further upside price progress signals institutional selling.

6. **Increase in consecutive down days.** For most stocks, the number of consecutive *down* days in price over a few weeks relative to *up* days in price will probably increase when the stock begins to come down from its top. You may see four or five days *down*, followed by 2 or 3 days *up*, whereas before you would have seen 4 days *up* and then 2 or 3 *down*.

Low volume and other weak action:

1. **New highs on low volume.** Some stocks will make new highs on lower or poor volume. As the stock goes higher, volume decreases, suggesting that big investors have lost their appetite for the stock.

2. **Greatest one-day price drop.** If a stock has already made an extended advance and suddenly makes its greatest 1-day price drop since the beginning of the move, consider selling if the move is confirmed by other signals.

3. **Living below the 10-week moving average.** Consider selling if a stock has a long advance, then closes below its 10-week moving average

and lives below that average for 8 or 9 consecutive weeks, unable to rally and close the week above the line.

Don't get shaken out too early. About 40% of stocks you buy will pull back near your initial buy point (also called the *pivot point*) sometimes on big volume for 1 or 2 days. Don't get scared out on this normal yet sharp pullback in price. As long as your loss-cutting price has not been reached (8% below what you paid for it), sit tight and be patient. Sometimes it takes a number of weeks for a stock to slowly take off from its launching pad. Big money can only be made by waiting.

Sparring with the Opponent: Arguments with the Ego

*"The way of the sword and the way of the Zen are identical,
for they have the same purpose, that of killing the ego."*

—YAMADA JIROKICHI

Learning to keep emotions under control is one of the most crucial elements to becoming a successful investor but one of the hardest things to achieve. When your money is on the line, it is very common to wrestle with a multitude of emotions and make investing mistakes as a result. Emotions that every investor must learn to deal with are hope, fear, and greed.

Hope

Jeannie McGrew has a natural bullish bias when it comes to the market. Part of this is because her general outlook is always positive. She's a very happy person, which is a wonderful trait to have in life but one that can get you into trouble in the stock market. Jeannie sometimes stayed invested when she shouldn't have because she was "so sure the market was going to continue to go higher." Because of this overly optimistic attitude, Jeannie gave back some very nice gains made in an uptrending market by not going to cash when the market began to correct. Since the vast majority of stocks move up or down with the general market, it's critical to pay attention to this.

Jeannie realized that a lack of discipline was the problem and decided that a remedy would be to "pay a huge amount of attention to the overall market direction, because this will determine your level of success." Now Jeannie makes sure to monitor the overall trend before making any investing decisions.

Fear

Fear of losing money is quite common in stock investing, particularly if someone is new to investing. When Brian Gonzales was relatively new to investing, he would nervously watch stocks that he owned throughout the trading day, because he was afraid they would go down and he'd lose money. When his IBD Meetup Development colleague Jason D'Amore was beginning to invest, he too admitted to "being very tentative about losing gains that I made. I sold a couple of positions very quickly after the stock went down a few percentage points, which ended up being too soon, because I was afraid of losing money."

To alleviate their fears and remove any possible emotional trading, they both set predetermined sell triggers through their brokerage accounts, which would be 4 to 5% below their original buy points on any stocks that they owned. By placing the trade triggers, their losses would be small if a stock purchase that they made didn't work out. It also meant they didn't have to watch their stocks anxiously during market hours. The key thing that both of them have learned is the importance of having a set of rules and staying true to them. Brian says, "Rules keep me grounded and help remove the fear and uncertainty." He has watched friends invest without any rules or system and has seen them lose large amounts of money in the market as a result. Brian says, "The 'throw a dart at a stock and hope it goes up' method of investing can be very dangerous."

Greed

Gennady Kupershteyn had been trading stocks since college in the early 1990s when, at the tender age of 18, he was given the nickname "Stock

God." While his friends were drinking beer downstairs, he was upstairs in his dorm room looking at stock charts. By 2005, his portfolio had grown to $2 million, but he says greed was beginning to set in, and Gennady started taking too many losses as a result. He admits he would sometimes make a significant amount of money and then give all of it back, because he wasn't keeping his sell rules.

Gennady's desire to make money also caused him to ignore the trend of the overall market. Because of the volatility that Gennady experienced with his portfolio, he adjusted his stop losses, the price at which he would sell a stock if it dropped below his purchase price. In a more choppy market, Gennady learned to keep a tighter leash on his positions and sell sooner. "Emotions can get the best of you," he said, "and bad decisions often lead to more bad decisions if you don't have your rules in place."

Never Fall in Love with a Stock

Kathleen Phillips had a sizable portfolio back in the 1990s and ran it up to a jaw-dropping amount. At that time, she held strong companies like Cisco Systems, Intel, Microsoft, and other tech titans. This was a dream portfolio that she thought would run up even higher. There was one problem. She had fallen in love with her stocks, because they had given her such large gains. Kathy didn't realize how bad a bear market could be and how much her stocks could correct when the entire market was under tremendous selling pressure. As a result, Kathy gave back a large portion of her gains.

Today, Kathy has a much greater understanding of market cycles and has a set of rules to make sure that she locks in gains and vows to "never fall in love with a stock again."

Bad Habits

Lee Tanner said his bad habits started in the 1990s, when investing was much easier and the market was more forgiving if you made a mistake. He picked some great stocks using the CAN SLIM strategy and made some very nice gains but was "quite sloppy and lazy on the sell rules." One stock that Lee had tremendous success with as a newer investor was JDS Uniphase. He bought the stock in 1997 and watched it soar through early November 1999. By that point, Lee was up 1,450% on his original investment. Lee was elated and quite generous that Christmas with gifts to friends and family.

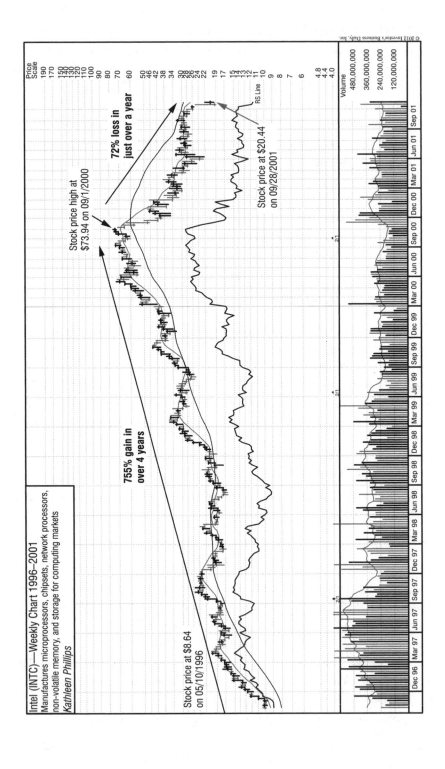

Intel (INTC)—Weekly Chart 1996–2001
Manufactures microprocessors, chipsets, network processors, non-volatile memory, and storage for computing markets
Kathleen Phillips

Stock price at $8.64 on 05/10/1996

755% gain in over 4 years

Stock price high at $73.94 on 09/1/2000

72% loss in just over a year

Stock price at $20.44 on 09/28/2001

RS Line

© 2012 Investor's Business Daily, Inc.

By late January 2000, Lee's position in JDS Uniphase was up more than 3,700% from a split adjusted initial position of $3.25 to over $125. This was a time of tremendous excitement. What Lee didn't realize, though, was that the stock had just gone through an enormous climax run—after which most stocks correct sharply.

Lee was surprised by the sharp pullback in JDS Uniphase and held the stock until it plunged all the way back down to around $20 in May 2001. He was so sure it would recover. Lee says his bad habits and "sloppy sell rules" had caught up with him. "Looking back," he says, "it is simply flabbergasting that I held this stock all the way down from $150 to $20."

Lee regrouped, attended several IBD Seminars, and went back to the basics. He knew that he needed to approach investing in a more disciplined way. Lee has learned that investing "is kind of like baking an apple pie. You have a recipe, and you need to follow it. You must follow the rules to take the emotions out of it." Lee says he learned this the hard way, but it's made him a better investor in the long run.

Arguments with the Ego

"Aloha Mike," as he is known in investing circles, followed every CAN SLIM Investing rule when he was a newer investor. This led to several years of substantial gains in the market, but the more successful he was, the more his ego became a problem, and he began breaking the sell rules. "Instead of taking a 7 to 8% loss in a stock, the supposedly smarter me was selling at 25 to 40% losses, because I was so sure I knew what I was doing."

Reviewing how much money he lost by not keeping the 7 to 8% sell rule "was a real shocker."

"Aloha Mike" faced the fact that every trade he made could be a possible mistake and that those mistakes must be corrected quickly, and all losses must be kept small.

A firm set of rules helped "Aloha Mike" have a concrete way to deal with the market that has nothing to do with his emotions. He has a plan for three roads that the market can take. "Stocks can go up, they can go down, or they can stay in a sideways trading range," he says. "Keeping the three roads in mind allows me to stay nimble and not get mentally stuck in one scenario when another fork in the road or the market may occur."

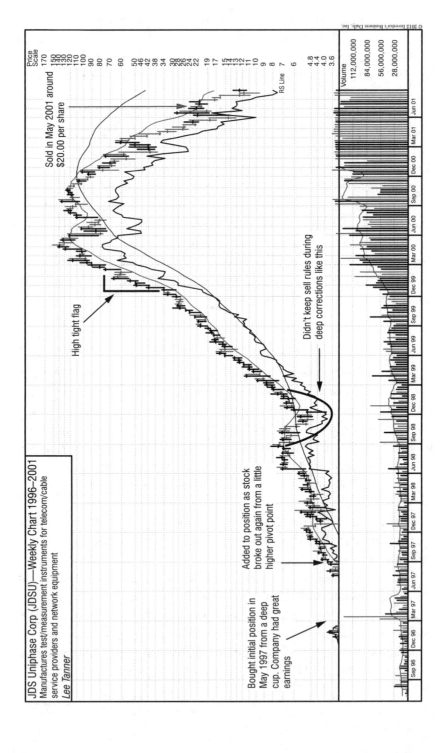

JDS Uniphase Corp (JDSU)—Weekly Chart 1996–2001
Manufactures test/measurement instruments for telecom/cable
service providers and network equipment
Lee Tanner

Bought initial position in
May 1997 from a deep
cup. Company had great
earnings

Added to position as stock
broke out again from a little
higher pivot point

High tight flag

Sold in May 2001 around
$20.00 per share

Didn't keep sell rules during
deep corrections like this

RS Line

Price Scale

Volume

© 2012 Investor's Business Daily, Inc.

His overall goal is to be in sync with the market and leave his emotions and ego out of the equation completely. The market "is like a ballroom dance: it leads, and we must follow. I try and look at what the market is telling me and ignore all the other voices including my own."

Mike Scott admits to having an ego also. Sometimes intraday volatility makes him want to buy or sell something. There are four things that he does to keep his ego and his emotions under control:

1. Stop looking at 5-minute intraday charts and watching a stock's move every minute during the trading day.

2. Wait until the end of the day to decide whether to buy or hold a stock, allowing decisions to be calm, rational, and less emotional.

3. Use a weekly chart as the primary way to analyze and make decisions. The weekly chart shows a longer period of time to analyze a stock's trend and lessens emotions associated with daily fluctuations.

4. Get up and walk away from the computer when these strategies don't work.

Mike takes walks or rides a bike during the trading session when he discovers that he wants to take action and is about to break some of his trading rules.

Years ago, Mike learned Zen meditation at the Zen Center in Los Angeles. Meditation is also something that he does to help him stay focused and relaxed.

Successful trading begins in the mind. The best traders find a way to relax and get focused, whether it's listening to music, taking a walk, exercising, or meditating. Taking time away from the market is important. A trader must get back to a grounded place in order to think clearly and operate from a nonemotional place.

• KEY POINTS •

- Check the market trend before making any trades.
- Consider setting sell triggers to keep losses small.
- Keep greed under control by selling most stocks at a 20 to 25% gain.
- In a choppy market, sell positions sooner.
- Never fall in love with a stock.
- Fix bad habits, and follow a set of rules to keep emotions under control.
- Find a way to relax and get focused.

Breaking Boards: Successful Trades and Lessons Learned

"The successful warrior is an average human being with laser-like force."

—BRUCE LEE

For a martial artist, breaking through wood boards and even cement blocks is less about brute strength and more about specific techniques. You must not break your form; if you do, fingers and wrists can be broken!

Investors can run into the same dangers if they try and create their own system or rules. The good news is that many traders have found success as a result of staying true to the CAN SLIM Investing System. The best part is that if you've had a successful trade once or twice, you can do it again using the same principles.

Keep It Simple

"Aloha Mike" is retired from the aerospace industry. He was able to achieve this by the age of 55 because of his success with the CAN SLIM strategy, which he began in 1987. He's very encouraging to newer investors and mentors a group of retirees as a way of giving back to the community. "The average person can definitely learn to invest successfully if they are willing to put in some time and effort," he says.

"Aloha Mike" says there are three key elements to investing:

1. **Market Timing.** Get in sync and stay in sync with the market direction.

2. **Stock Selection.** Find the great CAN SLIM stocks that are moving up.

3. **Money Management.** Start your positions small. Add if you're making gains.

"What you want to do is force-feed stocks that are outpacing the market," says Mike. "Never average down and add to stocks that are going against you."

One of Mike's best trades was with NVR Inc., the parent company of Ryan Homes, NVR Homes, and Fox Ridge Homes. Mike traded in and out of the home builder, capturing 300% of its 429% move.

"Aloha Mike" rewards himself with a new Hawaiian shirt every time he makes a 25% gain in a stock and says he has a closet full of them.

• KEY POINTS •

- Follow the market direction.
- Select the best CAN SLIM stocks that you can find.
- Start your positions small; add if you're making gains.

Wait for a Follow-Through Day: The Market Is Not a Casino

Gennady Kupershteyn's years of investing experience have taught him that there are optimum periods of time for owning stocks.

"After the market issues a follow-through day," says Gennady, "volatility usually quiets down, and it becomes much easier to hold stocks, particularly if you're following the rules. The key is to be patient and extremely selective. Within four weeks of a successful follow-through day, new high quality names will begin to break out.

"A lot of people have said to me that investing in the stock market is like gambling, but to me, the market is only like a casino if you treat it like one,"

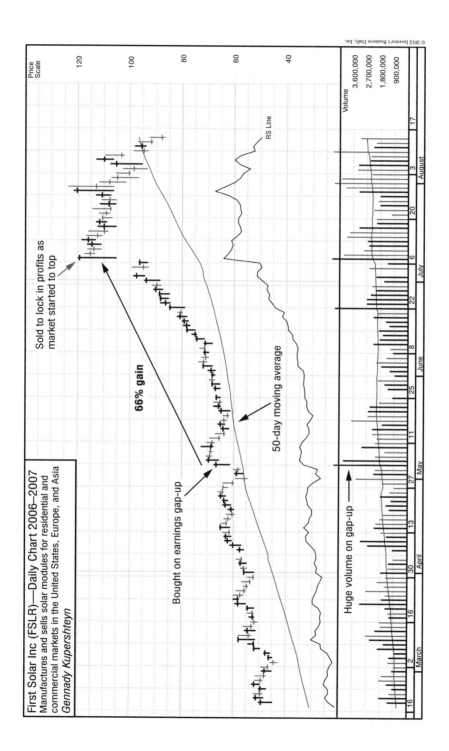

First Solar Inc (FSLR)—Daily Chart 2006–2007
Manufactures and sells solar modules for residential and
commercial markets in the United States, Europe, and Asia
Gennady Kupershteyn

66% gain

Sold to lock in profits as
market started to top

Bought on earnings gap-up

50-day moving average

RS Line

Huge volume on gap-up

Price Scale

Volume

says Gennady. "With investing, you're trying to put the odds in your favor. Unlike gambling in a casino, you can walk away from a trade with a small loss if it begins to go against you, because you're following a set of sell rules. But once you place your bet in the casino, try telling the dealer that you'd like a brand new hand because you don't like the way he dealt the cards."

Over the years, Gennady has taught and attended many IBD Meetup Groups. He found one great stock in 2007 by attending a New Jersey IBD Meetup. "For some reason, the energy stocks had escaped my radar," says Gennady. "When I heard the Meetup group discuss the triple digit earnings in First Solar, I did more research and ended up profiting nicely from the stock."

By being in the market at the right time and obeying his rules, Gennady has notched some nice gains over the years.

Dell. 1995–1997: 529% gain

First Solar. 2007: 66% gain

Fuqi International. 2009: 52% gain

Abercrombie and Fitch. 2010: 38%

• KEY POINTS •

- Wait for a follow-through day.
- Don't gamble in the stock market; keep a set of rules.
- Attend an IBD Meetup Group, and learn about stocks you may not be familiar with.

Finding Stocks with a Simple Daily and Weekly Routine and a Winning Attitude

Ken Chin says, "I go through the print version of IBD with a cup of coffee in the evening, circling stocks in various features of the paper that may be approaching a potential buy point. I'm a dentist, so during the day I'm pretty busy, but in between treating patients, I go to Investors.com and quickly check *Stocks on the Move* to see which stocks are moving up in heavy volume, signaling that institutions might be buying shares of a stock that I'm interested in.

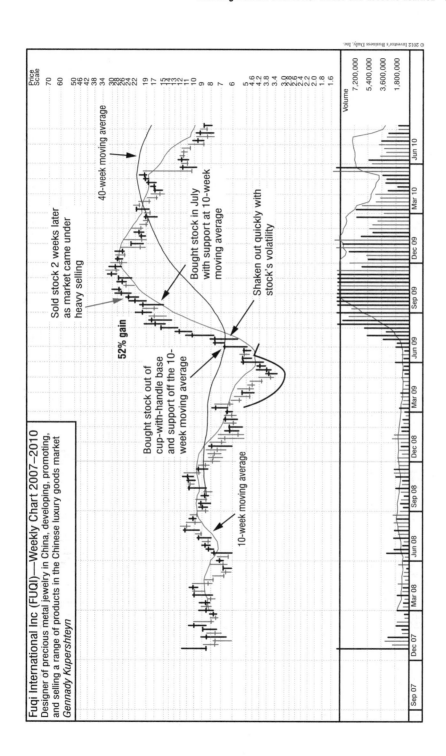

Fuqi International Inc (FUQI)—Weekly Chart 2007–2010
Designer of precious metal jewelry in China, developing, promoting, and selling a range of products in the Chinese luxury goods market
Gennady Kupershteyn

Sold stock 2 weeks later as market came under heavy selling

40-week moving average

52% gain

Bought stock out of cup-with-handle base and support off the 10-week moving average

Bought stock in July with support at 10-week moving average

Shaken out quickly with stock's volatility

10-week moving average

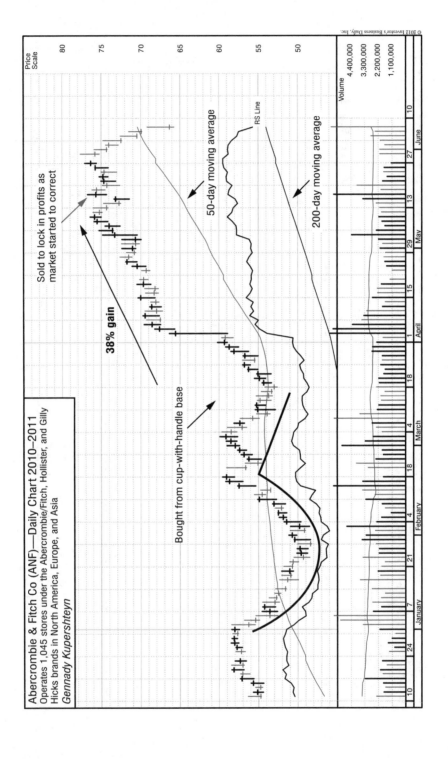

Abercrombie & Fitch Co (ANF)—Daily Chart 2010–2011
Operates 1,045 stores under the Abercrombie/Fitch, Hollister, and Gilly
Hicks brands in North America, Europe, and Asia
Gennady Kupershteyn

Sold to lock in profits as
market started to correct

38% gain

50-day moving average

200-day moving average

RS Line

Bought from cup-with-handle base

Price
Scale

80

75

70

65

60

55

50

Volume
4,400,000
3,300,000
2,200,000
1,100,000

© 2012 Investor's Business Daily, Inc.

24 10 January 7 21 February 4 18 March 4 18 April 1 15 29 May 13 27 June 10

"On the weekends," continues Ken, "I read through the Friday edition of the paper, paying special attention to *Your Weekly Review*, and the Monday version of the paper, which has the *IBD 50*. Both of these sections have mini charts with a description underneath them of the stock's base pattern and the potential buy point. This provides me with a quick and easy watch list of stocks.

"I also study *The New America* articles. As creatures of habit, we return to stocks that have made us money in the past and shun those that haven't. *The New America* articles have opened my mind to companies that I never would have considered because I didn't know enough about them."

Ken says, "'A mind once expanded will never contract to its original dimension.' I can't take credit for those inspiring words—they belong to Oliver Wendell Holmes—but IBD often prints these inspiring quotes in its *Wisdom to Live By* column. These quotes help me maintain a winning attitude, which is just as important as finding a winning stock. Without a winning attitude, you'll limit yourself on how far you can go."

That winning attitude has helped Ken achieve some stellar gains:

Baidu. 2010: 212% in 18 months

Apple. 2011: 91% in 18 months

• KEY POINTS •

- Check *Stocks on the Move* at Investors.com for stocks moving up on heavy volume, indicating institutional buying.
- Develop a nightly and a weekend routine for reading the paper.
- Study *The New America* articles to find potential big winners.

Follow the Market and Look for Setups and Breakouts

Randall Mauro is a portfolio manager for an investment firm in Colorado. He uses the CAN SLIM Investing strategy for his personal trading as well as for clients' portfolios.

"When looking for positions to invest in," he says, "I always start the process by gauging the strength of the overall market (the "M" in CAN SLIM),

THE NEW AMERICA

BAIDU INC. *Beijing, China*

Google's Fade In China Gives A Big Boost To Local Competitor

BY PETE BARLAS
INVESTOR'S BUSINESS DAILY

In the midst of a lackluster year for the stock market, **Baidu** continues to be the little engine that could.

Since Jan. 1, shares of China's top Web search service have more than doubled while stocks for most other technology companies are wallowing in the redo ver the same period.

Baidu(BIDU) has made a habit of beating analyst views on its quarterly profit and revenue results. The company's second-quarter report late last month was no exception.

But Baidu can probably thank Google(GOOG), the company's closest rival in the region, for at least some of the boost in its share price this year.

Google's Fate

Analysts say Baidu's shares will likely continue to trade on Google's June decision to curtail its searchable Web index in China to comply with the government's censorship laws. The move reduced Google's presence in what has become one of the fastest-growing Internet markets in the world while opening the door for Baidu to get a bigger share, says Ryan Jacob, portfolio manager for the Jacob Internet Fund, which owns shares in both Baidu and Google.

"Baidu is in a unique situation where not only has their growth been strong, but it's accelerating because of the situation with Google," he said. "The fundamental change

has been the drop-off of Google as a significant competitor."

Searches on Google in China are now limited to categories that don't require the company to censor its results. The reduction in its index also limits Google's ability to monetize

the results with ads, a key benefit to Baidu and its shareholders, says Mayuresh Masurekar, an analyst for Kaufman Bros. Masurekar rates Baidu a buy.

"For both users of search and for advertisers who spend on (ads)

there is no other place to go but Baidu," he said.

The Baidu story also appeals to investors still scrounging for a growth opportunity in a not how wise wretched market, says Alan B. Lancz, president of Alan B. Lancz & Associates, an investment adviser and money management company, which owns shares in both Baidu and Google.

"The Chinese market continues to grow, the economy is one of the strongest in the world and they lost their major competitor in Google," he said. "They probably could not have written a better script for 2010-2011."

And the story seems to keep getting better.

In the second quarter, Baidu held about 70% share of China's Web search market revenue, up from about 64% in the first quarter, says Analysys International, a research firm.

Meanwhile, Google's share of reve-

Baidu
ir.baidu.com

Ticker	BIDU
Share price	Near 86
12-month sales	$844 mil
5-year profit growth rate	98%

IBD SmartSelect Corporate Ratings

Composite Rating	99
Earnings Per Share	99
Relative Price Strength	98
Industry Group Rank	24
Sales-Profit Margins-ROE	A
Accumulation/Distribution	B

See Investors.com for more details

nue advertisers fell 0.9% from the fourth quarter.

Other metrics were equally compelling.

Revenue per customer in the second quarter also increased 38.9% vs. a year ago and 21.7% from the first quarter. In the first quarter, revenue per customer was up 34.1% vs. the year-ago period and up 3.5% from the fourth quarter.

In a July 21 conference call with analysts, Robin Li, Baidu's chief executive, said the company continues to capitalize on increasing numbers of advertisers jumping on its search service.

"We were able to monetize more effectively, and large companies and (small- and medium-sized) enterprises are spending more with us," he said. "The strength should continue as customers become more familiar with the platform's functions and see potentially higher ROI (return on investment)."

Li never mentioned Google. Neither did any of the other Baidu executives on the call.

But that's not surprising, says Kaufman Bros.' Masurekar.

"They have traditionally been focused on their own initiatives and their own performance, so they don't talk much about the competitive environment," he said.

Baidu had another welcome surprise for investors in the second quarter.

Traffic Acquisition

lost, says Lancz.

"It just makes the story that much more enticing and it's played out much better than most investors would have expected," he said.

China's online ad market is only a fraction of the market in the U.S., but is growing fast. By 2013, sales of online ads in China will reach $8 billion vs. $2.5 billion in 2008, says eMarketer, a research firm.

The number of Internet users in China is now 420 million vs. 100 million in 2005. Yet almost 70% of the country remains offline, Li said during the call.

Baidu is working on several ways to drum up more revenue, including online video and e-commerce services.

The company is also adapting its search service to mobile devices, which analysts concur should be a major growth area for the company.

Mobile Growth

However, Li cautioned that mobile is a work in progress because mobile phones are expensive in China, and the service is much slower than the PC-based Internet.

"During the past couple of years, we have seen a faster growth in mobile search traffic vs. PC-based search, but it remains a small percentage of our total traffic," he said.

Baidu could still face some local competition.

Alibaba Group, an e-commerce services company, recently purchased a 16% stake in Sogou, a search ser-

Going Online

Baidu, China's largest Internet search engine, is benefiting from the soaring number of Internet users

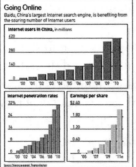

Internet users in China, in millions

Internet penetration rates

Earnings per share

Sources: Chinese government, Thomson Reuters

Going Online

Baidu, China's largest Internet search engine, is benefiting from the soaring number of Internet users

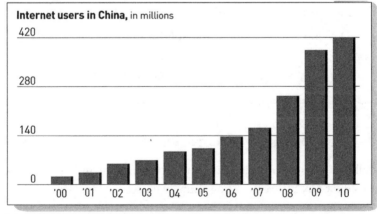

Internet users in China, in millions

420	
280	
140	
0	'00 '01 '02 '03 '04 '05 '06 '07 '08 '09 '10

Sources: Chinese government, Thomson Reuters

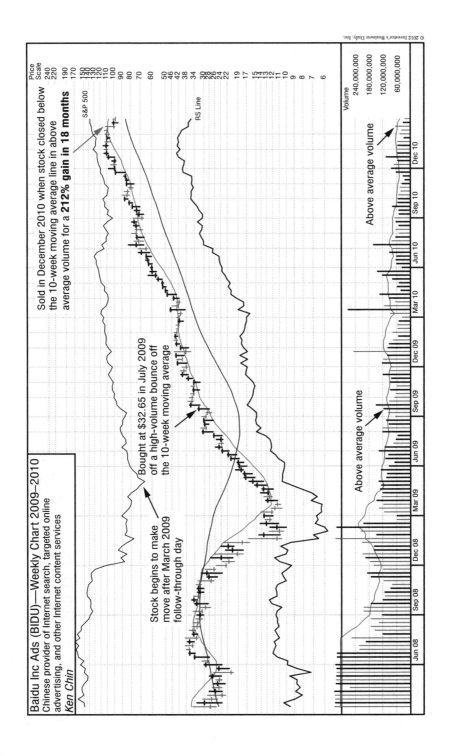

Baidu Inc Ads (BIDU)—Weekly Chart 2009–2010
Chinese provider of Internet search, targeted online
advertising, and other Internet content services
Ken Chin

Sold in December 2010 when stock closed below
the 10-week moving average line in above
average volume for a **212% gain in 18 months**

Bought at $32.65 in July 2009
off a high-volume bounce off
the 10-week moving average

Stock begins to make
move after March 2009
follow-through day

Above average volume

Above average volume

© 2012 Investor's Business Daily, Inc.

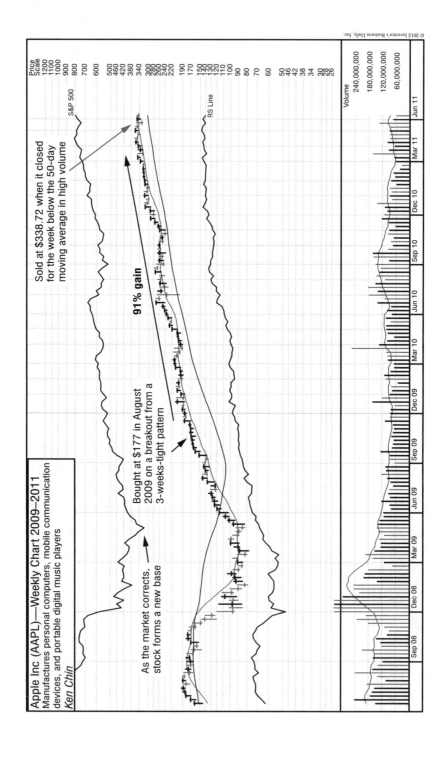

© 2012 Investor's Business Daily, Inc.

Apple Inc (AAPL)—Weekly Chart 2009–2011
Manufactures personal computers, mobile communication
devices, and portable digital music players
Ken Chin

Sold at $338.72 when it closed
for the week below the 50-day
moving average in high volume

91% gain

Bought at $177 in August
2009 on a breakout from a
3-weeks-tight pattern

As the market corrects,
stock forms a new base

S&P 500

RS Line

Price
Scale
1200
1100
1000
900
800
700
600
500
460
420
380
340
300
280
260
240
220
190
170
150
140
130
120
110
100
90
80
70
60
50
46
42
38
34
30
28
26

Volume
240,000,000
180,000,000
120,000,000
60,000,000

Sep 08 Dec 08 Mar 09 Jun 09 Sep 09 Dec 09 Mar 10 Jun 10 Sep 10 Dec 10 Mar 11 Jun 11 because as IBD research has shown, most stocks follow the direction of the general market and, as a result, investing in an uptrending market is the safest, easiest way to make money.

"Looking at a Nasdaq chart," he continues, "if you compare the price movements in early December 2011 with the previous few months, one could very easily see that things were getting quieter and less volatile. This told me that we were getting closer to a new uptrend and that the last quarter decline was nearing its end. On December 20, the market produced a follow-through day, and this indicated it was time to put our money to work."

Randall says, "Whole Foods Market moved strongly in step with the market. This stock had been a strong mover over the past year, but I felt it was ready to move again after a short consolidation. Whole Foods sells organic and natural foods to an educated consumer and has the "N" in CAN SLIM: the organic movement is something I believe to still be somewhat new to the mainstream consumer world. I had been watching it since September, when it made a new price high while the market was still near the bottom of its correction. And as I've learned from reading *How to Make Money in Stocks*, when a stock is making higher highs counter to the general market, it shows strength and could very well be a leader in the next market uptrend.

"Although it was too early to enter Whole Foods on December 20, since the stock was still completing its base pattern, I noticed that the price-volume relationship was starting to become much more tight and controlled compared to the previous few months. Volume was starting to dry up on the down days and subtly increasing on the up days. This is the type of action I like to see before a stock breaks out.

"On January 9, Whole Foods was within 1% of its high on the left side of the cup. Then the stock declined in low volume down to the 10-day moving average, which showed that institutional investors were holding onto their positions and not selling as the stock pulled back gently in price. Then, on January 17, Whole Foods broke out of its cup-with-handle base on volume that was 149% above average, and I bought the stock.

"The next week, the stock moved higher for a few days but then pulled back to the breakout price, which is common; 40% of stocks will pull back to the pivot. I wasn't worried since I saw that the pullback was orderly and on low volume (buy point). The stock gained 30% over the next 5 months and largely ignored the correction that the general market experienced in April, May, and June 2012.

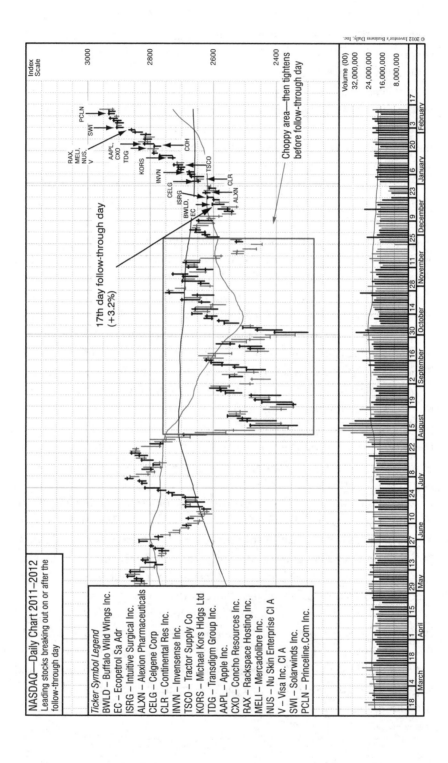

NASDAQ—Daily Chart 2011–2012
Leading stocks breaking out on or after the
follow-through day

Ticker Symbol Legend
BWLD – Buffalo Wild Wings Inc.
EC – Ecopetrol Sa Adr
ISRG – Intuitive Surgical Inc.
ALXN – Alexion Pharmaceuticals
CELG – Celgene Corp
CLR – Continental Res Inc.
INVN – Invensense Inc.
TSCO – Tractor Supply Co
KORS – Michael Kors Hldgs Ltd
TDG – Transdigm Group Inc.
AAPL – Apple Inc.
CXO – Concho Resources Inc.
RAX – Rackspace Hosting Inc.
MELI – Mercadolibre Inc.
NUS – Nu Skin Enterprise Cl A
V – Visa Inc. Cl A
SWI – Solarwinds Inc.
PCLN – Princeline.Com Inc.

17th day follow-through day
(+3.2%)

Choppy area—then tightens
before follow-through day

Index Scale

3000

2800

2600

2400

Volume (00)
32,000,000
24,000,000
16,000,000
8,000,000

© 2012 Investor's Business Daily, Inc.

"Everyone has a home run story to tell, but in the investing world, it's the singles and doubles that add up to real results consistently over time. To steadily make money in the market, you must stay focused on preserving capital and minimizing risk. Investing when the market tells you it wants to go up—and staying in cash when the market starts to give signs of a top—are the most important criteria to remain profitable over the long run."

• KEY POINTS •

- The most important part of investing is to determine the strength of the overall market. Read *The Big Picture* column daily.

- Investing in an uptrend is the easiest way to make money.

- Watch for stocks making new price highs counter to the general market; this shows strength.

- Search for stocks breaking out of base patterns or areas of consolidation after a new uptrend begins.

- Aim for singles and doubles for consistent results.

Using Leaderboard to Save Time

Kathleen Phillips likes Leaderboard, a streamlined list of IBD's top performing stocks, "because it focuses on current market leaders that are ready to break out from their base patterns. The Leaderboard charts are annotated, showing the base pattern and the buy point. This saves me a lot of time by focusing on the very best stocks in the market with top fundamental ratings. I have done very well with stocks from the Leaderboard list, including Baidu, LinkedIn, Monster Beverage, Rackspace Hosting, and Tractor Supply. Leaderboard saves me a lot of time, and I have a lot of confidence in the product because I know the top editorial staff at IBD picks stocks for the list."

Rackspace Hosting. 24% gain

Tractor Supply. 34% gain

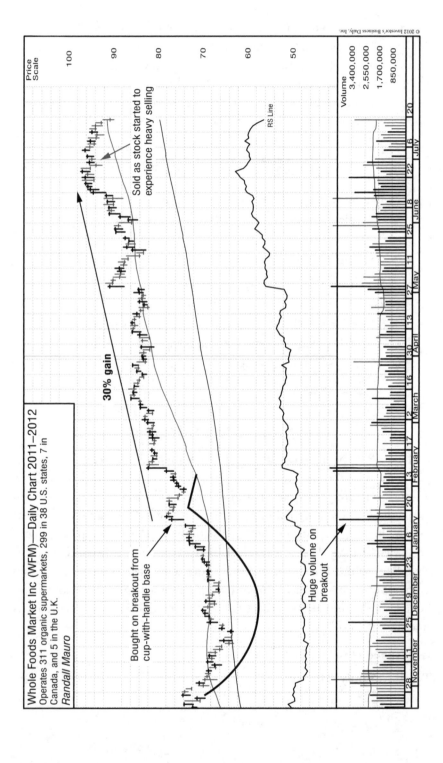

Whole Foods Market Inc (WFM)—Daily Chart 2011–2012
Operates 311 organic supermarkets, 299 in 38 U.S. states, 7 in
Canada, and 5 in the U.K.
Randall Mauro

30% gain

Sold as stock started to
experience heavy selling

Bought on breakout from
cup-with-handle base

Huge volume on
breakout

RS Line

Price
Scale

100

90

80

70

60

50

Volume
3,400,000
2,550,000
1,700,000
850,000

┌─────────── • KEY POINTS • ───────────┐

- Use Leaderboard to save time and find IBD's best performing stocks.
- Learn more about base patterns from Leaderboard's annotated charts.

└──────────────────────────────────────┘

Look for Fashion Trends and Fads

"Surfer Pat" Reardon started his investing adventure by picking up an IBD newspaper as an assignment for an Economics 101 class at a local community college. Pat said he had no idea how this assignment would impact and change his life.

His original goal was to take real estate and construction classes and begin a career "buying some fixer uppers, remodeling, and selling them."

Pat's curiosity about the stock market led him to read several books: *How to Make Money in Stocks*, by Bill O'Neil; *How I Made $2 Million in the Stock Market*, by Nicolas Darvas; and *Reminiscences of a Stock Operator*, by Edwin Lefevre. After reading these books, he completely changed his mind about wanting to go into construction. Pat decided he wanted to learn how to invest in stocks. And so he began investing.

"One of my early successes was with Skechers," he says. "Their company headquarters was in my hometown of Manhattan Beach. I saw moms and kids wearing the fashionable athletic shoes, so I checked the IBD Research Tables and saw that Skechers had top ratings. Then I looked at their chart and waited until the stock broke out of an area of consolidation on big volume. At the time, I was trading a very small amount of money, but I made 20%, and that got my attention. From then on, I was very excited about the possibilities to make money in the stock market.

"Another stock I found by paying attention to fads was Hansen's Natural, the makers of the Monster Energy Drink. The stock had big earnings and sales and was written about in several IBD articles. I saw institutional money with heavy volume on a chart going into the stock, and bought it."

Pat says his learning curve has been steady and gradual: "Going through several market cycles and gaining a better understanding of bull markets and the winners that appear in each new cycle helped me make some great profits in leading stocks.

Leaderboard Chart

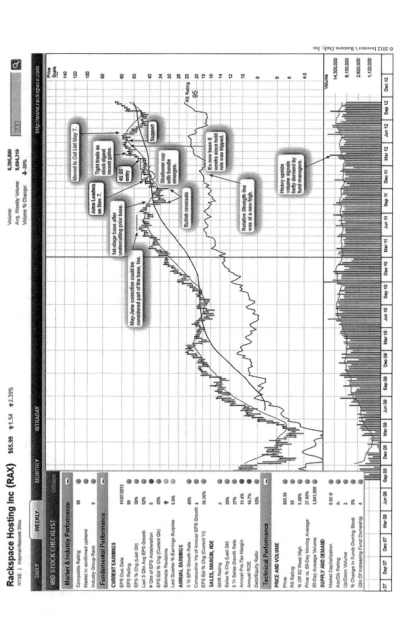

© 2012 Investor's Business Daily, Inc.

"My best trades were done when I bought correctly and sold because I did my homework and followed the rules."

Hansen's Natural. 156% + 33% gains (two separate buys)

NetEase. 100% + 60% gains (two separate buys)

• KEY POINTS •

- Look for fashion trends. What's new that everyone is wearing?
- Read books by legendary stock traders.
- Watch for food or drink fads.

Tune Out the News

Dave Whitmer is a U.S. Navy F/A-18 Fighter Pilot and TOPGUN graduate. He has been actively trading using the CAN SLIM System since 2000.

In March 2009, Dave was on the Aircraft Carrier USS John C. Stennis in the Western Pacific Ocean. "This allowed me to distance myself from all the news," he says. And much like legendary stock trader Nicolas Darvas, who was out of contact and away from the news while he traveled the world as a dancer in the 1950s, this would prove beneficial. Bill O'Neil also advocates tuning out the news and paying attention to what the market and leading stocks are actually doing.

Because of the ship's security network, Dave could not access Daily Graphs (now MarketSmith, a premium charting research tool and sister company to IBD) for research, so he had to rely on a good friend, John Mackel, to help him fill in the blanks when it came to chart analysis. Because he had such limited time and access to news, Dave wasn't influenced by media pundits who were saying the market would never turn around. Dave was interested in stocks that were showing strength and resilience despite the difficult market. He read about Green Mountain Coffee Roasters in *e*IBD™ (the digital version of IBD) and saw the stock setting up in a cup-with-handle base. Dave realized that as soon as the market turned around, Green Mountain Coffee Roasters would be a stock that he wanted to own.

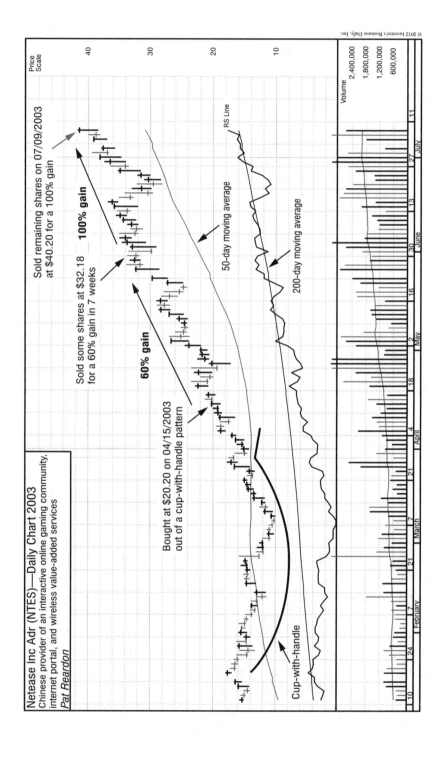

Netease Inc Adr (NTES)—Daily Chart 2003
Chinese provider of an interactive online gaming community,
internet portal, and wireless value-added services
Pat Reardon

Bought at $20.20 on 04/15/2003
out of a cup-with-handle pattern

Cup-with-handle

60% gain

Sold some shares at $32.18
for a 60% gain in 7 weeks

100% gain

Sold remaining shares on 07/09/2003
at $40.20 for a 100% gain

50-day moving average

200-day moving average

RS Line

Price
Scale

Volume

© 2012 Investor's Business Daily, Inc.

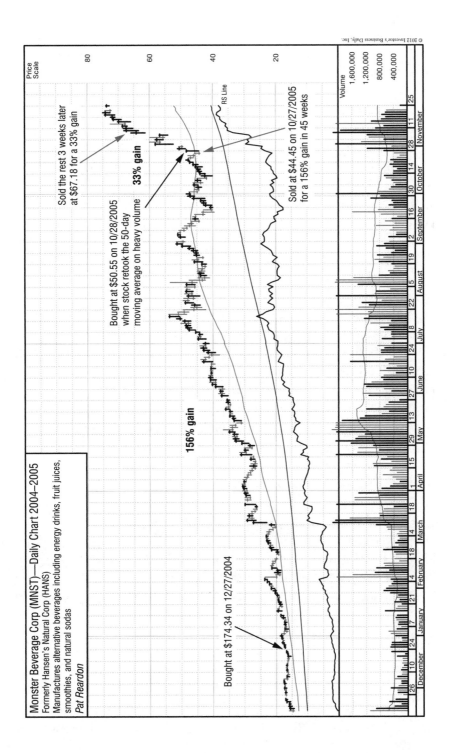

© 2012 Investor's Business Daily, Inc.

Monster Beverage Corp (MNST)—Daily Chart 2004–2005
Formerly Hansen's Natural Corp (HANS)
Manufactures alternative beverages including energy drinks, fruit juices, smoothies, and natural sodas
Pat Reardon

Sold the rest 3 weeks later at $67.18 for a 33% gain

Bought at $50.55 on 10/28/2005 when stock retook the 50-day moving average on heavy volume

33% gain

Sold at $44.45 on 10/27/2005 for a 156% gain in 45 weeks

156% gain

Bought at $174.34 on 12/27/2004

RS Line

Price Scale

80
60
40
20

Volume
1,600,000
1,200,000
800,000
400,000

The company had double digit earnings and sales growth as well as an innovative product, the Keurig Brewer, which makes individual cups of gourmet coffee. Dave bought the stock as it broke out of a classic cup-with-handle base pattern in March 2009, just as a new bull market was beginning.

"This was a very easy position to hold," he says. "Six weeks later, I was rewarded with a huge payoff. Along with a great earnings report, the company announced that their K-Cups would be available in Walmart prior to Mother's Day. The stock rocketed 37% on the announcement. Volume was 832% above average, showing enormous buying from professional investors.

"I hadn't faced a huge gap-up move when I already had an established position in a stock for a long time. I remember Charles Harris (portfolio manager for O'Neil Data Systems and instructor for IBD workshops) explaining in a seminar that one needs to hit the accelerator when you find a great stock." Dave says he likes to refer to it as "lighting the cans," which is fighter pilot terminology for igniting the afterburners. "So, due to the incredible gains made from the Walmart announcement to sell Green Mountain Coffee Roasters K-Cup products, I placed a market order to buy 25% more shares of the stock. By 11:30 p.m. that night, floating around on an aircraft carrier with a significant lag in the Internet, I realized that I had placed one of my best trades ever. Green Mountain Coffee Roasters closed that day 44% higher than the previous day."

Dave sat with Green Mountain till mid July, eventually closing out a gain of 78%. "I decided to exit the position due to a breach of the 10-week moving average," he says. "The stock recovered and went higher without me, but I was fine with locking in my gains."

• KEY POINTS •

- Tune out the news; pay attention to what the market and leading stocks are actually doing.
- Look for stocks setting up in a base while the market is in a correction.

Take Most Profits at 20 to 25%

Lee Tanner said he had a moment of clarity that significantly improved his trading after attending IBD's Level 4 workshop. The portfolio simulation

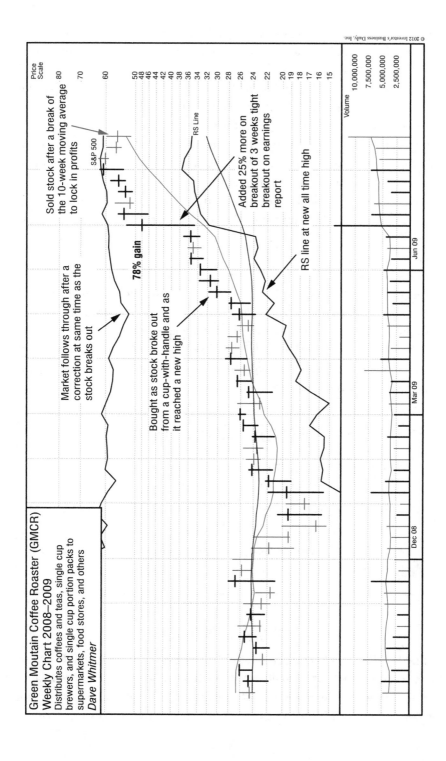

Green Moutain Coffee Roaster (GMCR)
Weekly Chart 2008–2009
Distributes coffees and teas, single cup brewers, and single cup portion packs to supermarkets, food stores, and others
Dave Whitmer

Market follows through after a correction at same time as the stock breaks out

Sold stock after a break of the 10-week moving average to lock in profits

78% gain

S&P 500

RS Line

Bought as stock broke out from a cup-with-handle and as it reached a new high

Added 25% more on breakout of 3 weeks tight

breakout on earnings report

RS line at new all time high

Price Scale
80
70
60
50
48
46
44
42
40
38
36
34
32
30
28
26
24
22
20
19
18
17
16
15

Volume
10,000,000
7,500,000
5,000,000
2,500,000

Jun 09

Mar 09

Dec 08

showed that most winning stocks should be sold after they are up 20 to 25%, because at that point, many stocks will pull back and form another base or area of consolidation or even top.

Lee tended to hold onto his stocks too long and gave back much of his gains prior to following this simple sell rule. Lee learned the only time you would hold onto a stock longer is if it makes a 20% move in 2 to 3 weeks after breaking out, in which case the stock must be held for at least 8 weeks. That's because market history shows that stocks like those tend to go on to make massive moves after moving higher so quickly.

One stock that evoked the 8-week hold rule for Lee was Crocs in 2007.

Lee says the market environment in recent years has not led to the "big trades" that previous markets offered, but he had a "barn burner" with Crocs in 2007, netting a gain of 140%.

Lee said he became aware of the stock because it appeared in an IBD *New America* article in October 2006. A few months after the stock made its IPO debut, it was mentioned in *The Big Picture* column and was a leader up in volume in the *Market Pulse* section of the paper.

"Before investing in the stock," says Lee, "I visited a local Macy's store and found that Crocs had its own special display section in the shoe department, so clearly the shoes were selling well."

• KEY POINTS •

- Sell most stocks for a 20 to 25% gain, unless they go up 20% in 2 to 3 weeks, in which case, hold for 8 weeks.
- Read *The New America* article to find potential winning IPOs.
- Visit a store and check out the merchandise a company is selling.

Learning to Profit from IPOs

In 2004, Mike Scott considered himself a "newbie" when it came to investing. He wanted to own Google but at the time didn't understand IPO bases, so he missed the September 2004 breakout. He bought the stock when it gapped up in April 2005. (A gap-up occurs when a stock makes a sharp move

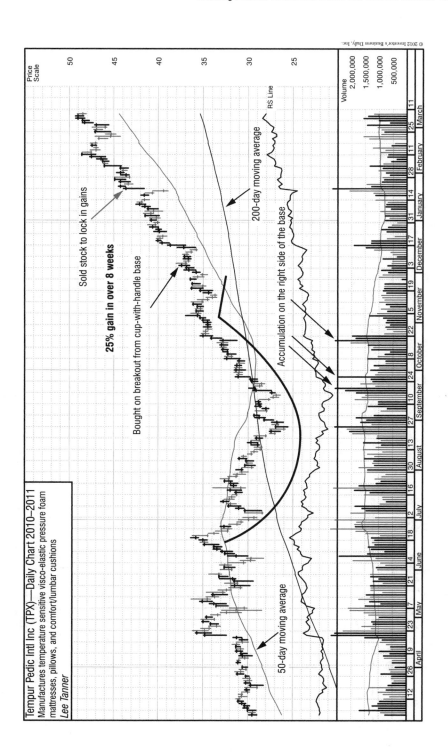

Tempur Pedic Intl Inc (TPX)—Daily Chart 2010–2011
Manufactures temperature sensitive visco-elastic pressure foam mattresses, pillows, and comfort/lumbar cushions
Lee Tanner

Sold stock to lock in gains

25% gain in over 8 weeks

Bought on breakout from cup-with-handle base

200-day moving average

Accumulation on the right side of the base

RS Line

50-day moving average

Price Scale

50
45
40
35
30
25

Volume
2,000,000
1,500,000
1,000,000
500,000

© 2012 Investor's Business Daily, Inc.

April May June July August September October November December January February March
12 26 9 23 7 21 4 18 2 16 30 13 27 10 24 8 22 5 19 3 17 31 14 28 11 25 11

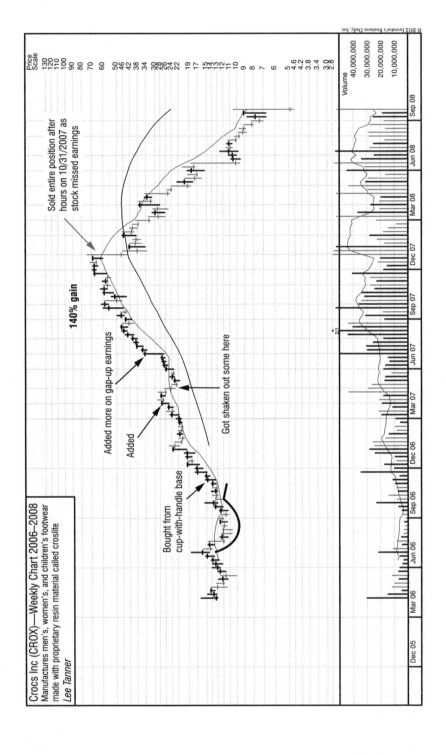

Crocs Inc (CROX)—Weekly Chart 2006–2008
Manufactures men's, women's, and children's footwear
made with proprietary resin material called croslite
Lee Tanner

140% gain

Sold entire position after
hours on 10/31/2007 as
stock missed earnings

Added more on gap-up earnings

Added

Got shaken out some here

Bought from
cup-with-handle base

up in price. The heavy buying that causes the gap in price is usually the result of a strong earnings report or other positive news.) "Buying gap-ups at that time was scary to me," says Mike. "Now I love them and often pay attention to stocks that gap up in price because I know that these stocks often end up going on to make big gains in the market."

Mike was able to learn from that mistake and made some nice gains in another IPO, Michael Kors. "Having subsequently learned how to buy an IPO base correctly from my Google experience," he says, "I didn't falter when it came to the Michael Kors IPO. I bought the stock on January 17, 2012, at $27.11. I had done my homework before the stock made its move and was waiting. Michael Kors was sponsored by three quality underwriters and had triple digit earnings and sales growth. The company's products were popular and widely sold in department stores such as Macy's. On January 17, Michael Kors had a gap-up, and I bought the stock. I added to my shares on three different occasions as the stock exhibited strength and moved higher, finally selling my position as the stock slid below the 10-day line for the first time in 8 weeks. I have learned that a stock that respects the 10-day moving average for a long time can be sold when it breaks that line." Mike had an overall gain of 74% in Kors.

• KEY POINTS •

- Watch for quality IPOs as they break out of their first base.
- Consider selling if a stock has stayed above the 10-day line during its run, then falls below it.

If You Have Big Profits from a Bull Market—
Sell if the Market Direction Changes

Anindo Majumdar was a software engineer for Cisco Systems in the mid-1990s. He said the company used to give employees stock options, so he became interested in seeing how the stock was performing. This was his first introduction to the stock market, and he viewed it as an exciting way to make some extra money.

Every 6 months or so, Cisco would give employees options, and since tech stocks were booming at the time, Anindo says it was pretty exciting to watch Cisco rocket higher.

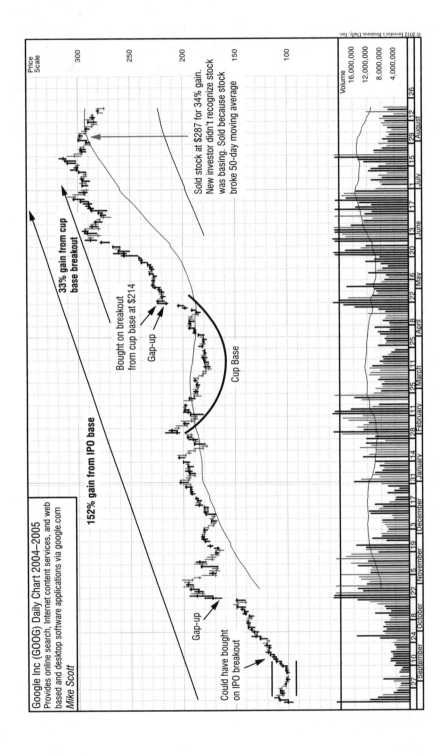

Google Inc (GOOG) Daily Chart 2004–2005
Provides online search, Internet content services, and web based and desktop software applications via google.com
Mike Scott

152% gain from IPO base

33% gain from cup base breakout

Bought on breakout from cup base at $214

Gap-up

Cup Base

Sold stock at $287 for 34% gain. New investor didn't recognize stock was basing. Sold because stock broke 50-day moving average

Gap-up

Could have bought on IPO breakout

Price Scale

© 2012 Investor's Business Daily, Inc.

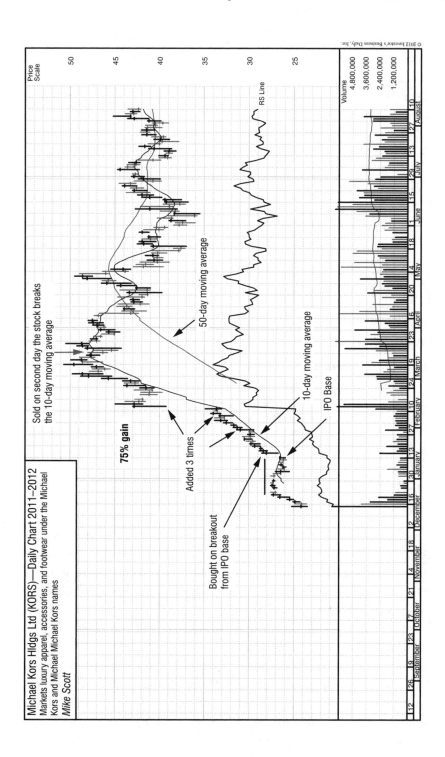

Michael Kors Hldgs Ltd (KORS)—Daily Chart 2011–2012
Markets luxury apparel, accessories, and footwear under the Michael
Kors and Michael Michael Kors names
Mike Scott

Sold on second day the stock breaks
the 10-day moving average

75% gain

50-day moving average

Added 3 times

Bought on breakout
from IPO base

10-day moving average

IPO Base

RS Line

Price
Scale

50

45

40

35

30

25

Volume
4,800,000
3,600,000
2,400,000
1,200,000

© 2012 Investor's Business Daily, Inc.

Anindo's wife saw the enormous gains in his account and urged him to take some money out of the market and buy a house. Fortunately, he listened.

In 2000, because Anindo had not yet really learned anything about investing or the CAN SLIM strategy, he says, "I lost the rest of my gains in Cisco because I did not have any sell rules as the market collapsed."

But because he was able to buy a house using the profits he made in Cisco, Anindo was interested in learning more about growth stock investing.

In 2003 and 2004, he attended several of IBD's advanced workshops and ended up making a lot of money in the market. "It cemented in my mind that this system works very well in a bull market and to always pay attention to the overall market trend," he says.

As a result of his studies, Anindo notched gains of:

Taser. 90%

Taser. 72%

Google. 31%

Intuitive Surgical. 27%

Hansen's Natural. 38%

• KEY POINT •

- Lock in big gains if the market direction changes.

Stay Focused

Tom Ellis says the only investing publication he reads is *Investor's Business Daily*. He doesn't subscribe to any other newsletter or service and isn't interested in what stocks other people own. "I also made a rule not to share with other investors what stocks I am invested in or how much," he says. "I have learned this lesson the hard way. When I listen to the news or other people's opinions, it causes me to make mistakes and not follow my plan. I begin to second guess my decisions."

Because of this intensity of focus, Tom is able to consistently make 20 to 25% gains in the market using only IBD and MarketSmith to find stocks.

On January 4, 2012, Tom noticed Continental Resources in IBD's *Stock Spotlight*. It was also featured in the paper's *Industry Themes* article.

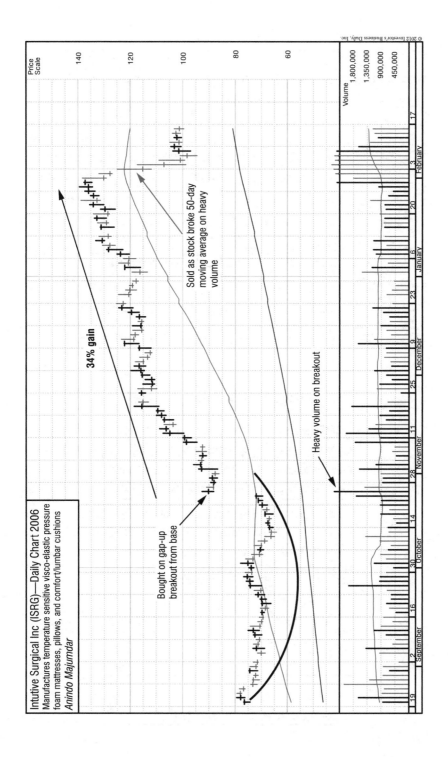

Intuitive Surgical Inc (ISRG)—Daily Chart 2006
Manufactures temperature sensitive visco-elastic pressure
foam mattresses, pillows, and comfort/lumbar cushions
Anindo Majumdar

34% gain

Sold as stock broke 50-day
moving average on heavy
volume

Bought on gap-up
breakout from base

Heavy volume on breakout

Price
Scale

140

120

100

80

60

Volume

1,800,000

1,350,000

900,000

450,000

B4 THURSDAY, JANUARY 5, 2012   **STOCK SPOTLIGHT**   INVESTORS.COM

Fracking Oils In Nice Spot, But Regulators Loom

BY PAUL WHITFIELD
INVESTOR'S BUSINESS DAILY

In the U.S. oil business nowadays, the optimistic camp rules.

At a Q3 earnings call in November, Continental Resources'[CLR] CEO Harold Hamm noted that "as they're saying in our business, the great oil fields keep getting better."

That's easy for Hamm to say because Continental has the largest acreage stake in the oil-rich Bakken region.

But the regulatory environment tempers the optimism. On Tuesday, the American Petroleum Institute slammed the Obama administration's energy policy as "on the wrong track" and "incoherent."

Recently, new regulations on fracking – a deep drilling method – emerged on the state level.

In mid-December, the Colorado Oil & Gas Conservation Commission reached a compromise on the disclosure of chemicals used in fracking. A lawyer for the oil industry called the compromise "workable." The rules take effect April 1.

Then on Tuesday, Arapahoe County commissioners backed off a plan to do its own regulating of the oil and gas industry. It will instead rely on Colorado's state agency. The last thing the oil industry wants is a plethora of rules from every local entity.

Continental's annual earnings have been strong but somewhat unstable. The five-year Earnings

Enlarged Stock Spotlight Chart

COMPANY XYZ (XYZ)   Group1   o$17.39

99 Comp. Rating 98EPS RS99 ROE8% 16.5M Shares

PROVIDES WEB-BASED TRAINING SERVICES FOR HEALTHCARE ORGANI-
ZATIONS AND PHARMACEUTICAL AND MEDICAL DEVICE COMPANIES

+25% Ann. EPS Gro   PE 62   Avg. Daily Vol 269,200   Debt 0%

Last Qtr Eps +100% ▲ Prior Qtr +33% ▼ Last Qtr Sales +24%

3 Qtrs EPS > 19%

Eps Due 2/22   15

R&D 11%   13

10

Acc/Dis 8+   8

Sup/Demand 75   6

APR   JUL   OCT   JAN 12

2250

750

That same day, the stock was added to Leaderboard, with a chart annotation showing a cup-with-handle base and a potential buy point of $73.08.

On January 5, Continental Resources broke out of its base pattern on volume that was 78% above average. Tom bought the stock and sold it 7 weeks later with a 25% gain.

Some of Tom's other successful trades in 2012 were

Select Comfort. 25% gain in 7 weeks

Herbalife. 25% gain in 11 weeks

Priceline. 25% gain in 5 weeks

• KEY POINTS •

- Don't get confused by reading too many different investing publications.
- Use IBD and MarketSmith to find winning stocks.

Celebrating Gains, Reviewing Mistakes

Townsend Baldwin began reading IBD in 2004 and was successful using the CAN SLIM Investing System to trade in and out of Nutrisystem, the maker of prepackaged diet products.

He first purchased Nutrisystem in July 2005 when he saw the stock hitting new price highs and sold when the stock made a 20% gain. Later that same year, after the stock came out of a cup-shaped base, Townsend bought Nutrisystem again, netting a 25% gain. He had enough capital invested in the stock to buy an apartment in New York City with the profits, so these two trades were very exciting and rewarding. But as Townsend looks back on the trades, he says he realizes that he missed out on even bigger gains. From his first purchase in July until the end of the year in 2005, Nutrisystem produced a 214% gain. Townsend had not yet learned how to handle a big winner.

From October 2004 through December 2005, Nutrisystem made a 2,100% move.

The company came public in 2000, but what was *new* about the company in 2004 and 2005, the "N" in CAN SLIM, was that Nutrisystem had *new* management and had found a *new* way to sell more of their products through heavy marketing, such as selling on the cable-shopping network QVC.

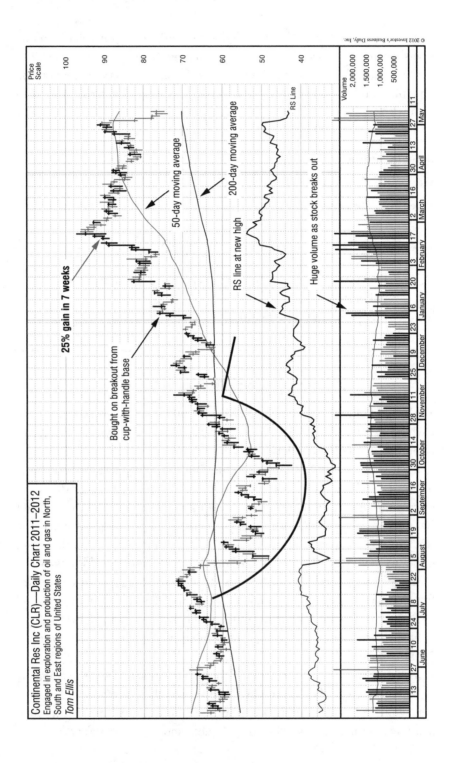

Continental Res Inc (CLR)—Daily Chart 2011–2012
Engaged in exploration and production of oil and gas in North,
South and East regions of United States
Tom Ellis

25% gain in 7 weeks

Bought on breakout from
cup-with-handle base

50-day moving average

200-day moving average

RS line at new high

Huge volume as stock breaks out

RS Line

Price
Scale

Volume

© 2012 Investor's Business Daily, Inc.

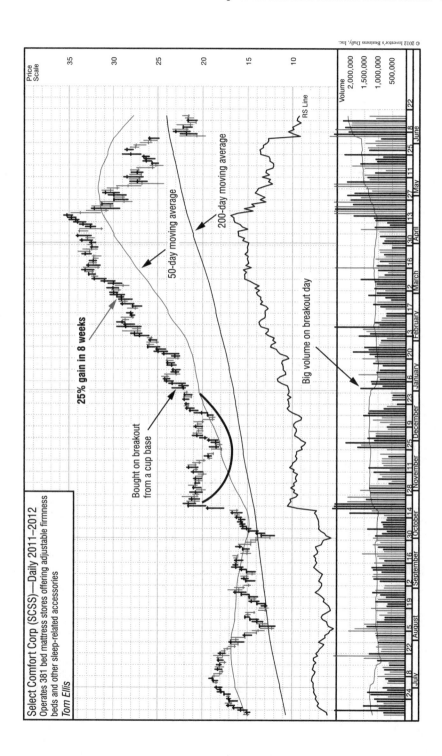

Select Comfort Corp (SCSS)—Daily 2011–2012
Operates 381 bed mattress stores offering adjustable firmness beds and other sleep-related accessories
Tom Ellis

Price Scale

35
30
25
20
15
10

25% gain in 8 weeks

50-day moving average

200-day moving average

RS Line

Bought on breakout from a cup base

Big volume on breakout day

Volume
2,000,000
1,500,000
1,000,000
500,000

© 2012 Investor's Business Daily, Inc.

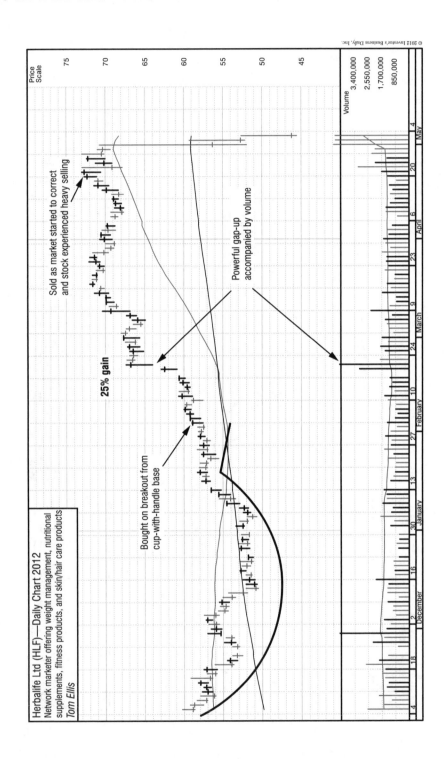

Herbalife Ltd (HLF)—Daily Chart 2012
Network marketer offering weight management, nutritional
supplements, fitness products, and skin/hair care products
Tom Ellis

Price
Scale

75
70
65
60
55
50
45

Volume 3,400,000
2,550,000
1,700,000
850,000

Sold as market started to correct
and stock experienced heavy selling

25% gain

Powerful gap-up
accompanied by volume

Bought on breakout from
cup-with-handle base

December   January   February   March   April   May

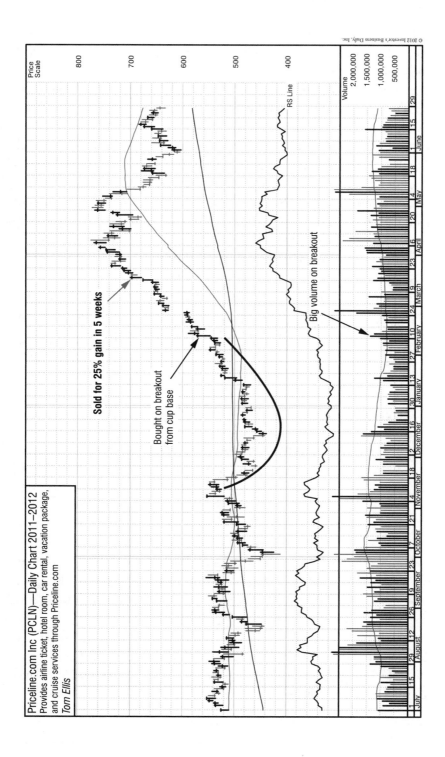

Priceline.com Inc (PCLN)—Daily Chart 2011–2012
Provides airline ticket, hotel room, car rental, vacation package,
and cruise services through Priceline.com
Tom Ellis

Sold for 25% gain in 5 weeks

Bought on breakout
from cup base

Big volume on breakout

RS Line

Price
Scale

800
700
600
500
400

Volume
2,000,000
1,500,000
1,000,000
500,000

© 2012 Investor's Business Daily, Inc.

This led to massive earnings acceleration and grabbed the attention of institutional investors, who bought shares of Nutrisystem, sending its stock price soaring.

In 2009, Townsend traded in and out of another stock, Baidu, which is the Google of China, netting gains of 40%, 15%, and 20%. Townsend said that reviewing his past trades gives him a chance to look at how he might have handled a stock differently. "Every trader makes mistakes," says Townsend, "but the most important thing I learned from my experience with Baidu was that I did not exercise the patience needed to pull out the 1,000% gain that the stock made. A CAN SLIM trader could have made those enormous gains with Baidu if one bought at the beginning of the new bull market in March 2009 and held onto the stock as it made its tenfold move. My plan is to find the super stocks of the future and capture the truly big moves that these stocks make, using the CAN SLIM strategy.

"If an investor embraces keeping losses small, lets winners run, and follows clear investing rules, then one can't help but be successful. Yet investing success takes hard work, understanding market psychology, and a willingness to study the overall market trend, but that's the easy part after one makes the commitment."

• KEY POINTS •

- Congratulate yourself on profitable trades.
- Review how you could have realized larger gains.

Treating Investing Like a Business

K. Basu was a "late bloomer to the dot.com rage" while he was in college. But he eventually started dabbling in the market and bought a stock that ran up 100% in a very short period of time. So he did what many young men would do: he took the profits and bought himself a car.

But when the tech bubble burst, he lost a lot of money in his account. At the time, he owned WorldCom, which eventually went bankrupt. He was very green and new to investing, so he didn't have sell rules in place when the stock began to collapse.

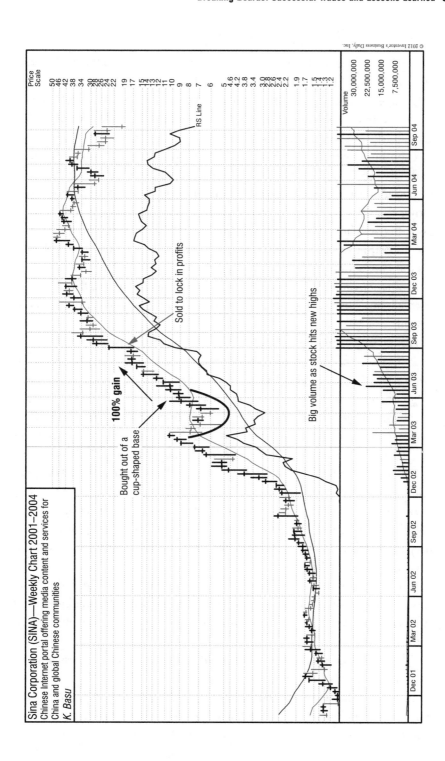

Sina Corporation (SINA)—Weekly Chart 2001–2004
Chinese Internet portal offering media content and services for
China and global Chinese communities
K. Basu

Bought out of a
cup-shaped base

100% gain

Sold to lock in profits

RS Line

Big volume as stock hits new highs

Price
Scale

Volume

Learning to Invest Enough Capital in a Big Winner

In 2002, a colleague at work introduced him to IBD and Bill O'Neil's book *How to Make Money in Stocks*. In 2003, he bought Sina Corp, a Chinese Internet gaming company, and made a 100% gain. K. Basu thought this was great; the only problem was, he didn't have a large enough position, so his actualized gains were relatively small.

Then he attended several advanced IBD workshops as well as the New York City IBD Meetup Group and met other like-minded investors who helped him learn how to follow the market every day, and how to be active rather than passive in the market. He considers this a turning point in his investing, and he is grateful for meeting some terrific people from that IBD Meetup Group that would become his mentors. They really helped change his thinking about his overall investing strategy.

From then on, K. Basu would treat investing more like a job than a hobby. He took investing more seriously and started doing better in the market as a result.

His advice to other investors is simple: wait for a follow-through day, and scale in slowly to see if the market is working or not. Then take most profits at 20 to 25%. "If you do those two simple things," he says, "your yearly returns will probably be 25 to 50% in a decent market."

In terms of follow-through days, K. Basu learned to see how stocks are working a week or two into the new uptrend. "If stocks are acting well and moving higher," he says, "then the follow-through day will probably work. But if stocks are faltering and not holding onto their breakout moves, the follow-through day will probably fail."

If the market is in a correction, he keeps it simple and looks at the *IBD 50* to see what the top 10 stocks are doing. Are they setting up in bases, preparing to break out, or stalling? It's a quick and easy way to gauge the health of the overall market.

K. Basu encourages other people who have a full-time job and says, "You can invest even if you're busy. Do your homework on the weekend, find stocks that are setting up, then put in your buy-stop orders on Sunday night with your brokerage firm.

"That way, your trades can be executed or sold when you're busy at work and you don't have to worry during the day."

"If you do the numbers and understand the value of compounding the gains that you make in the market, and you keep your losses small and follow the CAN SLIM rules, you can do extremely well over the long term."

```
┌─────────────────── • KEY POINTS • ────────────────────┐
```

- Treat investing like a business.
- Wait for a follow-through day, and then scale in slowly.
- Look at the *IBD 50*'s top 10 stocks during a correction to see if any are setting up in base patterns.
- Do homework over the weekend. Set trade triggers Sunday night through a brokerage account.

Paramjit Chumber

"I was living in England in the 1980s when Margaret Thatcher was the Prime Minister. At that time, a lot of the utility companies were being deregulated, and I did well investing with several of those companies as they began to become profitable. This was exciting and set a lifelong goal for me: I was going to become really good at investing no matter how long it took.

"In May 1999, I came to the U.S. but was busy getting settled and working a regular job, so I didn't become actively engaged in the markets until 2006. With my MBA background, I tried value investing, diversifying with 20 or more different stocks, bought some dividend stocks, and even tried to imitate some of the traders I saw on TV. I also tried options and swing trading. No matter which system I dabbled in, I watched my capital diminish."

"Through all of this, I realized you cannot rely on someone else's opinions; you must make your own decisions and be in control with a specific plan."

Paramjit became an IBD subscriber in July 2008, but this would prove to be a difficult time in the overall market.

He had a pivotal moment in 2011 when he saw Bill O'Neil speak to an IBD Meetup Group in Santa Monica, California. Bill mentioned Richard Wyckoff, a trader from the early 1900s who advocated controlling risks in any particular trade.

This changed Paramjit's outlook forever. He saw that trading needed to be treated like a business. From there, with his MBA background, he set forth a business plan with a set of rules that would include a monthly review of how he was doing.

He notes that sell rules are the most important and why it's critical not to get tied to a particular stock. "As the IBD saying goes, date the stock, don't marry it. If you don't think you can get something out of the transaction, you have no business going in."

Paramjit encourages other investors: "Don't feel embarrassed if the trade goes against you. It could be a lack of experience or problems in the overall market. Everyone makes mistakes. Keep losses small; if you're determined, you'll work through it. And remember to take most gains between 20 to 25%."

• KEY POINTS •

- Create an investing business plan and review trades on a monthly basis.
- Everyone makes mistakes. Keep losses small.

Have a Written Trading Plan

Steve Power has been an IBD subscriber since 2005. Although he understood the system and made money over the years, he's had ups and downs as a trader. The main thing Steve struggled with is that he felt the need to always be in the market. Now he realizes that there are windows of opportunity to capitalize on winning stocks, and there are periods of time when it is best to step to the sidelines.

Steve didn't really have a strong plan of action until his friend Tom Ellis, an experienced CAN SLIM investor, suggested that he write down a specific trading plan and stick to a regular routine. Steve is a Senior Representative for a multinational company, so most of his research is done on the weekends.

Steve's Weekend Routine

1. **Watch list.** This list includes approximately 10 to 30 leading stocks that have the best fundamentals, such as double- or triple-digit earnings growth, a high return on equity, and increasing revenue growth. If this stock list becomes unmanageable because there are too many stocks on it, create a second list for stocks that don't quite meet the top fundamental criteria.

2. **Buy list.** This is a list of 1 to 5 possible actionable stocks for the week. In some cases, buy triggers can be placed in advance of a breakout. In other

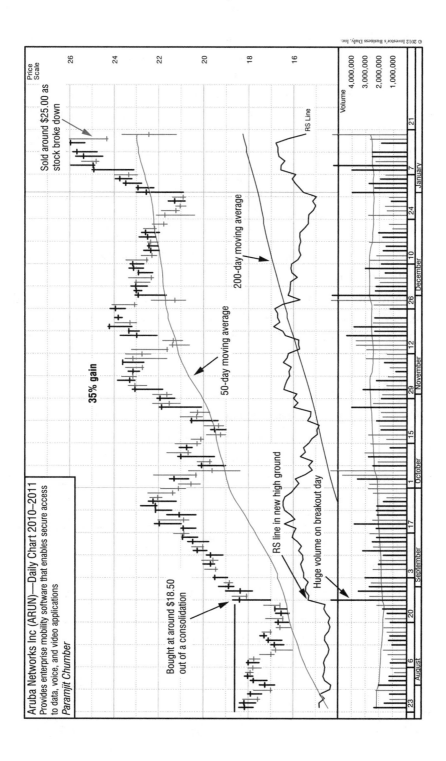

Aruba Networks Inc (ARUN)—Daily Chart 2010–2011
Provides enterprise mobility software that enables secure access
to data, voice, and video applications
Paramjit Chumber

Sold around $25.00 as
stock broke down

35% gain

50-day moving average

200-day moving average

RS line in new high ground

Huge volume on breakout day

Bought at around $18.50
out of a consolidation

RS Line

Price Scale

Volume

© 2012 Investor's Business Daily, Inc.

cases, the buy may be dependent on further base development. Try to keep at least one stock on this list. The most difficult thing is to keep this list small when a bull market is raging. Remember to streamline the list down to the very best stocks that you can find.

3. **Breakout list.** Keep track of stocks that break out from your watch list whether you bought them or not, and keep track of how they perform. This is a good indicator of overall market health.

4. **Stops.** Update stops (the price at which a stock would be sold if the trade doesn't work out, no more than 7 to 8% below the purchase price) on the spreadsheet weekly.

5. **New additions to watch list.** Download and review the *IBD 50* for new ideas twice a week. Run 1 to 2 MarketSmith screens looking for stocks with top earnings and sales.

6. **Maintain records.** Write in a market journal at least once a week and every time a trade is made. Record trades in a portfolio performance spreadsheet, and keep this updated to determine market exposure, risk, profits, and so on.

Steve's Daily Routine

1. Read *The Big Picture* column, and check the overall market trend.
2. Check stock lists (watch list, buy list, breakout list).
3. Record trades, and update portfolio of positions currently held.
4. Reprioritize the list with potential buy points if watch list stocks are preparing to break out.
5. Set buy or sell triggers with your broker if a new stock appears that you want to buy or if a stock that you own flashes a sell signal.
6. Read IBD articles for new ideas.
7. Write in a market journal every time a trade is made.

Steve says the system "works well when applied correctly. I try to make trading as mechanical as possible to take the emotions out of it."

From Running a Pension Fund to Individual Investing

In the 1960s, Kent Damon worked as a security analyst for First City National Bank of New York, now known as City Bank. After that, Kent was

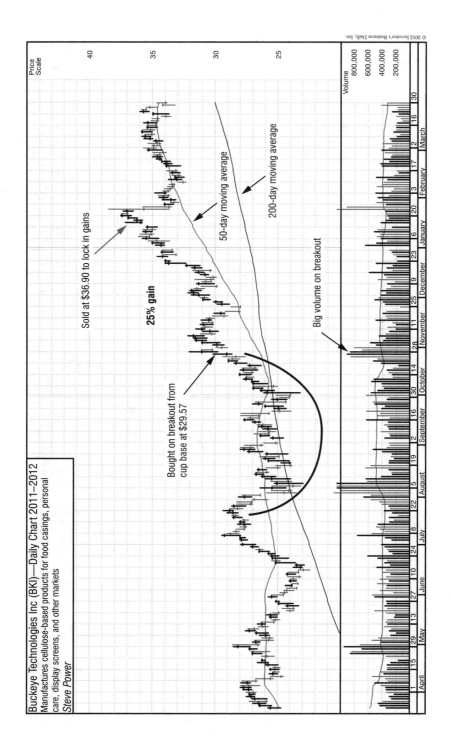

Buckeye Technologies Inc (BKI)—Daily Chart 2011–2012
Manufactures cellulose-based products for food casings, personal care, display screens, and other markets
Steve Power

Sold at $36.90 to lock in gains

25% gain

50-day moving average

200-day moving average

Bought on breakout from cup base at $29.57

Big volume on breakout

Price Scale

© 2012 Investor's Business Daily, Inc.

Volume

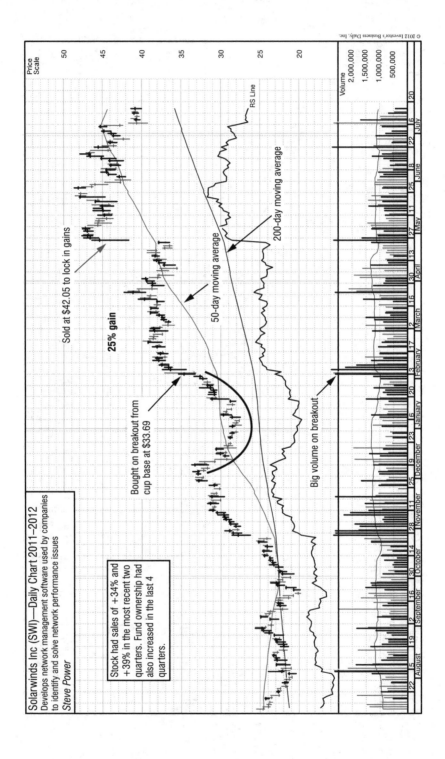

© 2012 Investor's Business Daily, Inc.

Solarwinds Inc (SWI)—Daily Chart 2011–2012
Develops network management software used by companies
to identify and solve network performance issues
Steve Power

Stock had sales of +34% and
+39% in the most recent two
quarters. Fund ownership had
also increased in the last 4
quarters.

Sold at $42.05 to lock in gains

25% gain

Bought on breakout from
cup base at $33.69

50-day moving average

200-day moving average

RS Line

Big volume on breakout

Price Scale

50

45

40

35

30

25

20

Volume
2,000,000
1,500,000
1,000,000
500,000

an oil analyst for six years before moving to Atlantic Richfield, where he was in charge of Investor Relations. In 1995, he joined Arco and was appointed senior vice president responsible for overseeing its pension fund and all of the fund's investments.

Kent had a team of 30 analysts working for him, each of whom was designated a different amount of money as portfolio managers depending on their level of experience and performance.

The fund bought mostly growth stocks and was guided by instructional lessons on chart reading by Bill O'Neil, who would talk to Kent's team from time to time and help them learn what traits to look for in the market's biggest leaders.

For five years in a row, from 1985 to 1990, Arco performed in the top 10% of all U.S. pension funds while following many of the CAN SLIM Investing strategies.

In 1993, Kent was named president of Arco Asia Pacific and relocated to Hong Kong, where he lived for many years.

He retired and returned to the United States in 2001 and began subscribing to IBD. Kent feels he has come full circle from being a young investor in the 1960s who bought big name growth stocks, to overseeing Arco's pension fund, back to individual investing using the CAN SLIM strategies.

Kent says he "relies very heavily on IBD's *Big Picture* column to stay in step with the overall market direction. IBD puts all of the market and stock information in an easy, useful form with all the fundamental data listed."

He tends to hold big winners if he has a cushion and the fundamentals are still strong. Kent is willing to hold a stock through a normal pullback provided that the chart doesn't show heavy institutional selling. He bought Apple in late 2010 and owned it through September 2012.

Kent helps other investors as the IBD Meetup leader in Montecito, California, and says going through the lessons "is helpful and reminds me to stick to the rules also."

• KEY POINT •

- Hold big winners if you have a cushion as long as the stock is going through a normal correction and isn't showing signs of heavy institutional selling.

Don't Be Too Hard on Yourself and Learn Patience

In 1995, Jahandar Kakvand was doing some engineering research in the library and ran across *How to Make Money In Stocks* by accident. He became an avid IBD reader after reading the book and, as a result of his success in the market, quit his engineering job and became a full-time investor in 1999.

He dispels some of the myths that surround investing, one myth being that it's just like gambling. "Individual investors have a tremendous advantage," he says. "They can move in and out of the market much faster than institutional investors, and if you take the right precautions and follow some simple rules, you can do very well.

"Accept the fact that you're going to make a lot of mistakes, particularly if you're new to investing. In the beginning, it's like a baby learning to walk. You have to try and try again, no matter how many times you fall down. Be patient with yourself. If you are making progress with your positions, hang in there.

"Some of the key things to remember are not to try and fight the market. You must respect the market trend above everything else."

Jahandar had success with Baidu in 2007. "Back in 2007, IBD had been writing about the stock many times, which brought it to my attention. I bought the stock at $132 in June 2007 and sold it in October 2007 at $320, when the stock had a big reversal day on high volume, netting a 142% gain."

• KEY POINTS •

- Accept the fact that you're going to make a lot of mistakes.
- Be patient with yourself.
- Don't try and fight the market trend.
- Read IBD articles to find winning stocks.

Find a Community of Like-Minded Investors

Jerry Powell heard Bill O'Neil speak at an IBD Meetup event in Anaheim in 2011 and said it made a significant impact on his trading. "Bill laid everything out in a very logical way that made sense to me."

The CAN SLIM rules are something that appealed to Jerry, and he learned the importance of going to cash if the market was in a downtrend. Jerry says he also learned why "the buy and hold strategy will kill you."

Jerry had been successful trading options but was concerned about his 401(k). When investing in his "nest egg for the future," he uses the paper and Investors.com to locate potential big winners and invests in CAN SLIM stocks.

Jerry has learned to keep his losses small and sticks to the 7 to 8% sell rule without fail.

He bought Apple shortly after the follow-though day on December 21, 2011, knowing the importance of buying stocks after a follow-through day in order to capture the moves of the best performing stocks. He bought Apple at $396 and sold April 11, 2012, at $624, logging in a gain of 57%.

His strategy is simple: follow the overall trend of the market by reading *The Big Picture* column in IBD daily, look for the market's biggest leaders through the many features found in IBD, and buy them as they break out of price consolidations. Take most profits at 20 to 25%, and stay in touch with other investors to help discuss the general market as well as leading stocks.

Jerry started a Facebook trading group as a way of sharing information with other like-minded investors. He says that trading is a very isolating thing. "It's easy to get too elated or down on yourself with your trades. You need to communicate with other people to stay balanced."

Jerry is also a member of the IBD Diamond Bar Meetup Group and says the quality of teaching and intelligent participation within the group has helped him solidify many of the CAN SLIM principles.

• KEY POINTS •

- Follow the overall market trend by reading *The Big Picture* column.
- Look for the market's biggest leaders through the many features in IBD.
- Join an IBD Meetup Group.

John Mackel

John is a lawyer and the leader of the Pasadena IBD Meetup Group, one of the most active IBD Meetups in the country. In order to keep the conversation going between monthly meetings, John formed a Google Group, which is basically a way for members to communicate with one another via e-mail through threaded conversations.

Meetup members can simultaneously e-mail everyone in the group and discuss the market or stocks. These e-mails get sent out to everyone in the group who opts to participate. John finds this a terrific way to update members about stocks that are breaking out or perhaps breaking down as well as answer questions from the group about stocks or the overall market. Other seasoned traders regularly contribute to the conversation to help newer investors engage and learn.

John also e-mails annotated charts of stocks that are setting up with comments concerning the stock's fundamentals or technical action. John says that teaching and helping other investors on a daily basis keeps him in touch with the market's current action as well as how the leaders are performing.

Before leading the IBD Pasadena Meetup group, John says he was "excited to find knowledgeable CAN SLIM traders at the Santa Monica IBD Meetup. During two years of attending these Meetups, I not only developed some great friendships but also honed my skills and increased confidence in my trading."

As a busy attorney, John says he sometimes misses a stock that is breaking out of a base pattern, but he realizes that a good stock will usually offer other entry points, like a pullback to the 10-week line. He also notes that in a good rally, there will usually be several quality stocks to buy, so if he misses one stock, there will be others breaking out. John usually owns no more than six stocks at a time and tries to narrow that down to the few that are performing the best.

"I find most of the stocks that I trade by reading IBD," he says. "As I'm reading through the paper, I keep MarketSmith open so I can study the chart of a stock that looks interesting."

John looks back fondly at the trade that got him excited about investing. "EMC, the computer data storage company, was my first big trade. When I look back, I realize how lucky I was to capture a 400% gain and yet how much I still had to learn.

"I first learned about the stock from an article in IBD and then met one of EMC's executives at a trade show who got me really excited about the company's growth potential.

"Not knowing much about sell rules, I didn't sell the stock as it topped in late 2000, but I had read in IBD that leaders were breaking down and distribution days were increasing, so when EMC dove below the 200-day moving average, I sold my entire position."

• KEY POINTS •

- Consider forming a Google group for e-mail discussions with other investors.
- Big winners will offer several entry points.

Switching Careers: Trading Full Time

Debra Kloote's father first got her interested in the stock market in the 1990s. She started out investing in mutual funds but by 1999 was investing in individual stocks. Although Debra had some success, she wasn't really following the market or stocks closely enough.

All of that changed when she found the Clearwater, Florida, IBD Meetup Group. She began attending the free monthly meetings and understood more about the paper and Investors.com. By this time, she was really ready to focus and learn.

In March 2011, an IBD Meetup leader from Naperville visited the Clearwater group and talked about switching careers. For years, Debra had been an accountant working in the corporate world, but she really wanted to spend more time trading and turn investing into a full-time job. This Meetup discussion made her realize that was a real possibility.

Later that year, Scott O'Neil, Bill O'Neil's son and president of MarketSmith, spoke to the Clearwater IBD Meetup Group and said something that really resonated with Debra: "Don't give the market your money unless it deserves it."

Debra attended some of IBD's advanced level workshops and began to do a post analysis of every trade she had made for the past three years. Doing this analysis really helped her learn where she needed to make improvements in her trading.

She wasn't upset with her past trades but looked at them as valuable learning experiences. She says, "Mistakes equal learning. Reviewing what I did wrong keeps me from making the same mistakes again."

Debra saw the market changing quickly in January 2012, and recognized the "window of opportunity was there with the beginning of a new uptrend.

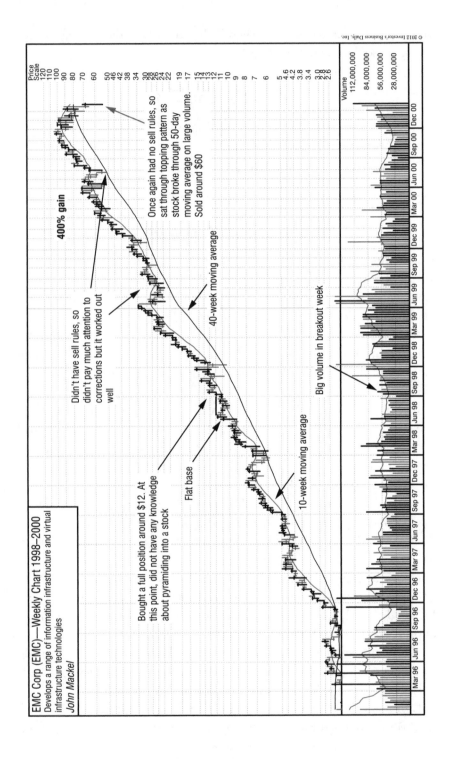

EMC Corp (EMC)—Weekly Chart 1998–2000
Develops a range of information infrastructure and virtual infrastructure technologies
John Mackel

Price Scale: 120, 110, 100, 90, 80, 70, 60, 50, 46, 42, 38, 34, 30, 28, 26, 24, 22, 19, 17, 15, 14, 13, 12, 11, 10, 9, 8, 7, 6

400% gain

Bought a full position around $12. At this point, did not have any knowledge about pyramiding into a stock

Flat base

Didn't have sell rules, so didn't pay much attention to corrections but it worked out well

Once again had no sell rules, so sat through topping pattern as stock broke through 50-day moving average on large volume. Sold around $60

40-week moving average

10-week moving average

Big volume in breakout week

Volume: 112,000,000, 84,000,000, 56,000,000, 28,000,000

5, 4.6, 4.2, 3.8, 3.4, 3.0, 2.8, 2.6

Mar 96, Jun 96, Sep 96, Dec 96, Mar 97, Jun 97, Sep 97, Dec 97, Mar 98, Jun 98, Sep 98, Dec 98, Mar 99, Jun 99, Sep 99, Dec 99, Mar 00, Jun 00, Sep 00, Dec 00

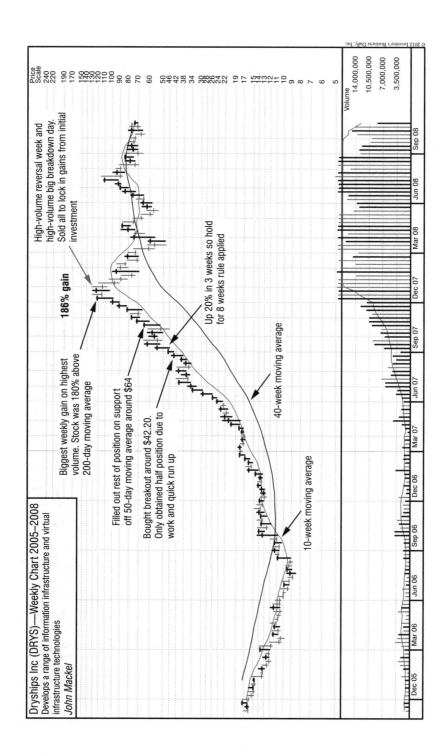

Dryships Inc (DRYS)—Weekly Chart 2005–2008
Develops a range of information infrastructure and virtual infrastructure technologies
John Mackel

High-volume reversal week and high-volume big breakdown day. Sold all to lock in gains from initial investment

Biggest weekly gain on highest volume. Stock was 180% above 200-day moving average

186% gain

Filled out rest of position on support off 50-day moving average around $64

Bought breakout around $42.20. Only obtained half position due to work and quick run up

Up 20% in 3 weeks so hold for 8 weeks rule applied

40-week moving average

10-week moving average

Price Scale
240
220
190
170
150
140
130
120
110
100
90
80
70
60
50
46
42
38
34
30
28
26
24
22
19
17
15
14
13
12
11
10
9
8
7
6
5

Volume
14,000,000
10,500,000
7,000,000
3,500,000

Dec 05 Mar 06 Jun 06 Sep 06 Dec 06 Mar 07 Jun 07 Sep 07 Dec 07 Mar 08 Jun 08 Sep 08

© 2012 Investor's Business Daily, Inc.

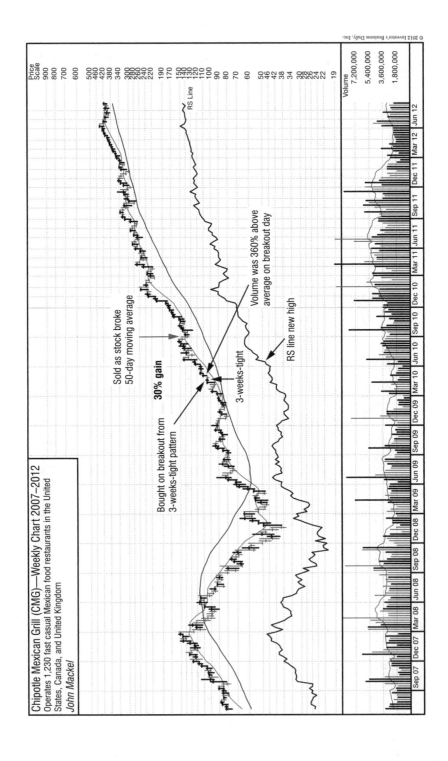

Chipotle Mexican Grill (CMG)—Weekly Chart 2007–2012
Operates 1,230 fast casual Mexican food restaurants in the United States, Canada, and United Kingdom
John Mackel

Sold as stock broke 50-day moving average

Bought on breakout from 3-weeks-tight pattern

30% gain

3-weeks-tight

Volume was 360% above average on breakout day

RS line new high

RS Line

You must be ready to take advantage of leading stocks as they are breaking out, and the overall market is acting strong." Debra started her journey of being a full-time investor.

She logged gains of:

Tractor Supply. 23% in 11 weeks

Apple. 33% in 13 weeks

MasterCard. 21% in 11 weeks

• KEY POINTS •

- Do a post analysis of trades, and find ways to improve.
- Always be ready for a new uptrend so you can capitalize on stocks that break out as a result.

Learning to Capture the Big Winners

Jeff Heimstaedt was in his senior year at Pepperdine University in Malibu when a fraternity brother invited him to his parent's home for dinner. Jeff met a successful stock broker at the dinner who described the stock market as a great place for someone young to make money, if they were willing to work hard. The financial possibilities and the intellectual challenge appealed to Jeff, so shortly after college, he got a job with Merrill Lynch.

He became aware of IBD through a co-worker and read *How to Make Money in Stocks*, which introduced him to a fact-based investing system that made sense. Jeff said as well as reading the paper on a regular basis, he started subscribing to Daily Graphs (now MarketSmith) and would pick the chart book up at noon every Saturday as a way to find companies that were setting up in base patterns. "At the time," he said, "there was no Internet, and very few charting services were around, so Daily Graphs was extraordinary."

From 1998 to 1999, Jeff was buying a lot of the "hot" tech stocks like Yahoo as they broke out of price consolidations. His overall strategy was to buy stocks at the pivot, but if the trade went against him more than a point or two, he would sell them.

From January 1998 until February 2000, a period of 26 months, Jeff's account increased over 750%.

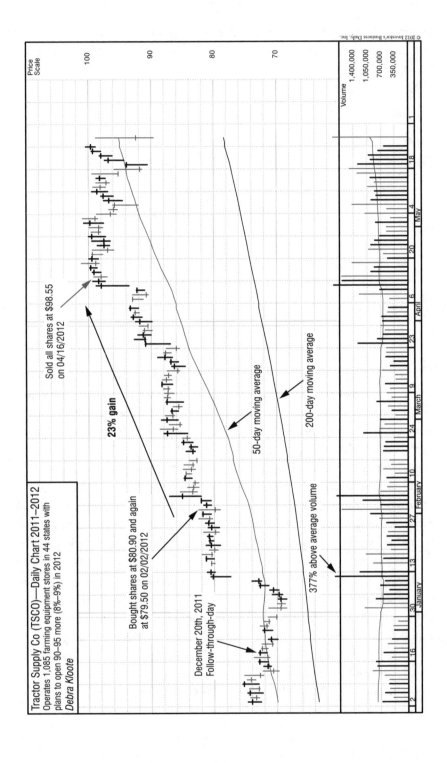

© 2012 Investor's Business Daily, Inc.

Tractor Supply Co (TSCO)—Daily Chart 2011–2012
Operates 1,085 farming equipment stores in 44 states with
plans to open 90–95 more (8%–9%) in 2012
Debra Kloote

Sold all shares at $98.55
on 04/16/2012

23% gain

Bought shares at $80.90 and again
at $79.50 on 02/02/2012

December 20th, 2011
Follow-through-day

50-day moving average

200-day moving average

377% above average volume

Price Scale

Volume

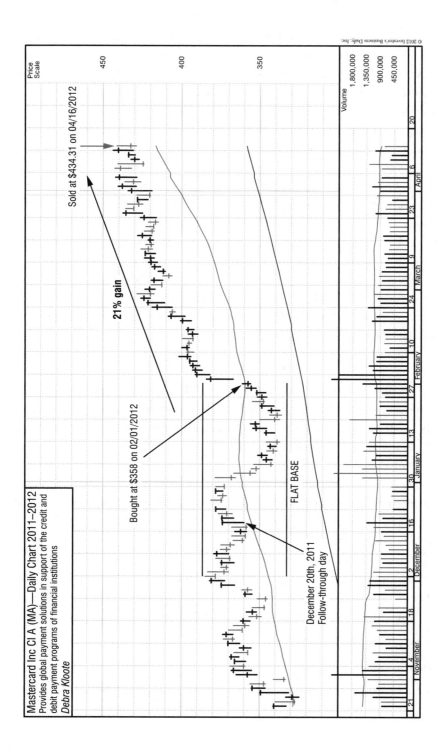

Mastercard Inc Cl A (MA)—Daily Chart 2011–2012
Provides global payment solutions in support of the credit and
debit payment programs of financial institutions
Debra Kloote

Sold at $434.31 on 04/16/2012

21% gain

Bought at $358 on 02/01/2012

FLAT BASE

December 20th, 2011
Follow-through day

Price
Scale

450

400

350

Volume

1,800,000
1,350,000
900,000
450,000

© 2012 Investor's Business Daily, Inc.

Jeff's daily routine starts the night before, when he reads through eIBD, the digital version of the paper. He looks for ideas and focuses on companies that are different and stand out. He is very focused on the "N" in CAN SLIM and prefers newer companies with products or services that are in big demand by consumers.

During the trading session, Jeff uses a MarketSmith screen to track stocks that are up on volume and determines whether any of these stocks warrant immediate attention if they are breaking out of bases. On days when the market is in an uptrend but opens lower, he likes to see which stocks can buck the trend and turn up first. This has helped Jeff find several winners over the years.

As Jeff reflects on his learning curve as an investor, he mentions the first IBD workshop that he attended in 1990, and what an impact it made on him as well as how much it helped his trading. Through the years, Jeff has attended all of IBD's advanced workshops and says, "There have been so many important things that I have learned. Each workshop has its gems—the take home lessons—and I continue to learn."

"One of the biggest things I know now is that I did not exploit the big winners that came out of the 1980s and 1990s, such as Cisco Systems, Microsoft, Intel, Dell, and Home Depot. These were the change-your-life type of stocks, and although I netted some nice gains in the tech boom of the 1990s, I was too inexperienced as an investor to understand how to hold these stocks and capture their massive gains.

"But I am excited, because I believe that we are on the cusp of another secular bull market. Bill O'Neil and Chris Gessel discussed this possibility during a webinar in August 2012. I'm trying to adapt my trading style so that I can truly exploit the big stocks that will make enormous gains when this new era happens.

"I have been able to handle Apple reasonably well over the past three years, pyramiding my original position to over five times my initial purchase."

Some of Jeff's biggest winners over the years:

Crocs. 2007: 223% gain

Baidu. 2007: 61% gain

Apple. 2009–2012 (still holding the position mid-September): 444% gain

<hr>

• KEY POINTS •

- During the trading session, look for stocks moving up on unusual volume using a MarketSmith screen or by checking *Stocks on the Move* at Investors.com.
- Focus on the "N" in CAN SLIM, newer companies with products or services that are in big demand by consumers.

Using IBD to Trade Options

Dave Whitmer

Friday, June 29, 2007, Dave was standing in line for an iPhone. He purchased one of the last ones in a mall on the outskirts of Pittsburgh. "It was the first Apple product that I had ever bought," Dave says. "I spent the entire weekend playing with it and could not believe how much better it was than the hype. I had the luxury of having Navy friends all over the country, and they told me that there were lines around the block at every Apple store. Because of my understanding of the 'N' in CAN SLIM, I knew that high demand for the iPhone would drive Apple's earnings and sales higher and create institutional demand for the stock. So I decided to buy Apple July call options at the open on Monday for $1.20 a share on its pullback to the 21-day moving average. I closed out the option position at $9.00 per share as the stock went over $140 in price. This was a 750% gain in just two and a half weeks. Conviction in the product gave me the confidence to execute this trade."

Jeannie McGrew

Jeannie reads IBD's *Big Picture* column every day to make sure she stays in sync with the overall market trend. In December 2011, when the market began a new uptrend, Jeannie waited to see if the follow-through day would work and leading stocks were breaking out of sound base patterns. In January 2012, when she observed that the overall trend was acting strong and leading stocks were holding onto their gains, she bought SPY calls. Jeannie started off with $300,000 in her account and increased it to $410,000 in less than three months for a 36% gain. She says, "The most important thing is to manage your risks and keep your losses small."

• KEY POINTS •

- The *Big Picture* column is a great way of understanding the market's current trend.
- Use *Stocks on the Move* at Investors.com and in IBD to find stocks that are rising or falling on unusual volume for various options strategies.

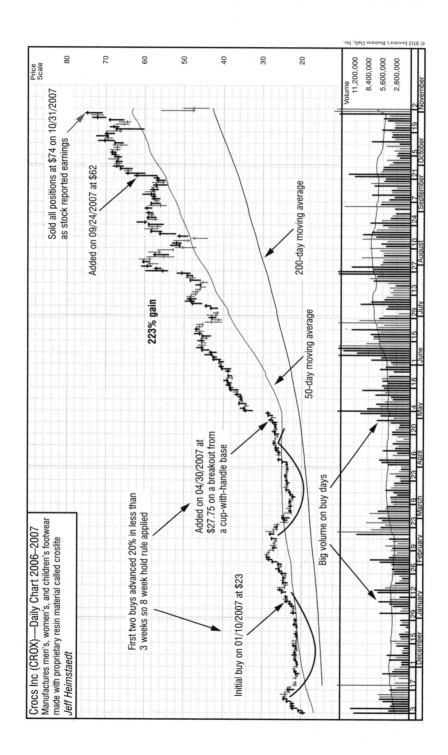

Crocs Inc (CROX)—Daily Chart 2006–2007
Manufactures men's, women's, and children's footwear
made with proprietary resin material called croslite
Jeff Heimstaedt

Sold all positions at $74 on 10/31/2007
as stock reported earnings

Added on 09/24/2007 at $62

223% gain

200-day moving average

50-day moving average

First two buys advanced 20% in less than
3 weeks so 8 week hold rule applied

Added on 04/30/2007 at
$27.75 on a breakout from
a cup-with-handle base

Big volume on buy days

Initial buy on 01/10/2007 at $23

Price
Scale

80
70
60
50
40
30
20

Volume
11,200,000
8,400,000
5,600,000
2,800,000

© 2012 Investor's Business Daily, Inc.

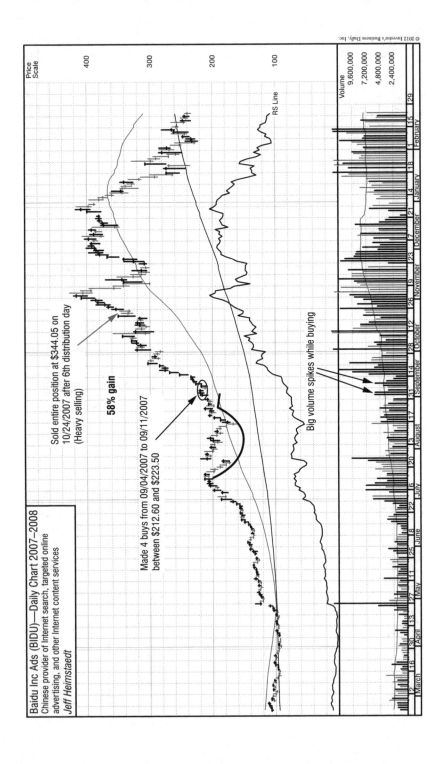

Baidu Inc Ads (BIDU)—Daily Chart 2007–2008
Chinese provider of Internet search, targeted online
advertising, and other Internet content services
Jeff Heimstaedt

Sold entire position at $344.05 on
10/24/2007 after 6th distribution day
(Heavy selling)

58% gain

Made 4 buys from 09/04/2007 to 09/11/2007
between $212.60 and $223.50

Big volume spikes while buying

RS Line

Price Scale

400
300
200
100

Volume
9,600,000
7,200,000
4,800,000
2,400,000

© 2012 Investor's Business Daily, Inc.

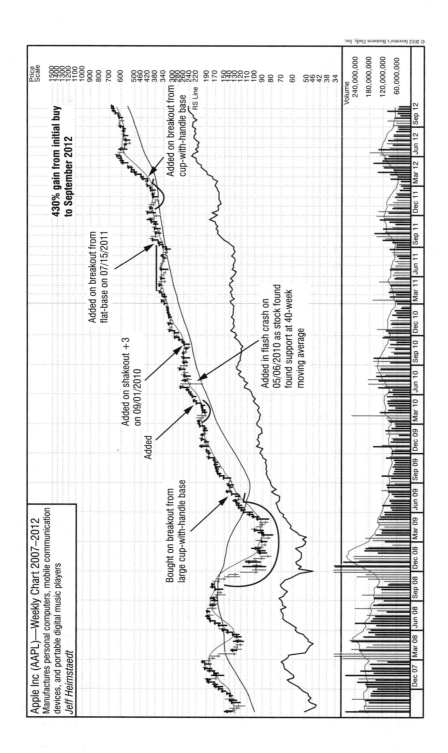

Apple Inc (AAPL)—Weekly Chart 2007–2012
Manufactures personal computers, mobile communication devices, and portable digital music players
Jeff Heimstaedt

430% gain from initial buy to September 2012

Added on breakout from flat-base on 07/15/2011

Added on breakout from cup-with-handle base

RS Line

Added on shakeout +3 on 09/01/2010

Added

Added in flash crash on 05/06/2010 as stock found support at 40-week moving average

Bought on breakout from large cup-with-handle base

Price Scale
1500
1300
1200
1100
1000
900
800
700
600
500
460
420
380
340
300
280
260
240
220
190
170
150
140
130
120
110
100
90
80
70
60
50
46
42
38
34

Volume
240,000,000
180,000,000
120,000,000
60,000,000

Dec 07 Mar 08 Jun 08 Sep 08 Dec 08 Mar 09 Jun 09 Sep 09 Dec 09 Mar 10 Jun 10 Sep 10 Dec 10 Mar 11 Jun 11 Sep 11 Dec 11 Mar 12 Jun 12 Sep 12

Black Belt Testing: Life-Changing Moments in Investing

"No matter how tall the mountain, it cannot block the sun."

— CHINESE PROVERB

There is an ancient fable about a Zen master who was out for a walk with one of his students and pointed out a fox chasing a rabbit. The master said, "The rabbit will get away from the fox." "Not so," replied the student. The master insisted, "The fox is faster, but the rabbit will elude him." When the student asked why, the master replied, "Because the fox is running for his dinner, while the rabbit is running for his life."

Barbara James

Barbara had been following IBD and investing for several years when she suddenly lost her husband of 30 years to a heart attack. A year and a half later, she was laid off from a major corporation where she was an executive secretary. Barbara was nearing retirement and thought it was unlikely that she would be hired at the income level she had been receiving. She also knew Social Security would never take care of her financial needs.

An Uptrending Market and Focusing on the Rules Pays Off

Knowing she would be laid off from her job in 2004, Barbara paid off her house and car loans using the extraordinary profits she had made from trades during the booming 1990s: 1,300% in EMC, 200% in Gap, 254% in Oracle, 235% in Intel, and 44% in Cisco.

Though she went through a very difficult emotional period after losing her husband and being laid off from her job so soon afterward, Barbara has advice for investors facing similar challenges. "Have self-confidence in your own abilities," she says, "but you must study, and you must learn to read charts. Chart reading is a visual art. What do you see? What is the chart telling you? Then act accordingly. You also have to let the overall market trend be your guide as to whether it is a good time to be in stocks or not." Barbara modestly adds that she had no financial background whatsoever. "I sold real estate and was a secretary, so if I can become a successful investor, anyone can."

Barbara says she learned the most from the IBD workshops, which she has attended regularly throughout the years, and always walks away having learned something new: "It is the continual process of learning that is so beneficial. And the paper is also full, every day, with educational materials to help people become better investors and better chart readers."

A Good Routine Can Be Profitable

Barbara follows a solid routine every morning, and this assures her that she won't miss a market leader as it's breaking out.

1. In the pre-market, Barbara checks *The Big Picture* column and the *Market Pulse* to see if the market is in an uptrend or a downtrend. Barbara circles leaders that are up in volume from this section and adds them to her watch list.

2. Next, she runs two MarketSmith screens.

   a. The first screen that Barbara runs is the William J. O'Neil screen, which brings up stocks with the CAN SLIM criteria. Barbara clicks through the charts that appear on this list to see which ones may be setting up and nearing a potential buy point.

b. Then she runs a screen for stocks up on big volume because this tracks what the institutional investors are buying.

3. Barbara then reviews Leaderboard and finds the list saves her time because "it's a very focused list of the market's current leaders."

4. Finally, Barbara looks at *Stocks on the Move* at Investors.com, another screen that highlights stocks that are rising or falling in heavy volume, showing where institutional money is flowing.

What Barbara is looking for are stocks that show up on several of these different lists. That might be an indication that she has found a stock that could make a big move.

Barbara says, "The key is creating a routine that works for you, something you will continue to do on a consistent basis, every day." Part of her routine also includes a morning phone call with a trading buddy. They talk about the general market together and look through charts in search of breakouts.

Barbara does best in the market when closely following the CAN SLIM rules and takes most profits at 20 to 25% and cuts every loss at 7 to 8% from her buy point. In a more volatile market, she will cut losses at 5 to 6%.

In 2009, Barbara had profits of:

Fuqi International (FUQI). 42%

Green Mountain Coffee Roasters (GMCR). 21%

F5 Networks (FFIV). 15%

Silver Wheaton Corp. (SLW). 39%

SPDR Gold Shares (GLD). 17%

and, in 2010, profits of:

NetApp (NTAP). 21%

SanDisk Corp. (SNDK). 27%

In Earnings Season, Always Know Your Stock's Release Date

That same year, Barbara admits to having a "favorite pet stock" with F5 Networks (FFIV) and bought the stock three times. In April, she sold for a profit of 12% and in November for a profit of 22%.

But the third time for F5 Networks was not the charm. Barbara broke one of her rules and bought the stock right before earnings. F5's earnings disappointed expectations, and the stock dropped 26%. She said it was a stinging reminder to never buy stocks right before earnings because anything can happen. A stock can soar on good earnings or dive precipitously on disappointments. Barbara had let a nice gain in F5 Networks evaporate. She states that because she had done well with the stock previously, it caused her to not be as diligent as she usually is in writing down earnings dates for stocks that she owns.

One of Barbara's greatest joys is in helping newer investors. She works part time for IBD at the many Money Shows that are held throughout the year. Barbara sits down one-on-one with attendees and goes over her routine to find winning stocks as well as showing people how to use the paper more effectively. Barbara feels she is helping women and retired investors who are worried about their financial situation as they grow older. Sadly, she has heard many heartbreaking stories from people who did not have a sell rule and suffered devastating losses of 40 to 50% in their retirement savings.

Barbara relates her own story and how she overcame financial challenges and encourages them to learn the CAN SLIM strategy to help them change their lives for the better.

Barbara says, "I manage my own stock portfolio accounts, both my main trading and IRA accounts. There was a pretty big learning curve involved that went beyond studying and learning to read charts. The biggest obstacle I had to overcome was developing self-confidence in my abilities. My success in these accounts has without question proven that I am capable of managing my own money better than any stock broker or financial money manager that I had tried. This was a major breakthrough in my thinking process. Any time I handed my account over to a money manager, they did not do nearly as well as I did. I can now say no one will manage my money better than I will."

Her stock market profits pay for annual month-long trips to exotic locations around the world. She has traveled to India, Asia, Costa Rica, Africa, Australia, New Zealand, and Eastern Europe, among other places.

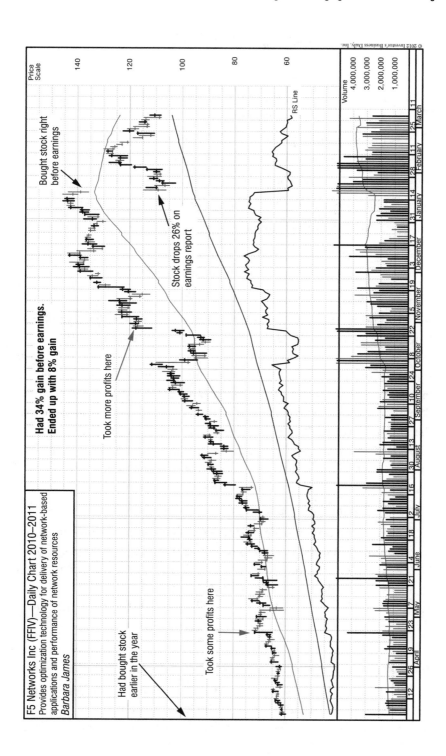

F5 Networks Inc (FFIV)—Daily Chart 2010–2011
Provides optimization technology for delivery of network-based
applications and performance of network resources
Barbara James

**Had 34% gain before earnings.
Ended up with 8% gain**

Bought stock right
before earnings

Took more profits here

Stock drops 26% on
earnings report

Had bought stock
earlier in the year

Took some profits here

RS Line

Price
Scale

140

120

100

80

60

Volume

4,000,000
3,000,000
2,000,000
1,000,000

© 2012 Investor's Business Daily, Inc.

March February January December November October September August July June May April March

---

• KEY POINTS •

- Learn to read charts.
- Let the overall market trend be your guide, whether it's a good time to be in stocks or not.
- Follow a daily routine to stay in sync with the market and leading stocks.
- Take most profits at 20 to 25%.
- Cut every loss 7 to 8% from the price paid for the stock.
- Never buy stocks right before earnings.

Jerry Samet

Jerry had been a professional investor in the stock market for several years before coming across the CAN SLIM Investing System. After the crash of 1987, which left many investors stunned, a friend handed Jerry a copy of *Investor's Business Daily*. After seeing the quality of the paper and the information that was in it, Jerry bought *How to Make Money in Stocks* and devoured the book. Suddenly, a lot of things made sense about the market that he had never realized before, even as a professional trader.

By the time the bull market of 1991 started, Jerry formed an investment firm with a partner and began to experience tremendous gains using the system.

A Stock That Triples in Price Can Still Go Up

Jerry had his first eye-opening experience with growth stock investing when he bought ECI Telecommunications. The stock had already tripled in price before he bought it in August 1991. Jerry sold ECI in March 1992 for a gain of nearly 200%. Before he learned CAN SLIM Investing, Jerry "thought anyone would be crazy to buy a stock that had already tripled in price *before* they bought it."

The Unexpected

In 1992, Jerry found himself in a very difficult and stressful situation. His partner had died of a heart attack, leaving him the burden of managing $10 million by himself. Jerry says he was never really the corporate type. Addressing questions or concerns from clients at all hours of the day was something he found increasingly difficult because it disrupted the trading day. Besides, it was psychologically draining. Some of his clients wanted to be in the market all the time, even if the environment wasn't right. By 1994, Jerry made the decision to stop managing money professionally and returned all of the money to his investors. But by this point, he also had enough confidence in the system from several successful trades to begin investing his own money full time.

Lessons from the Trenches

In October 1999, Jerry bought Qlogic (QLGC) and made 150%. He could have increased his profit even more but sold too late after the stock topped. At that time, Jerry wasn't as experienced about how to handle a climax top. This is when a stock has a rapid price run up for one to two weeks after an advance of many months and then rolls over. This climactic activity usually occurs in the final stages of a stock's advance.

The reason Jerry was able to buy Qlogic is because of his experience with ECI Telecommunications. He bought Qlogic after it had already tripled in price, which is almost exactly what ECI had done. This taught him a very valuable lesson: winning stocks repeat themselves with similar patterns and behaviors.

Jerry learned another valuable lesson with EMC in 1999. He bought the stock at $68 but got shaken out and took a loss. He sold at $61. But the stock went on to build a cup-with-handle base. Jerry learned to keep watching stocks that didn't work the first time he tried to buy them, because big winners often give you another chance.

In November, he bought EMC again as it came out of a base at $75 and sold it at $112 in 2000 for a 49% gain.

Then, in 2003, Jerry bought J2 Global Communications (JCOM) in March and sold it in October after a two-for-one split for a 198% gain.

He learned that it was important to bag gains early in a bull market cycle. That's when market leaders really pop and the big money will be made.

Recovering from a Setback

Then a hard blow came for Jerry due to several factors, including what he feels was overconfidence in his trading abilities. He lost half his money in a drawdown. For a serious trader, losing a large amount of money can be the darkest moment, filled with self-doubt and disillusionment.

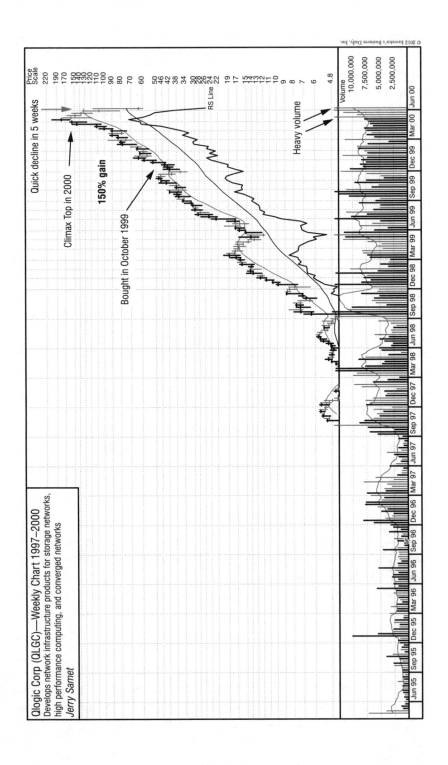

Qlogic Corp (QLGC)—Weekly Chart 1997–2000
Develops network infrastructure products for storage networks, high performance computing, and converged networks
Jerry Samet

Quick decline in 5 weeks

Climax Top in 2000

150% gain

Bought in October 1999

RS Line

Heavy volume

Price Scale
220
190
170
150
140
130
120
110
100
90
80
70
60
50
46
42
38
34
30
28
26
24
22
19
17
15
14
13
12
11
10
9
8
7
6
4.8

Volume
10,000,000
7,500,000
5,000,000
2,500,000

Jun 95 Sep 95 Dec 95 Mar 96 Jun 96 Sep 96 Dec 96 Mar 97 Jun 97 Sep 97 Dec 97 Mar 98 Jun 98 Sep 98 Dec 98 Mar 99 Jun 99 Sep 99 Dec 99 Mar 00 Jun 00

© 2012 Investor's Business Daily, Inc.

Over the years, Jerry had attended IBD workshops multiple times, so he went back and studied the workshop books. The first egregious error was in not cutting losses sooner. As Jerry examined his trading mistakes, he learned that the emotions of euphoria when he was doing well in the market as well as being too distraught when a trade went against him were damaging to his trading. He studied and worked hard with a trading coach that specialized in psychological barriers and learned to keep a more even keel and be calmer in his everyday approach to the market.

He found out that the most dangerous time is when you're doing really well in the market, because you get sloppy: "The market will prove to you that you're getting cocky."

Jerry has been very successful in the market since adjusting his trading. He mentions with a chuckle, "If things are going well and I'm really excited, it's a good indication the market may be topping."

Now when he is doing well, Jerry calmly takes some gains off the table and takes his family on a vacation. He found that it is important to reward yourself at least in some small way when you've had some success. This keeps overconfidence in control.

One of the biggest lessons Jerry has learned is that you can make a lot of money in a rally only to give it back in a correction. This can be extremely frustrating. "One of the hardest things is to stay out of a correcting market," he says. "Although you can get some of the biggest up days in a bear market, and this makes it tempting to go back in, you buy some stocks and take small losses, then buy a few more stocks, and then take a few more losses. Pretty soon, if you do that enough times, even if you are cutting your losses, you'll often lose a decent amount of money."

To keep from giving back gains that he made during an uptrend, Jerry refuses to buy stocks if there are only three or four stocks that are making decent gains in the market. He is looking for true confirmation in the market, and that means that 10 to 15 or more stocks must be setting up and looking good. "If the market doesn't look strong, you have no business getting in."

The Leaders Index

To help him determine if the market was in a good phase or a so-so phase, Jerry set up what he calls his "leaders index," which is a mixture of 20 to 25 stocks from 15 different industry groups. Jerry does this early in every new uptrend. He creates the list by searching for stocks that look strong as a new uptrend is beginning.

Many of these are stocks that have already broken out. Stocks that are a bit extended are great candidates, because Jerry knows from market history that these are the stocks that are most likely to go higher. Stocks making new highs tend to go higher.

Jerry looks for stocks with strong fundamentals, big earnings and sales, and a great new product or service that is in demand.

He follows this "leaders index" as a gauge of the general market and updates its performance on a daily basis. Jerry e-mails the daily results of the index to several IBD Meetup Groups. He says that sharing the results helps him stay "honest about what the market is actually doing." Jerry also helps teach at several IBD Meetup Groups and always enjoys the exchange of ideas.

He says, "I can wear Hawaiian shirts and shorts to work, come and go as I please, take a vacation when I want, have the luxury of spending more time with my family, and I don't have a boss telling me what to do. It suits my personality well."

• KEY POINTS •

- Winning stocks repeat themselves with similar patterns and behaviors.
- Keep watching stocks that don't work out the first time they are bought. They may offer another opportunity.
- It's important to get in early in a new bull market cycle. That's when market leaders really take off.
- If you're doing very well in the market, be sure to keep emotions under control.
- Reward yourself in some small way if you've had success.
- Stay out of a trendless market; small losses add up.

Mike Hicks

Mike first became interested in stocks through business courses taken in college. His first job was at a CPA firm that had a library and a couple of books on equities. After reading a few books, he decided to dabble in the market.

The Early Years

Mike thought cheap stocks looked interesting, so he bought Ramada Inn when it was under $5. He made a 13% gain, which seemed pretty good for his first stock pick. But he quickly learned that duplicating that success was going to be difficult.

Through the years, he was confused by all the information that was out there and didn't understand which methodology he should be following.

Mike had continually tried to be a bottom fisher because he never had the confidence to buy a stock that was so far up from what he thought was a low-risk entry price. As a result of continually buying cheap, low-quality stocks that weren't showing earnings growth, he frequently lost huge percentages on his individual stocks as well as having a meager overall portfolio performance.

In 1989, an architect friend introduced him to IBD. Mike stared for a few moments at the paper and all of its detailed information. "I was so absolutely amazed that I almost had to sit in a chair," he says. "This is what I had been looking for all my life." He made a plan in the back of his head that investing would be his retirement career.

Mike continued to be a subscriber to IBD, but time was in short supply because he was busy with his own CPA firm. So although Mike bought stocks here and there, he didn't get serious about investing until 2002.

Mike began focusing on stocks that showed a rare combination of traits: strong volume demand and stellar fundamentals. These are the market leaders that exhibit earnings and sales that are far outperforming the market averages, which is why they kept showing up in various features in IBD week after week during their massive runs.

The Breakthrough

Garmin (GRMN) was one of the first successful stocks Mike bought in December 2002, using the CAN SLIM Investing System. He bought the stock as it was coming out of a cup-with-handle base and logged a 74% gain.

After a particularly grueling tax season in 2003 and buoyed by his success with Garmin, Mike decided to really study the CAN SLIM System intensely. He sat in his office for an entire weekend and printed out a huge amount of educational pieces from Investors.com. As he read through the material, he had an epiphany. Mike was beginning to put all the pieces together: he needed to focus on stocks that had great fundamentals com-

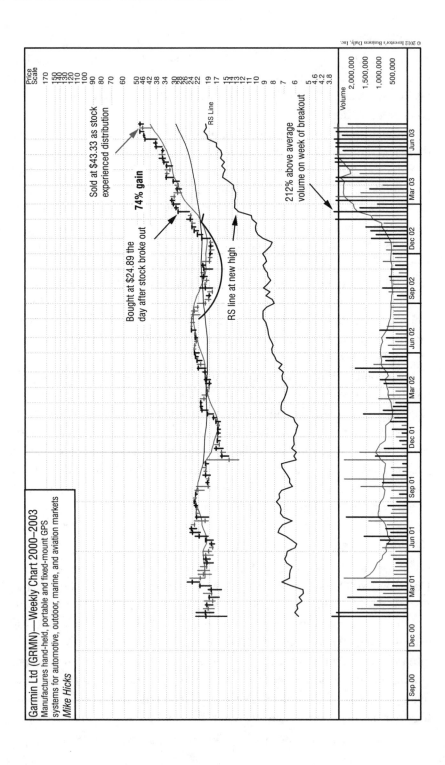

Garmin Ltd (GRMN)—Weekly Chart 2000–2003
Manufactures hand-held, portable and fixed-mount GPS
systems for automotive, outdoor, marine, and aviation markets
Mike Hicks

Sold at $43.33 as stock
experienced distribution

74% gain

Bought at $24.89 the
day after stock broke out

RS line at new high

RS Line

212% above average
volume on week of breakout

Volume

© 2012 Investor's Business Daily, Inc.

bined with the right chart action. These were stocks that had at least double-digit earnings numbers and were breaking out of areas of price consolidation on big volume.

Mike also began to read all of the books Bill O'Neil had on his recommended reading list: *How I Made $2 Million in the Market* by Nicolas Darvas, *The Battle for Investment Survival* by Gerald Loeb, *My Own Story* by Bernard Baruch, and *Reminiscences of a Stock Operator* by Edwin Lefevre.

The Life Changer

In May 2003, Mike was reading an IBD *New America* article and learned about a stun gun called Taser. He realized that this could be a big winner because of the development of a nonlethal weapon that would improve a police officer's options to capture and detain suspects. He bought Taser (TASR) in September 2003 and sold it in October for a 105% gain in 30 days. This was a very exciting moment for Mike; he had done well with Garmin and now had a triple digit gain with Taser. His confidence was soaring.

But Mike was frustrated as Taser continued to rocket higher—another couple hundred percentage points—and he realized he had sold too early, though IBD analysis hadn't indicated this. His heart sank, but, realizing his mistake, he started looking for a proper new entry point. In December 2009, the stock formed a series of rare high tight flags. This is when a stock has a fast advance of 100 to 200% in 4 to 8 weeks. Then a stock moves sideways for 3 to 5 weeks before making another run. High tight flags are very rare and only seen in the market's biggest winners. After this formation, stocks usually make a massive move upward.

Mike bought the stock back again. His position was significant as he pyramided into the stock and added to his position. Then Mike did something that is hard to do: he sat tight with a volatile stock. When a stock gyrates and is a bit of a wild thing in daily price swings, it can be difficult to sit with. This will test your nerves, but it's where a set of rules comes into play. You sit with a stock that has proven itself to be a true market leader. Taser never went below its buy point, so Mike held onto it, despite some wild price fluctuations.

Then he saw some climax activity in the chart. The stock had gone up a tremendous amount, and Mike realized that this might be a dangerous time. He knew from his studies that all stocks top out at some point. On April 19, Taser was due to report earnings after the close. Lawsuits and bad news were beginning to creep up, and there were other yellow flags, such as

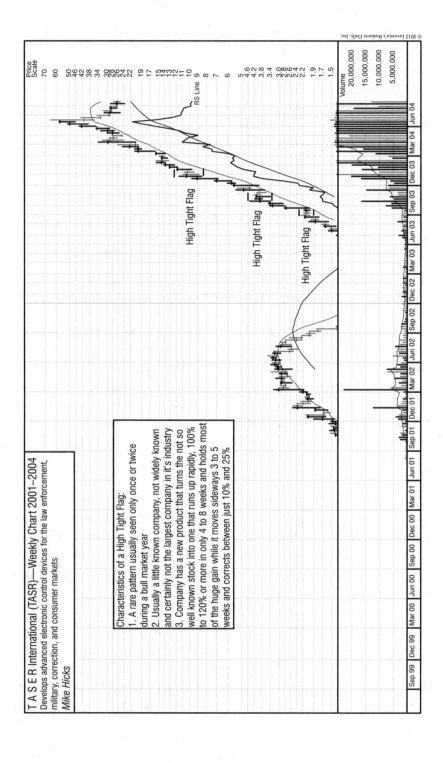

TASER International (TASR)—Weekly Chart 2001–2004

Develops advanced electronic control devices for the law enforcement, military, correction, and consumer markets

Mike Hicks

Characteristics of a High Tight Flag:

1. A rare pattern usually seen only once or twice during a bull market year

2. Usually a little known company, not widely known and certainly not the largest company in it's industry

3. Company has a new product that turns the not so well known stock into one that runs up rapidly, 100% to 120% or more in only 4 to 8 weeks and holds most of the huge gain while it moves sideways 3 to 5 weeks and corrects between just 10% and 25%

High Tight Flag

High Tight Flag

High Tight Flag

RS Line

© 2012 Investor's Business Daily, Inc.

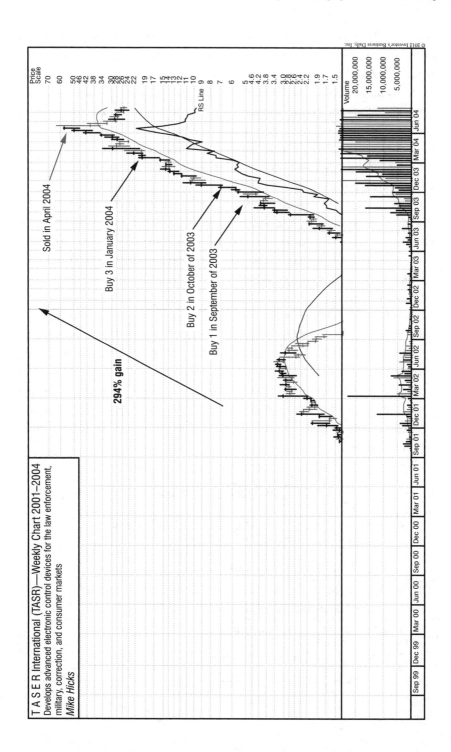

T A S E R International (TASR)—Weekly Chart 2001–2004
Develops advanced electronic control devices for the law enforcement,
military, correction, and consumer markets
Mike Hicks

Price Scale

Sold in April 2004

Buy 3 in January 2004

294% gain

Buy 2 in October of 2003

Buy 1 in September of 2003

RS Line

Volume

© 2012 Investor's Business Daily, Inc.

excessive stock splits. Mike made note of this and called his broker that afternoon. He took his entire gains off the table. After Taser released earnings and disappointed analysts' expectations, the stock cratered 29%.

Mike had sold exactly at the right time and had bagged a 294% gain in a stock on top of earlier gains of 105%. This was a very emotional moment for Mike. He closed the door to his office and sat in his chair as tears welled up in his eyes. It was a life-changing moment. Mike had made a six-figure profit in a stock, and he could now pursue his retirement dream of selling his CPA firm and turning to investing full time.

Having a huge gain was both a blessing and a curse, however. After the success Mike found with Taser, he felt every stock would be a huge winner and, as a result, has had a tendency to be a home run hitter since then. The problem he found is that not all market environments produce giant gains like Taser.

Mike has since learned to take profits at 20 to 25% instead of giving back hard-earned profits.

One thing that helps him stay in step regularly with the market and reduce his mistakes is teaching. In October 2003, after Mike's first big gain in Taser (TASR) of 105%, he formed an IBD Meetup Group in his hometown of Clearwater, Florida. He said this was one of the best decisions he has made in his stock market career. He has found other people who are passionate about the market and who invest the same way. Mike has also enjoyed helping a number of newer investors get started and enjoys watching their success.

• KEY POINTS •

- Focus on stocks with strong fundamentals breaking out of areas of consolidation on big volume.
- Sit patiently with a stock that is a true market leader.
- Don't try to be a home run hitter all the time. Not all market environments produce gains like Taser's.
- Read *The New America* article.
- Look for unique products that are in big demand.

Ed Hornstein

Ed was raised in a middle class family in the suburbs of Long Island, New York. Throughout his childhood, his exposure to the stock market consisted of watching his father buy stocks on "hot tips." Every stock that his dad bought was supposedly going to be a ten bagger and make him a multimillionaire. However, the reality was that his father would lose a small fortune in the stock market by listening to whatever stocks were being pumped by his broker. Ed's experience of watching this completely turned him off to the markets.

Ed borrowed $100,000 in loans to pay for law school and quickly came to the realization that in order to pay off the loans, he would need to land a job with a firm that could afford to pay a six-figure salary to starting associates.

As he entered law school, it became quickly apparent that he was surrounded by extremely talented and intelligent people. Ed figured that several had IQs that dwarfed his and that if he was going to obtain the grades necessary to land a job with one of those large firms, he'd have to outwork them. He spent the first year of law school either in the classroom or pulling all nighters in the library. That work ethic paid off: Ed finished his first year near the top of his class and was recruited to work for a highly ranked law firm in its New York office for the summer.

Ed never paid much attention to the stock market during law school and completely missed the tech bubble and explosion in Internet stocks in 2000. But after he graduated and began working, Ed decided it might be prudent to invest some of the money he was making. He knew that he needed to learn a thing or two about stocks before committing capital, so he read a few books about value investing and other stock market strategies. None of it made much sense to him, especially after seeing people buy cheap stocks only to lose most of their money.

A few months later, Ed was in a bookstore and noticed a copy of *How to Make Money in Stocks* sitting on a table. He picked up the book, browsed through it, and decided to purchase it. Little did he know at the time that this decision would forever change his life.

The key principles all made sense. Shortly thereafter, he purchased *The Successful Investor*, which really resonated with him. He realized that his friends and family could have kept the small fortunes they made in the late 1990s if they had followed some simple sell rules.

Throughout the rest of 2002 and 2003, Ed read Bill O'Neil's books multiple times: *How to Make Money in Stocks*, *The Successful Investor*, and *24 Essential Lessons for Investment Success*. These books were intended to make the rules and guidelines register with investors in a deeper way.

Testing His Wings

In March 2003, a new bull market began, and Ed started trading stocks. He quickly turned $50,000 into nearly $300,000 until the market corrected in early 2004. Reading and understanding CAN SLIM Investing, however, was entirely different than its application. By the end of the correction, because he didn't stay out of the market while it was heading lower, Ed lost every penny that he'd made. When he did his post analysis, he realized that he did not follow the CAN SLIM sell rules he had studied.

Ed spent the next three years of his life immersed in mastering CAN SLIM and learning every detail he could about the system and how to use it effectively. Besides studying, Ed also traded his own account and made "almost every mistake that a trader can possibly make. The market can evoke emotions in everyone, causing one to break rules, overreact, and make mistakes." Because Ed had no mentors, he had to learn everything by trial and error and experience. Instead of becoming disenchanted when he would lose money on a stock, however, he would mark up a chart to see the reason for his mistake. And he constantly reviewed them so he wouldn't make the same mistakes again.

Hitting His Stride

At the end of 2005, Ed had his first "big stock experience." Ed missed out on Google's first two base breakouts, but when the stock gapped out of a base on October 21, 2005, he bought what was a rather large position for him at the time. He had studied models of past breakaway gaps of former leaders, and he knew this was a high probability play, despite many pundits saying the stock was overvalued. He spotted volume accumulation on a weekly chart and saw the continued demand as it ran up. On January 20, 2006, Ed locked in a large profit by implementing one of his sell rules, which is to sell a stock if it breaks its 50-day moving average on heavy volume.

Ed noted, "Holding onto a big winner is sometimes hard, and that's why you have to know everything about a stock and a company, because if you don't know much about the product, its useful place in the market, why sales

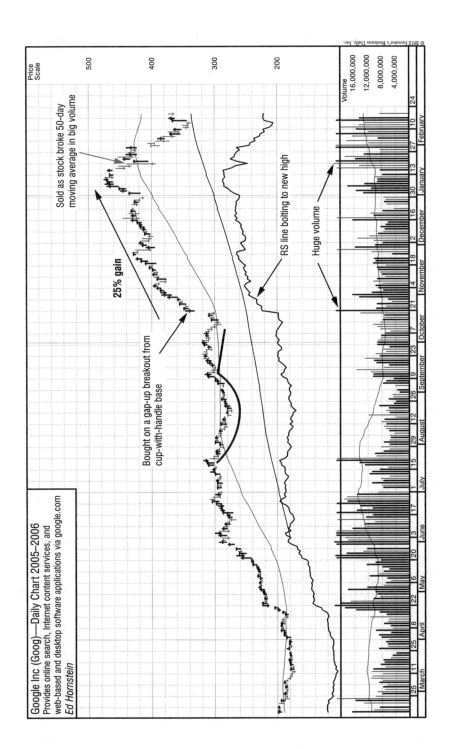

Google Inc (Goog)—Daily Chart 2005–2006
Provides online search, Internet content services, and
web-based and desktop software applications via google.com
Ed Hornstein

Sold as stock broke 50-day
moving average in big volume

25% gain

Bought on a gap-up breakout from
cup-with-handle base

RS line bolting to new high

Huge volume

Price
Scale

500

400

300

200

Volume
16,000,000
12,000,000
8,000,000
4,000,000

© 2012 Investor's Business Daily, Inc.

24 | February | 10 | 27 | January | 13 | 30 | December | 16 | 2 | November | 18 | 4 | October | 21 | 7 | September | 23 | 9 | August | 26 | 12 | July | 29 | 15 | June | 1 | 17 | May | 3 | April | 20 | 6 | March | 22 | 8 | 25 | 11 | 25

may increase, or why its product or services may be in demand, the more likely you are to get shaken out of it. Conviction is definitely key to holding onto a big winner. You have to ask yourself, 'Why is this company likely to be successful in the future? Does it have a remarkable product or service that is revolutionary in its industry?'"

Another important factor that Ed looks for is liquidity. He wants a stock that big funds would buy, and more thinly traded stocks don't capture the attention of the big institutional investor.

By 2006, Ed had made enough money with CAN SLIM Investing that he decided to follow his new passion, the stock market. He had always dreamed of owning his own business and was further motivated by reading about all the successful entrepreneurs in the *Leaders and Success* column in IBD.

Freedom to Follow His Passion

Although he had virtually no clients and no experience managing profes-sional money, he felt that if he followed his passion, continued to work hard, and stayed true to the principles of CAN SLIM Investing, he could make it a full-time career.

At the end of 2007, Ed said good-bye to the law firm where he had begun his career and launched his own money management firm. He slowly built his client base, and when the market crashed in 2008, he had his clients' money safely in cash. Although he didn't know how severe the crash would be, he recognized the breakdown of leading stocks and the large amount of selling in the financial stocks. That made him realize cash was the safest place to be.

A new bull market began in March 2009, and during that year, Ed's firm did so well that he decided to launch a hedge fund in January 2010. The fund did well in 2010, but in 2011, Ed faced a more difficult period. For the first time since he started managing money, he wasn't performing up to peak. After he went back and analyzed the entire year, he realized that port-folio concentration was the problem, and he needed a new set of manage-ment rules for choppy, difficult markets.

He made a "threshold rule": if the market issued a follow-through day, he would go in no more than 20% invested, unless the stocks in his portfolio made a gain of 2%, then he could go in a little deeper. Even if he was tempted to buy more than he should, having portfolio management rules would keep him out of a choppy market.

Even though 2012 was an easier environment to trade in, having the 20% threshold rule helped Ed outperform the S&P by nearly double through September 2012. Ed seeks to "constantly learn through post analysis and make new rules that will help him as a trader."

Ed also noted that no matter how good you get at investing, you're going to have a bad year at some point, so it's important to fix mistakes. He said that he learned a lot more in the difficult 2011 period than in easier up years. "Don't be afraid of your mistakes, but make rules to fix them."

He continues to be a student of the market, studying and learning. Ed also likes to go to a local mall and see what people are buying. He was able to make a nice profit from Chipotle Mexican Grill when he noticed one open near his old law firm and saw lines 45 minutes long for healthy fast food.

Ed says that had he not read *How to Make Money in Stocks* nine years ago, he might still be a lawyer, working long hours and being unhappy with his profession. Instead, now, not only does he have his own hedge fund where others trust him to manage their money, but when he wakes up in the morning to go to work, he is excited and passionate about every waking hour he spends analyzing the market and trading. "My life is much more fulfilling than I could imagine as I have much more free time to spend with my family and three-year-old son. Mr. O'Neil, I thank you for making this all possible."

Google. 25% gain 2005

Vmware. 80% gain 2007

Dryships. 91% gain 2007

Michael Kors. 80% gain 2012

LinkedIn. 100% gain 2012

Priceline. 50% gain 2012

Apple. 28% gain 2012

• KEY POINTS •

- Sell a stock if it falls below the 50-day moving average on heavy volume.

- Ask why a company you are considering buying is likely to be successful in the future. Does it have a remarkable product or service that is revolutionary in its industry?

- Gap-ups can be bought on a stock that has established itself as a market leader and has top fundamentals. The gap-up should be on heavy volume.

- Be a continual student of the market.

Becoming a Master: Continually Studying the Market

"Study the past if you would define the future."

—CONFUCIUS

In martial arts, becoming a master isn't a destination, but more of a journey. It is a continual quest for knowledge and improvement through practicing and trying to improve on weaknesses.

The most successful investors are constantly studying and looking for ways to improve their prior performance. Examining past trades and former stock market winners can often give clues about how to find successful trades in the future.

Daily Journal and Post Analysis

Katrina Guensch is a mediation lawyer who lives in Florida. As part of her ongoing quest to become a better trader, she keeps a daily journal so that she can go back and understand what she was thinking at the time about the market and leading stocks. If she has a busy work week, Katrina will catch up and make sure that at the very least, she writes in her journal on a weekly basis. By putting her thoughts down on a regular basis, she can go back and see what her perspective was at the time about stocks that she owned as well as the general market.

Katrina also does an extensive post analysis of her trades. She prints out daily and weekly charts when she buys or sells a stock. This provides her with a chart diary that includes her reasons for buying or selling a stock and what the fundamentals were at the time, such as earnings, sales, and return on equity.

Post Analysis Guidelines

The primary purpose of any post analysis is to formulate specific rules that address your unique weaknesses.

Your post analysis should lead you to a better understanding of the nature and essence of your trading successes and failures.

1. Throughout the year, print daily and weekly charts upon buying or selling a stock.

2. Once a year, organize the charts for the previous 12 months based on performance.

3. Analyze your largest percent gainers and largest percent losers.

4. As you study your individual trades, ask yourself these questions:

   - Did I break any rules?
   - Did I enter the position correctly?
   - What percentage of the portfolio ended up in leading groups and stocks?
   - Did I buy at the right time?
   - Did my emotions cause me to sell?
   - Did I miss big opportunities by selling too early?
   - Was I heavily on margin? Did I handle the additional risk correctly?
   - Did I miss obvious clues to sell or fail to sell at the right time?
   - Did I evaluate my individual stock and portfolio risk for each decision?
   - What happened to my stocks after I sold them?

Don't complicate the process by having too many rules. Focus on your top one or two weaknesses. Remember, the point of your analysis is to formulate your rules. Use your analysis to establish rules for yourself. Write your rules down to reinforce them.

Back Testing

Lee Tanner does market simulations to compare how well he actually did in a particular time period with what he might have been able to achieve. He learned this technique from an IBD Level 4 workshop in 2004. He says, "The great thing about back testing is there are no emotions involved, but one can practice what they might have done in similar market circumstances."

To do his analysis:

1. Lee goes back in time, using the date change feature in MarketSmith, to a time period shortly before a new market rally started and builds a "theoretical" watch list of stocks as objectively and realistically as possible by using:

   • His old watch list of stocks that were setting up, as well as notes or IBD articles that he saved from that time period

   • eIBD features from the time period, especially the *IBD 50*, the *Big Cap 20*, and the 85-85 index

   • Stocks that were on Leaderboard at that time

2. Lee goes through the market and the stocks that are on his theoretical watch list day by day, week by week, looking at charts and trying to find the big winners. He finds this part of the simulation particularly useful because he can see the charts as they looked at the time, not as they look in the present.

   Lee makes simulated buy and sell decisions for stocks in the theoretical portfolio the way he normally would in real time while keeping a record of:

   • All the watch list stocks for each week of the simulation that were bought and put in the theoretical portfolio

   • The market direction for that time and the distribution day count during the simulation

- A trading log with appropriate notes on why he bought each stock
- The stocks that he decided to trade in the mock portfolio and the gain or loss for each one

3. Then he compares his theoretical portfolio results to his actual portfolio and sees where he can make improvements.

Studying Historical Charts

Tom Ellis has read *How to Make Money in Stocks* five or six times cover to cover. He scanned the 100 charts that appear in the beginning of the book and put together a spreadsheet that contains every cup-with-handle base pattern and the pages where the chart pattern appeared in the book.

He did the same thing for all of the other base patterns so that he could go back and study each pattern in detail.

Tom realized the importance of learning to read charts well from something that Bill O'Neil wrote in a pamphlet titled, *How to Recognize Great Performing Stocks.* Bill said, "You must learn how to read and interpret daily, weekly, and monthly price and volume charts because they can tell you if a stock is behaving properly or not and shows whether the stock is under accumulation (institutional buying). Charts measure the actual supply and demand for a stock and indicate the best time to begin buying as well as the more risky times to continue holding a stock. Reading charts well and recognizing when stocks are coming out of base patterns gives investors an enormous advantage in finding the next big winners when combined with superior fundamentals like strong earnings and sales."

Whether it's Tennessee Coal from 1898 or Apple in 2004, chart patterns of the biggest winners are the same, cycle after cycle.

Tom also saves PDFs of *e*IBD each day so he can go back and study charts of the market's biggest winners. By saving the paper each day, he can also look up what the fundamentals were of a stock at that time.

• KEY POINTS •

- Keep a daily or weekly journal for stocks that you own as well as thoughts on the general market.
- Do a post analysis of all your trades.
- Back test to see how you might have traded stocks differently.
- Study historical charts of the big winners from the past so you can recognize the same patterns in the present.

Chart Patterns Remain the Same Whether Tennessee Coal from 1898 or Apple in 2004

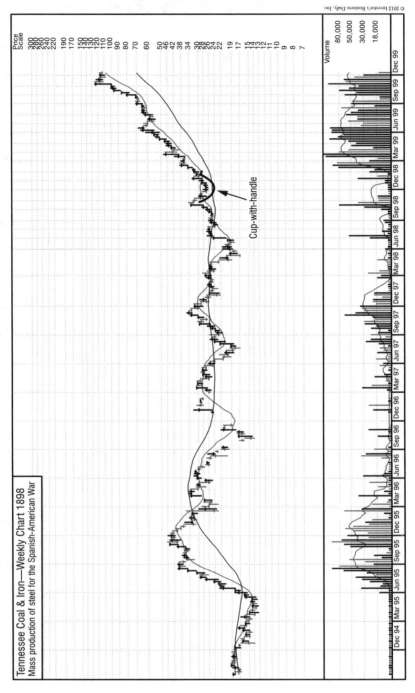

Tennessee Coal & Iron—Weekly Chart 1898
Mass production of steel for the Spanish-American War

Cup-with-handle

© 2012 Investor's Business Daily, Inc.

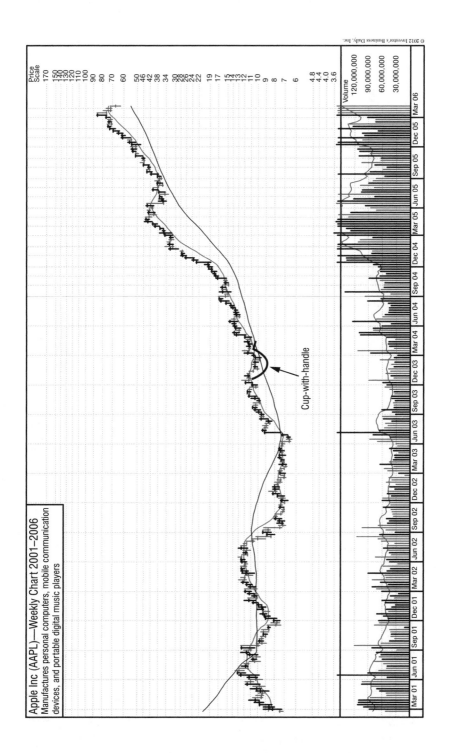

Apple Inc (AAPL)—Weekly Chart 2001–2006
Manufactures personal computers, mobile communication devices, and portable digital music players

Cup-with-handle

© 2012 Investor's Business Daily, Inc.

• CHAPTER •

Black Belt Trading: Investing Like a Pro

*"Champions aren't made in gyms. Champions are made
from something they have deep inside them—a desire,
a dream, a vision. They have to have the skill, and the will.
But the will must be stronger than the skill."*

—MUHAMMAD ALI

It is said that a black belt is a white belt that never quit. Only through persever-ance and indomitable spirit can one achieve the highest level in martial arts. It is the same with investing. The top traders develop skills through hard work, discipline, following a daily routine, and controlling emotions. The journey is not always easy, and there will be trials along the way, but anyone can achieve this level if they are willing to put in the work.

Kevin Marder

Kevin started investing in 1985 with a very simple strategy: he bought blue chip stocks from the Dow Jones Industrial Average that had earnings growth of 20% per year.

In July 1987, Kevin noticed that the market was selling off, and so, being a risk-averse investor, he sold many of his positions. But he had no idea what was coming. Kevin turned on the TV on October 19th, the morning of the "Black Monday" crash, and saw that the Dow had dropped 500 points, more than 20%, and that the entire world market was collapsing. He immediately sold his last short-term position, which was Royal Dutch, an oil and gas company. Although Kevin had been more fortunate than many investors, he felt a bit stunned. It was a serious and devastating day for a multitude of traders, and the crash hit many Wall Street firms hard, driving some out of business altogether.

In the aftermath of the crash, Kevin realized he didn't know how to time the market. His strategy worked in the 1980s because stocks were in a bull market. But now times were different. In 1990, he happened to come across *Investor's Business Daily* and saw an ad in the paper for *How to Make Money in Stocks*. Kevin bought the book, and as he read through the chapters, he began to see how the markets worked historically. For Kevin, this was a watershed moment. Midway through the book, he felt as though someone had turned a light bulb on in his mind. He put the book down, and he began to pace the living room floor, thinking about what he had just read and what a difference it would make in his trading.

The Learning Curve

Kevin attended several of IBD's advanced investment seminars and found that the CAN SLIM strategy fit his personality well, particularly the "N" in CAN SLIM, which stands for something new. He had always been intrigued by new things, whether they were related to cars, fashion, musical styles, companies, or a host of other things. Operating in the aggressive growth sector would allow him to watch firsthand the progress of many companies that were on the cutting edge. These were the names that would crank out the heaviest advances in the stock market because they had customers beating a path to their doorstep.

Kevin began subscribing to the Daily Graphs charting service that IBD offered and would drive down to the printing plant every Saturday morning

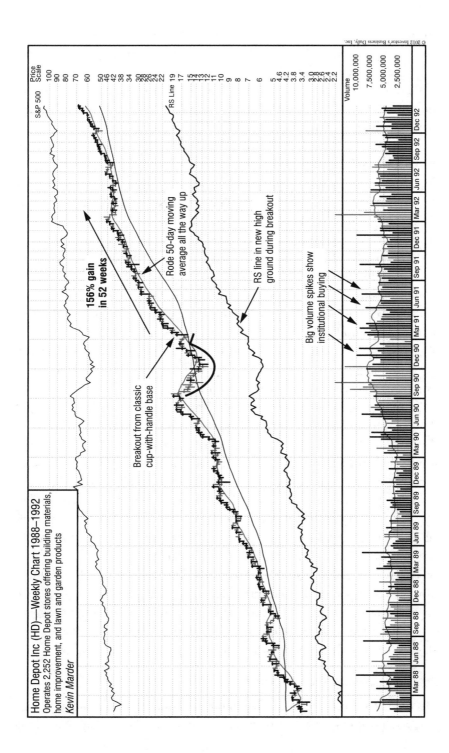

Home Depot Inc (HD)—Weekly Chart 1988–1992
Operates 2,252 Home Depot stores offering building materials, home improvement, and lawn and garden products

Kevin Marder

156% gain in 52 weeks

Rode 50-day moving average all the way up

Breakout from classic cup-with-handle base

RS line in new high ground during breakout

Big volume spikes show institutional buying

© 2012 Investor's Business Daily, Inc.

to pick them up. He says, "All the hardcore stock jocks showed up on Saturday mornings at the plant to get their charts early. You felt like you were part of a secret club."

One of the biggest technical indicators that Kevin learned to pay attention to on charts was the RS (Relative Strength) line. Kevin learned that what was important was the slope of this line. If the line was upward sloping and hitting new highs, it meant that the stock was outperforming the S&P 500. Conversely, if the line was downward sloping and drifting into newer lows, the stock was underperforming the major indexes. He was looking for the truly big growth stocks that were far outperforming the major indexes, so this indicator was something he would continue to focus on as he looked at charts.

Early in 1991, Kevin recognized that a new bull market had begun. He was able to use the CAN SLIM Investing strategy in "full bloom." Companies like Microsoft soared as people gobbled up its state-of-the-art software. Home Depot experienced blistering growth by coming out with a chain of innovative home improvement stores offering discount prices. Cisco Systems became an earnings juggernaut by developing technology used to link groups of individual computers together. In each case, these companies had carved out a whole new market.

In the spring of 1993, Kevin would learn a big lesson. He had bought Microsoft out of a base, but the breakout failed, and the stock fell 10%. Kevin didn't sell. Microsoft dropped some more and was down 15% from where he bought it. Kevin held onto the stock and kept telling himself what a really great company Microsoft was and that it would recover. He finally sold the stock after it was down 20%. Kevin realized he had not adhered to the CAN SLIM sell rules. Since then, Kevin relies on technical analysis alone to sell a position, and he has never sold a stock with more than a 7 to 8% loss except for the rare news-related gap-down.

He also realized that there are two problems in hanging onto losers. First, you can take a potentially devastating hit to your account if you allow a small loss to grow into a big one. Second, you can tie up your money in a laggard stock instead of selling a losing stock and putting your money into a winner. This is particularly important at the beginning of a new bull market.

Taking Advantage of New Technology

By 1995, it seemed obvious to Kevin that the Internet was going to change the way investors could get quotes and other information, but everything was very new. The Internet was in its infancy. Kevin began by publishing bond market commentary on the Internet, but his heart was in the stock market. He wanted to share all that he had learned about making money in stocks.

In early 1996, he cofounded DBC Online. This was among the first websites where the individual investor could find quotes and news information about what was happening in the market. In the early days, Kevin's intraday market updates served as the site's home page.

CBS bought half of DBC Online in 1997 and named it CBSMarketWatch. In January 1999, the company went public. The IPO was priced at 18 and opened at 80. It ran up as high as 150 during the first day. This was the second-best opening-day performance for any IPO in history.

The website became a huge hit and is now a widely recognized site for online news and market data with over one million viewers per day from 70 countries around the world.

As part of Kevin's market commentary, he interviewed top traders. In particular, he sought out other traders of the O'Neil method. Among his favorite interviews were Bill O'Neil, David Ryan, Greg Kuhn, and Cedd Moses Through what he had learned from the "O'Neil approach," Kevin was able to write about the market in a way that others found enlightening. Kevin's real-time commentary was seen around the world on USAToday.com, AOL, Yahoo, and other outlets. For Kevin, this was tremendously exciting. His foundation of how the market worked was built on what he had learned from reading *How to Make Money in Stocks*.

Kevin learned from his interviews that the top traders "become successful by putting their personal opinions aside and listening to the market's message. In fact, keeping one's ego in check is one of the most important aspects of trading. This becomes particularly difficult when someone who is a success in another field—say medicine, law, business, or sports—believes his success will translate to a superb trading career." As Bill O'Neil had often said, "The market doesn't know who you are, doesn't know how bright you are, and doesn't know what great college you attended. It simply doesn't care." Kevin added, "The highly successful lawyer walks into the game expecting to clean up. Often, he is the one who gets cleaned."

Always Be Prepared for the Next Opportunity

Kevin's biggest lessons from interviewing Bill multiple times for MarketWatch have been about the general market trend.

"I learned from Bill that, no matter how grim the economy or the market may appear, you must always do your daily analysis of the averages and leaders," says Kevin. "This is because a new bull phase begins when things are at their worst, and investor sentiment is quite bearish. The initial breakouts in a new bull phase often occur in the growth stocks that end up being your genuine leaders in the ensuing move up. So making sure you get in early in a new trend is important. This is especially critical because once these new leaders break out, they can run a good amount before pausing to form their next base.

"This means if you enter after the initial breakout, you are likely entering when the price is materially extended past its most recent base. And entering an extended stock is risky because there is no technical support below to cushion any normal pullback that might occur.

"I learned this lesson in the July to October 1990 bear market. Instead of doing my daily analysis, I did not look at a single chart for months. Only after everything was obvious after the mid-January 1991 lift-off did I realize a new bull market had begun three months earlier. As the saying goes, you snooze, you lose."

Learning how a market tops proved to be as important as getting in on a new bull run. "My first triple-digit percentage month was February 2000," says Kevin. "I did this by holding 15–17 stocks, nearly all in the explosive technology sector. As it turned out, this was the final blow-off phase of the most powerful bull market in 70 years, though of course no one knew this at the time. In early March 2000, I noticed institutions beginning to exit the stocks that I held. This showed up on price charts as distribution days (heavy selling) in the leadership names. By taking quick action, I moved my account to a 100% cash position by March 14, which was two trading days after the March 10, 2000, top. A day later, on March 15, I mentioned this in a column of mine on a major website."

Kevin's long-term record has outperformed the S&P 500 by a multiple of 10 (net of a management and performance fee), according to audited reports by Big Four CPA firm Ernst & Young LLP.

Kevin says that he is "grateful to Bill O'Neil for learning so much about the market early in his career, because it significantly impacted my professional journey through the market. I believe Bill has influenced more of this era's most outstanding stock pickers than anyone else." Kevin's gratitude and respect for Bill can be felt more in the silences following these statements than anything else.

• KEY POINTS •

- Check the relative strength line. If it slopes up and hits new highs, it's beating the S&P 500. True market leaders far outperform the major indexes.
- Rely on technical analysis alone to sell a stock.
- Never take more than a 7 to 8% loss from your purchase price.
- Sell underperforming stocks in your portfolio, and put the money into a winner.
- Read interviews of top traders.
- Put aside personal opinions, and listen to the market's message.
- No matter how grim the economy or market may appear, always do your analysis of the major indexes and the leaders.

Kier McDonough

Kier's first job out of college was with a large brokerage firm. He was trained to be a stock broker but didn't really learn very much about stocks: "They teach you to be a salesman and follow the internal analysts' recommendations."

In 1990, Kier got to know a broker from another firm who was a very good stock picker. When Kier inquired how he found stocks for his portfolio, the broker handed Kier *Investor's Business Daily* and recommended that Kier read *How to Make Money in Stocks*.

As Kier read through the book, he began to see how successful investing really worked. Before reading *How to Make Money in Stocks*, Kier was using a number of bad investing strategies. He bought when the market was trending down, didn't cut his losses short, and had no idea how to isolate which stocks were leading in the current market. Kier was excited as he read and reread the book, because he "had found a solid framework to help him keep in sync with the market and leading stocks."

Kier attended his first IBD Workshop in 1992 and felt empowered from the education. He began to employ the strategies and started to have success in the market both personally and professionally. Kier moved from a large investment firm to a smaller boutique company and became a manager for a team that had diversified investments. One thing that was exciting about this smaller firm was its concentration on the new economy, which included the more innovative companies focused on technology and the consumer. Many of these newer companies had CAN SLIM traits.

Latching onto a Big Winner

In 1995, Kier bought Centennial Technologies, a Massachusetts company that made PC computer cards that provided increased storage capacity.

Earnings soared 262% and sales rose 62% for the March quarter. Because of those stellar numbers, the stock broke out of an area of price consolidation and zoomed 17% on volume that was 838% above average. Kier recognized the large institutional money that was going into Centennial and began pyramiding into the stock and added to his position.

Centennial would become the number one performing stock on The New York Stock Exchange in 1996. Kier sold the stock when it went on a climax run at the end of December 1996. Centennial ran up 65% in 5 weeks and was 170% above its 200-day moving average, which is excessive. After a 21-month run, Kier locked in a gain of 475% in Centennial.

Kier personally held a sizeable position in the stock and had bought a significant amount for his investors. Kier says, "The gains from this stock had a big impact on my business, my net worth, and validated that the rules of CAN SLIM Investing, when followed correctly, do indeed work."

After the bear market of 2000–2003, Kier realized that trading wasn't going to be as easy as it had been in the 1990s. He decided to go to IBD's Level 3 and Level 4 Workshops to further his market knowledge. Kier listened to the recordings from those workshops over and over and met other high level traders. He found it very helpful to exchange ideas about the market with other investors and continued to keep in touch with several of them.

In 2005, IBD was looking for a national speaker from the Boston area. Kier wanted to audition for the position because he felt it would be a tremendous learning experience. He was given a PowerPoint presentation from the IBD Education Department as the basis for his audition. Kier knows you only get one chance to make a first impression, so he spent two months writing a script and practicing before flying out to California to audition in front of an IBD speaker approval committee. The hard work paid off: Kier was unanimously approved and began teaching workshops for

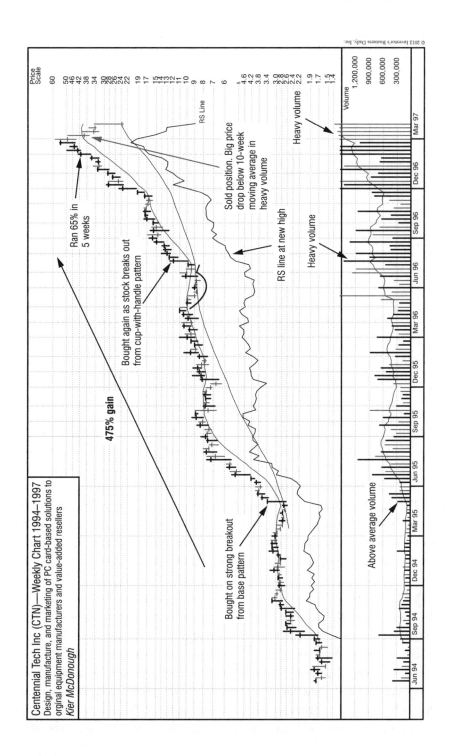

Centennial Tech Inc (CTN)—Weekly Chart 1994–1997
Design, manufacture, and marketing of PC card-based solutions to orginal equipment manufacturers and value-added resellers
Kier McDonough

475% gain

Ran 65% in 5 weeks

Bought again as stock breaks out from cup-with-handle pattern

Bought on strong breakout from base pattern

RS Line

Sold position. Big price drop below 10-week moving average in heavy volume

RS line at new high

Heavy volume

Heavy volume

Above average volume

Price Scale
60
50
46
42
38
34
30
28
26
24
22
19
17
15
14
13
12
11
10
9
8
7
6
5
4.6
4.2
3.8
3.4
3.0
2.8
2.6
2.4
2.2
1.9
1.7
1.5
1.4

Volume
1,200,000
900,000
600,000
300,000

Jun 94
Sep 94
Dec 94
Mar 95
Jun 95
Sep 95
Dec 95
Mar 96
Jun 96
Sep 96
Dec 96
Mar 97

© 2012 Investor's Business Daily, Inc.

IBD nationally. Preparing to teach each workshop was "like spring training, where I had to go over the principles and basics for every event. Good habits became deeply imbedded and second nature." Kier taught over 30 workshops for IBD and really enjoyed helping other investors learn and profit from the system.

Watch for Shoe Trends

Kier discovered a shoe company called Crocs in October 2006 that had an impressive 13 quarters in a row of triple-digit sales. The last two quarters had an EPS (earnings per share) growth of 330% and 120%. Sales had vaulted 232% and 309% in the last two quarters. Stocks that exhibit extraordinary earnings and sales numbers like that capture the attention of professional investors. Part of Kier's research was to look for solid institutional sponsorship in any new position he might take.

Jeff Vinik, a successful hedge fund manager, owned 1.8 million shares at the time, which was up from 468 shares in the prior quarter. Kier knew that a top performing hedge fund manager increasing the size of his position was another strong indication that Crocs might make a major move. He bought the stock out of its IPO base and added to his position as the stock ran up. Kier was sitting on a gain of 378% when Crocs reported earnings on October 31. The stock sold off hard in after-hours trading due to disappointing guidance for the next quarter that was well below expectations. Kier saw the stock crashing (trading down sharply), called his trader, and sold his entire position immediately in after-hours trading, locking in a gain of 362% from his original purchase.

Through his studies of past big market winners, as well as his experience with Crocs, Kier has found that shoe fads can cause a stock to make an explosive move based on a new trend or style. Some examples that Kier has studied are Reebok, L.A. Gear, and Decker's Outdoor, the maker of Uggs.

The Solar Craze

In March 2007, Kier bought First Solar, the maker of photovoltaic solar panels. The group was extremely strong at that time, as demand for alternative energy sources soared. Kier bought the stock as it bounced off the 10-week moving average line but got shaken out shortly thereafter when First Solar dropped below that line on heavy volume. He decided to sell the position at that time because earnings were coming out later that week, and one of Kier's rules is to not hold positions going into earnings announcements if he

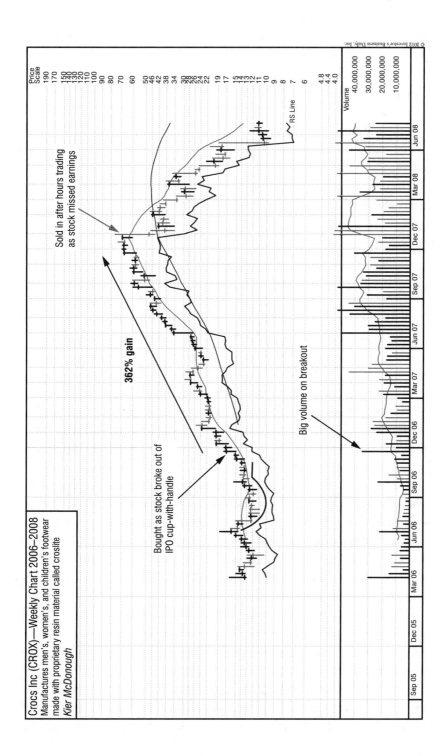

Crocs Inc (CROX)—Weekly Chart 2006–2008
Manufactures men's, women's, and children's footwear
made with proprietary resin material called croslite
Kier McDonough

Sold in after hours trading
as stock missed earnings

362% gain

Bought as stock broke out of
IPO cup-with-handle

Big volume on breakout

RS Line

Price
Scale
190
170
150
140
130
120
110
100
90
80
70
60
50
46
42
38
34
30
28
26
24
22
19
17
15
14
13
12
11
10
9
8
7
6

Volume
40,000,000
30,000,000
20,000,000
10,000,000

4.8
4.4
4.0

Sep 05 Dec 05 Mar 06 Jun 06 Sep 06 Dec 06 Mar 07 Jun 07 Sep 07 Dec 07 Mar 08 Jun 08

© 2012 Investor's Business Daily, Inc.

doesn't have a profit cushion. The stock then proceeded to double but did-n't offer a good entry point. Kier was patient and waited for First Solar to form another base, and then he bought the stock again. He sold the stock when it once again dropped below the 10-week line on heavy selling vol-ume, locking in a gain of 83%.

In 2008, Kier formed a hedge fund and significantly outperformed the general market by being almost entirely in cash for much of that year's bear market. The Nasdaq was down 40% that year, and Kier kept the losses in his fund to under 5%. The rules of CAN SLIM pushed Kier to seek the safety of cash during that devastating market correction.

Kier's investment rules for his new fund would be very similar to what he had learned from his years of teaching for IBD. His top-down approach would include the health of the general market, followed by searching for dynamic companies with new products or services that were in leading industry groups. The fund would focus on top-notch earnings and sales numbers followed by technical analysis of chart patterns and price and vol-ume as an indicator of demand for leading stocks. The overall goal of the fund was to isolate the top 1 to 2% of stocks in the market that could become true market leaders.

He made rules that the fund could hold up to 15 positions at a time, but the market exposure would increase only as previous positions showed prof-its. Margin would be used when the fund was fully invested and showing sig-nificant gains. The concentration level on any given security would be up to 30%.

Other rules for the fund included taking most profits at 20 to 25%, although true market leaders could be held for larger moves. Risk manage-ment rules would be strictly adhered to in order to protect against losses, such as a strict sell rule 7 to 8% below the initial cost of the equity. Cash lev-els could be as much as 100% to protect assets in difficult markets. These rules were time-tested by Bill O'Neil since the 1960s and have led to better results in the market.

In 2009, Kier underperformed and found that buying off the bottom was difficult. The market had gone through a very turbulent time, and most traders were cautious. He found most base patterns were badly damaged, "making it difficult to see what was setting up properly."

In 2010, Kier was able to find leading stocks more easily that were work-ing in conjunction with the overall market. Some of the stocks Kier was able to notch decent gains in were Priceline, Apple, and Chipotle Mexican Grill.

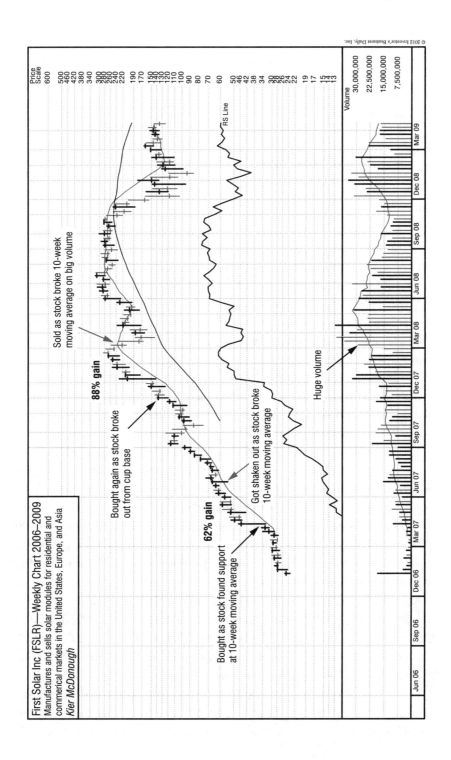

First Solar Inc (FSLR)—Weekly Chart 2006–2009
Manufactures and sells solar modules for residential and
commericial markets in the United States, Europe, and Asia
Kier McDonough

Sold as stock broke 10-week
moving average on big volume

88% gain

Bought again as stock broke
out from cup base

Got shaken out as stock broke
10-week moving average

62% gain

Bought as stock found support
at 10-week moving average

RS Line

Huge volume

Price
Scale
600
500
460
420
380
340
300
280
260
240
220
190
170
150
140
130
120
110
100
90
80
70
60
50
46
42
38
34
30
28
26
24
22
19
17
15
14
13

Volume
30,000,000
22,500,000
15,000,000
7,500,000

Jun 06 Sep 06 Dec 06 Mar 07 Jun 07 Sep 07 Dec 07 Mar 08 Jun 08 Sep 08 Dec 08 Mar 09

His Winning Routine

Kier looks for an average daily trading volume of at least 700,000 (average daily dollar volume of $70,000,000) and tends to drift toward consumer stocks that he really understands.

During the trading day, Kier runs various screens while he is watching the overall market. He also does an extensive analysis of past big market winners. He knows that the patterns of big winners from the past repeat themselves over and over: "Like Bill O'Neil always says, the more you know what past winners look like, the more likely you are to spot a new winner as it is emerging in the current market."

In the evening, Kier reads *e*IBD, the digital edition of the paper, and says, "The entire paper is a resource tool that has continually evolved and improved throughout the years." Every single day, Kier creates a spreadsheet of the *Stock Spotlight* feature from the paper because he's found that the "big leaders of any market uptrend will appear in this list."

The *New America* article is another IBD feature that Kier uses regularly: "The paper has many sections that help an investor isolate new emerging companies. My most profitable trades have always appeared somewhere in IBD."

Leaderboard is another product Kier uses to "have another set of eyes and research focused on the same investment philosophy as I do. As a speculator, you should not care who comes up with the idea but rather how you can capitalize on it."

Kier finds actionable ideas with Leaderboard that dovetail with his own research: "The annotated charts are an excellent reference tool for beginners or even professional investors like me. I also find the cut list helpful during downtrending markets to look for ideas to short."

Kier uses the weekends for studying. He scanned and enlarged the 100 charts that appear in beginning pages of *How to Make Money in Stocks* and studies one or two of them each week. It's the desire to find the next big winner that motivates and excites him.

Kier believes in giving back and likes helping others learn more about the market. For the past six years, Kier has taken on two interns from Boston University every semester and teaches them about stocks and the overall market. He also remains involved in his local IBD Meetup community, teaching lessons several times a year over the last four years.

In searching for the next big winner, Kier notes, "Big leaders take time to develop. Most big moves typically take 12 to 18 months to occur. One has to be willing to sit through intermediate corrections that are often 20 to 25%

to capture the big returns. That's why patience and discipline are, in my opinion, key characteristics of successful speculators."

• KEY POINTS •

- Many of the market's biggest winners will have triple-digit earnings and sales.
- Watch for shoe fads.
- The patterns of the big winners from the past repeat themselves over and over.
- In the evening, read *e*IBD as a resource tool for finding the market's leaders.
- Develop patience and discipline.

Jim Roppel

Jim is the founder and managing partner of a hedge fund in the Chicago area. When you talk to Jim, his energy and enthusiasm for the market is obvious. He notes, "Opportunities in the stock market are endless if an investor is willing to do their homework, stay disciplined, and learn to be patient."

Shortly after graduating college, Jim began his financial career as a stock broker. At the time, his dad invested in biotech and drug companies. Jim thought he would try investing in medical stocks as well. His initial buys moved higher, however, when a stock's price cratered due to a bad earnings report, or when a company didn't get approval for one of their drugs, the drawdown was severe. Since Jim hadn't yet developed sell rules, he lost a great deal of money.

For several years, Jim would struggle as a stock broker, continuing to look for a winning system, even trying value investing, but he didn't have much success with any new strategy. He was determined to succeed, though, so he kept reading various books and publications on investing.

In Search of Excellence

In 1990, Jim came across *How to Make Money in Stocks* at a bookstore and was immediately intrigued. He also found *Investor's Business Daily* and began reading it every day. Jim became such an avid fan of the paper that he would wait till midnight for the truck to deliver the papers to a local distribution center. As part of the learning process, Jim cut out weekly charts from the newspaper and glued them to the back of copier paper box lids. Then he leaned the box lids against the wall and studied the charts over and over. (These were big names in the market like Amgen and Cisco Systems.) He also cut out the New High list from the paper. Looking at this list gave Jim an indication of the overall market health. If leading stocks were continuing to hit new price highs, the market was robust.

That same year, Jim attended his first IBD Seminar with Bill O'Neil and David Ryan. Jim started really understanding the importance of fundamental criteria as well as technical buy and sell signals. He bought every cassette tape that IBD produced and would listen to these educational tapes on the way to and from work every day.

Jim realized that one of the biggest mistakes he had been making was a lack of defined sell rules. The second major problem was that he didn't have the proper selection criteria for picking stocks. He also hadn't learned to get rid of the underperforming stocks in his portfolio and move more money into the stocks that were working well. Once he began to implement a few simple rules, his portfolio returns turned around almost overnight.

Jim has attended IBD Workshops once a year and sometimes three times a year since 1990. He wanted to gain a thorough understanding of the investing strategy and base pattern recognition in order to spot potential leading stocks that were breaking out of sound patterns. He knew that buying stocks just as they are coming out of those areas of price consolidation was crucial to making large gains. Jim went over and over his notes from the workshops to cement the finer points of the system. He wanted to make money, and his desire to succeed completely overshadowed his previous challenges.

Learning from a Missed Opportunity

In 1993, Jim observed New Bridge Networks as it went up 600% in just under a year. He saw that it was highlighted frequently in IBD and was upset that he missed a big winner. But it gave Jim complete faith in the CAN SLIM Investing System and made him ready to commit some serious capital.

In 1995, Ascend Communications appeared in the paper almost every day. This was a true market leader with triple-digit earnings and sales growth. Jim had bought the stock and was sitting on a nice gain when Ascend suddenly broke below the 50-day moving average on heavy volume in October. He sold his entire position, but by the end of the trading day, Ascend closed back above the 50-day moving average. Jim realized that he had made a mistake in selling the stock, but he didn't go back in. The shakeout had rattled him. Ascend went on to rocket higher in the following months, and Jim missed some big gains.

After that, Jim made a rule that if he gets shaken out of a position, he must go back into a stock on the same day if the stock retakes the 50-day moving average. This benchmark line is a place where large institutional players will often come in to support a position that they hold, so it is a sign of strength if a stock retakes that line with heavy volume on the same day that it falls below it.

Know When to Go to Cash

By 1999, Jim had made over a million dollars trading, but this was the roaring 1990s, just before the tech bubble burst. Things seemed a little too good to be true, and that was the understatement of the decade. The market avalanche was about to begin.

In 2000, Jim was running a $150 million account for Morgan Stanley. He saw that the market wasn't acting right: Leaders were topping, many with dramatic climax runs. From January through early March, Qualcomm zoomed 42% in four days, Qlogic surged 75% in 11 days, and Yahoo rocketed up 90% in less than a month. This was abnormal activity. The number of climax runs that were occurring all at the same time was a warning sign to the seasoned investor that the market was topping. Jim went completely off margin and sold all of his holdings. He remembers being in a hotel in Arizona on St. Patrick's Day, all in cash, celebrating his gains. Then the crash came. Jim had avoided catastrophic losses and saved his clients and his firm enormous amounts of money as a result of heeding what he had learned from *How to Make Money in Stocks* and what he was reading in IBD at the time about the overall trend and the action of leading stocks.

After the top, people were sending Jim large amounts of money to invest, thinking that it was a great time to enter the market, but Jim let the money sit in cash, because he knew the trend was down: "When it is obvious to the masses and they begin to jump into the market with both feet, you know you've reached a major market top." Clients would call, begging him to buy Cisco Systems after it was down 40%, thinking it was a bargain, but Jim knew that buying a stock that was doing a nosedive was like trying to catch a falling knife. Cisco ended up losing 85% of its value. IBD's research shows that former leaders correct 72% on average. That is why a buy and hold strategy is very dangerous.

Dealing with a Prolonged Downtrend

The next three years were very difficult as the ensuing bear market wore on from 2000–2003, although there were a few tradable rallies. A professional trying to make money in the market found this a most challenging time.

Although Jim knew from looking at market history that things would get better eventually, the prolonged bear almost wore him out. It was so bad that people who worked in his office couldn't wait till Friday. Watching the market week by week was excruciating and often depressing.

About the time that Jim started to seriously worry that if things didn't turn around soon, he'd be "selling donuts at the local coffee shop," the market direction changed, and a new uptrend began. It really hit home to Jim that it is often during the darkest hour that the market will bottom and begin to turn up. Since then, he has welcomed bear markets, knowing they clear the decks for new leadership and powerful bull markets. New winners are born, and Jim knows he'll be there to profit from their enormous moves.

New Up Trends Bring Exciting Leaders

In December 2003, he bought Research in Motion, the maker of the Blackberry. Jim was excited about the stock because of the new technology. People could leave their office and keep up with work and e-mails. The stock's earnings soared as a result. Research in Motion is a stock that Jim would profit from a few years down the line also.

Jim bought Google in 2005. The company had the "big stock criteria" that Jim always looks for: something completely new and innovative. Google's search engine would transform the way people searched for information on the Internet.

Jim also saw something very unusual with Google's up/down volume ratio, which was 2.9. This ratio tracks the trading volume when a stock is rising in price and compares it to the volume when the stock is falling in price. A ratio greater than 1.2 shows positive demand for a stock. At 2.9, the demand for Google's shares was off the charts. Jim had found while doing research on the biggest winners from the past that they might have an up/down ratio of 1.9 or higher, but 2.9 was the highest he had ever seen (up/down volume can be found in Stock Checkup at Investors.com).

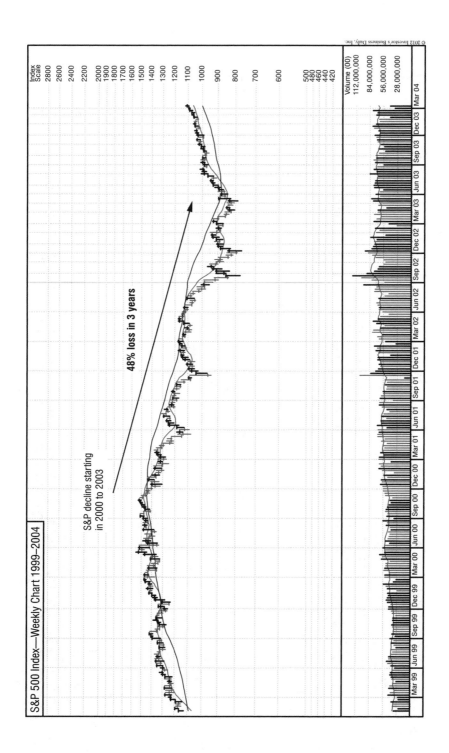

S&P 500 Index—Weekly Chart 1999–2004

S&P decline starting in 2000 to 2003

48% loss in 3 years

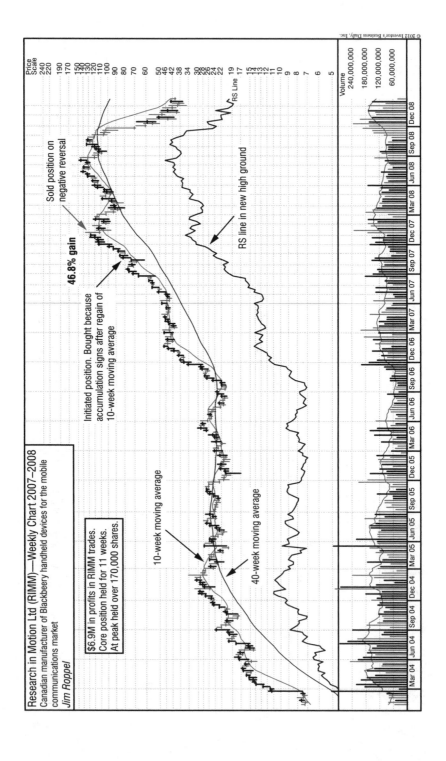

Research in Motion Ltd (RIMM)—Weekly Chart 2007–2008
Canadian manufacturer of Blackberry handheld devices for the mobile communications market
Jim Roppel

$6.9M in profits in RIMM trades.
Core position held for 11 weeks.
At peak held over 170,000 shares.

10-week moving average

40-week moving average

Initiated position. Bought because accumulation signs after regain of 10-week moving average

46.8% gain

Sold position on negative reversal

RS line in new high ground

RS Line

© 2012 Investor's Business Daily, Inc.

The Google of China

Baidu, which is the Google of China, first came to Jim's attention after it came public in February 2005. He didn't buy the stock because its initial base looked faulty, but he kept following it because of the unique story and because many of the market's biggest winners will have come public within the prior eight years of their big price moves.

By 2007, Baidu had more quarters of earnings and sales data, so Jim could do a better analysis of the company. As Jim did his research, he thought that Baidu looked too good to be true. "It just seemed too perfect."

Starting in the June 2007 quarter, Baidu had earnings growth of 100% and sales growth of 120%. These were massive earnings and sales numbers, and that is why Jim was able to have conviction in the stock and why he bought shares aggressively. Earnings in the following quarters were 75%, 61%, 100%, and 114%. Sales rose 118%, 125%, 130%, 122%, and 103%.

With more than 1.6 billion people in China and only a small number on the Internet at that time, Jim knew that the stock had enormous potential. Baidu also had government protection and virtually no competition. Several mutual funds, banks, and other institutional investors like Fidelity were taking large positions in Baidu, and this gave Jim greater confidence in the company.

Jim thought that Baidu was likely to have the same success that Google had as an Internet search engine. There was an exploding environment in China with a whole new group of people using the Internet. Barriers were beginning to break down in the Communist regime, and Baidu would go on to become a truly giant market leader.

Market Leaders Get Hit Also in a Downtrend

Even so, as the market turned south late in 2007, Baidu was hit along with several other market leaders. Jim sold his entire position in Baidu, knowing that even the best stocks correct when the market heads lower.

The market went down dramatically from late 2007 until March 2009. The Nasdaq suffered a loss of over 50% due to the banking and housing debacles. But Jim had been through a period like this before with the 2000–2003 bear market, and he knew that eventually the economy would pick up and that new innovative companies would emerge.

Baidu Hints of a New Uptrend

Starting in February 2009, Jim noticed that Baidu was beginning to move up again. The stock advanced 13 weeks in a row, which indicated that institutional money was accumulating shares. He also noted that the RS line (relative strength line) was heading into new high ground, something that is often seen in the biggest market leaders. This meant that Baidu was outperforming the S&P 500. Subsequently, on March 12, 2009, the general market began a new uptrend. With the market acting well, Jim reestablished a position in Baidu.

On October 26, 2009, Baidu announced that it was going to change to an advertising platform called Phoenix Nest. The stock sold off heavily on the news because analysts thought earnings were going to be affected by the switch to a different platform. The next day, the stock gapped down 18% and fell below the 50-day moving average. Jim owned a large number of shares and was down several million dollars in his account. He sold a sizeable amount of his position down to the "being able to sleep at night level" and waited to see how Baidu would do in the following weeks.

Baidu traded sideways for 10 weeks but bounced off the 50-day line with heavy volume. Baidu said that the Phoenix platform would solve problems they were having with advertisers, which turned out to be good news. Institutional money went back into Baidu, and so did Jim Roppel.

Watch for Excessive Stock Splits

Baidu had a 10-for-1 stock split in June 2010. Jim reduced his position, knowing that oversize splits can sometimes make a company more lethargic by creating a substantially larger number of shares. He sold another part of his position as the stock broke the 50-day line in June and the final portion in June 2011 after the stock again pulled below the 50-day line. Jim has a sell rule that if a stock has a severe break of the 50-day moving average on heavy volume after a long run, then it must be sold.

Jim ended up making just under $30 million with his trades in Baidu. This illustrates the importance of handling a big winner correctly once you find it. Many people might discover a winning stock but end up selling it too soon or make the mistake of not going back into the stock after being shaken out of it. But this is necessary if you're going to capture the market's biggest leaders. And these stocks are the ones that can really change your life if you handle them correctly.

Sitting on His Hands with a Leading Stock

Jim's overall strategy is to hold a stock for a year, though this isn't cast in stone. He knows that a big winner may have four pullbacks to the 50-day

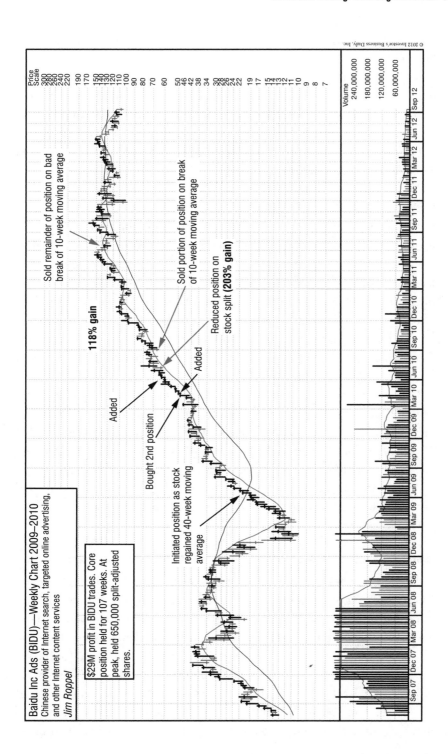

Baidu Inc Ads (BIDU)—Weekly Chart 2009–2010
Chinese provider of Internet search, targeted online advertising, and other Internet content services
Jim Roppel

$29M profit in BIDU trades. Core position held for 107 weeks. At peak, held 650,000 split-adjusted shares.

Sold remainder of position on bad break of 10-week moving average

Sold portion of position on break of 10-week moving average

Reduced position on stock split **(203% gain)**

118% gain

Added

Added

Bought 2nd position

Initiated position as stock regained 40-week moving average

line along its massive run. He is mentally prepared for a pullback of 20 to 26% with a truly big winner but notes that "you have to literally sit on your hands and stay disciplined as a stock pulls back." He knows that the equity curve in his hedge fund can come down 20% or more, but this is where the professional investor must have the confidence to sit through pullbacks in order to get the big monster moves. Jim does a lot of research on a company before he buys shares, and this allows him to have the conviction to hold through periods of pullbacks.

Finding the Biggest Winners

Jim is looking for the rare stocks that will make enormous moves. When he is establishing a position in a stock, he could be investing $15 million or more, making liquidity extremely important. Ideally, the average daily dollar volume should be two hundred million or higher (calculated by multiplying the number of shares a stock trades by the stock's price per share). These are also stocks that are more likely to have institutional support from mutual funds, banks, and pension funds. Jim says part of the "magic sauce for finding the market's biggest winners is high liquidity combined with soaring earnings growth."

Baidu went on to make a move of 1,000% from March 2009 to July 2011. This only occurs when the stock is a complete game changer and dominates in its field. The biggest winners have something—a product or service that no one else has. Apple had the iPod, iPhone, and the iPad. Hansen launched the Monster Energy Drink. eBay became a multibillion dollar company with its online auction site, which offers a variety of goods and services. The exciting thing is these innovative companies show up in every new bull market cycle.

Look for a Unique Product Hitting the Market at an Opportune Time

Jim found another game changer with Netflix in 2010. Netflix knocked Blockbuster out of business. The United States was in a recession, but people could order movies from Netflix, stay home, and watch them without any late fees. Noting the company's exceptional fundamentals and innovative business model, Jim bought Netflix in August 2010 and held for the big run, selling his final shares in April 2011 and netting an $8.9 million profit.

Jim's fund was heavily margined on May 3 going into an earnings report for OpenTable. When the company reported earnings, the stock gapped down significantly on huge volume. Other leading stocks began to break

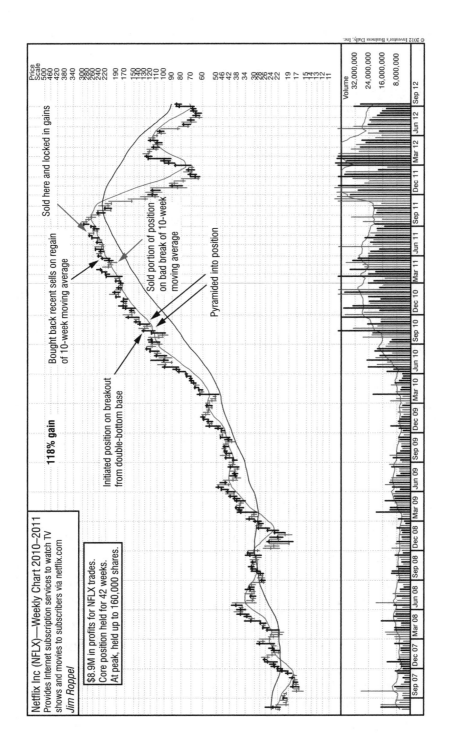

Netflix Inc (NFLX)—Weekly Chart 2010–2011
Provides Internet subscription services to watch TV
shows and movies to subscribers via netflix.com
Jim Roppel

118% gain

$8.9M in profits for NFLX trades.
Core position held for 42 weeks.
At peak, held up to 160,000 shares.

Sold here and locked in gains

Bought back recent sells on regain
of 10-week moving average

Sold portion of position
on bad break of 10-week
moving average

Initiated position on breakout
from double-bottom base

Pyramided into position

© 2012 Investor's Business Daily, Inc.

down on heavy volume, signaling some potential trouble for the market. Jim reduced his market exposure by 50% and was able to preserve the gains in his account by moving entirely to cash within a couple of days.

For the rest of 2011, the market was choppy and difficult to trade. Jim allowed himself to get swayed by all the problems in Europe, so in December 2011, when the trend of the market changed and began to head up again, he was late to the game.

Staying in Sync with the Market

Jim notes that identifying the market trend is the trickiest yet most critical part of investing. "You have to stay in sync with the market and not argue when leading stocks begin breaking out and heading higher, because it is then and only then that you are positioned to make a lot of money in the market."

Despite mistakes, Jim has complete confidence that he will capture a piece of several new leaders in every cycle: "There are huge winners in every bull cycle, and the more you use the CAN SLIM Investing System, the more your confidence builds that you'll be able to find and profit from a big winner."

Jim is modest and self-effacing in discussing his successful career, reminding investors that he loses money on at least half the stocks that he buys, but he keeps his losses small and says that "it only takes a few big winners, if you handle them correctly, to significantly improve your life financially."

• KEY POINTS •

- Pay attention to stocks that appear in IBD almost every day.
- If you get shaken out of a stock that drops below the 50-day moving average, consider going back in if it retakes that line by the end of the day.
- Look for stocks with the "big stock criteria," something completely new and innovative that is in big demand.
- Many of the market's biggest winners will have come public within the prior eight years of their big price moves.

- Take note of stocks going up several weeks in a row, showing institutional buying.
- Watch for too many stock splits. Several splits or an oversized split can sometimes make a company more lethargic by creating a substantially larger number of shares, which makes it harder for the stock to rise in price.
- Learn to handle a big winner once you find it.
- Many of the market's biggest winners will have high liquidity combined with soaring earnings growth.
- The market trend is the most important part of investing. Stay in sync with the market so you are positioned to profit from a market uptrend.

Eve Bobach

In 1995, Eve was browsing through a bookstore looking for stock investing ideas and happened to pick up a copy of *How to Make Money in Stocks*. She had always found the complexity and speed of change in the markets fascinating and was immediately hooked by growth stock investing possibilities.

Later that year, Eve attended her first advanced IBD Seminar and was excited to meet Bill O'Neil in person. She took her copy of *How to Make Money in Stocks* up to Bill after the workshop and asked for his autograph. He signed, "Buy the best companies with great earnings, coming out of bases." It's something Eve has never forgotten and often reads to remind herself of what to look for in the very best stocks.

Over the years, Eve has attended dozens of IBD Workshops. She says they "reinforce everything that is in Bill's book." From them, she has learned what to look for in the technical patterns and key fundamental factors in leading stocks.

In early 1996, Eve bought Whole Foods Market after the stock followed through on a high-volume breakout from a cup-with-handle base and made some nice gains. At the time, Whole Foods had only 35 stores, with plenty of opportunities to expand. Some of the key fundamental numbers included: latest quarter earnings +41%; latest quarter sales +24%; and Accumulation/Distribution Rating A. (This rating measures whether a stock is under institutional accumulation or buying. The rating goes from A to E, with A being the highest.) Whole Foods was one of Eve's earlier successes, and it's a stock that she would profit from more than once. Eve admits to being a bit of a health food nut, so she was familiar with the store long before it became a household name. It helped her have conviction in the company and its possibilities.

This success taught Eve a valuable lesson: whenever possible, she visits the store of a company that she is evaluating, or buys a product to see what she thinks of it. She admits to having a closet full of various products purchased for market research, such as the K-Cup coffee makers that Green Mountain Coffee Roasters sells, Lululemon athletic gear, and Michael Kors accessories.

Jim Roppel met Eve through mutual friends and recruited Eve to assist with a new small cap growth fund that he started in 2011.

It Takes a Structured Approach

Eve is very methodical in her approach to the market and investing. She is structured and analytical while following a relatively straightforward routine. She has streamlined the process to what is most essential.

Eve checks the global markets, futures, and pre-market prices and news on stocks in the portfolio as well as watch list stocks to see how they are doing before the market opens.

After the market opens, Eve watches the major indexes and the action of market leaders. Throughout the day, she monitors the 100 or so stocks that she feels might have the potential to become leaders and runs screens to find stocks with exceptional fundamentals that are rising on unusual volume.

An hour and a half before the market close, Eve closely monitors the action of the indexes, market leaders, and stocks on her watch list. Key reversals can happen late in the trading day, so she pays close attention during this critical time.

After the close, Eve takes a break and works out. She runs or does Pilates and feels this is a healthy way to recharge after the market action. Eve also enjoys spending time with her family and friends; this helps put everything into perspective.

In the evening, Eve reads through *e*IBD and does more online research. She is always looking for new trends and future leading stocks.

If the market has started a new uptrend, Eve tracks the stocks that broke out after the most recent follow-through day. The stocks that break out early and perform the best a few weeks after a new uptrend begins are the ones that may lead the new rally. Eve also monitors how the breakouts act to determine the health of the rally. If a number of breakouts stall or begin to fall below their pivot points, it may lead to a failed rally attempt.

To help assess the health of the market, Eve also monitors distribution and accumulation days on the major indexes as well as price performance and duration of the current rally relative to other market cycles.

Eve conducts a post analysis of her trades and has found that one of the worst mistakes is to take a small profit in a big market leader. These are the stocks that should be held for the bigger run. Eve bought eBay out of its IPO base but was shaken out and never went back in, missing out on the stock's big move.

Once you have found a market leader, it's important to put enough capital into it to make substantial profits. Your best-performing stock should be your largest holding. eBay taught Eve a lesson.

As a result, she has learned to always be prepared to buy a stock back if it subsequently turns around and starts to make another move.

Avoiding Emotional Trading

In order to control possible emotional trades made in the heat of the market action, Eve has her rules written out and nearby. When she makes a trade, she asks herself what rule is making her buy, sell, or hold onto a stock.

One way to remove emotional trading is to buy on the daily charts and sell on the weekly. The daily action tells you when a stock is breaking out, but the weekly shows the big picture that is valuable in assessing how a stock is acting. To capture the significant moves, it's important not to be shaken out by the day-to-day market gyrations, instead focusing on the intermediate trend. A weekly stock chart helps put this into perspective.

Eve feels it's important when entering a position to write out some hold rules and have sell points established ahead of time. This takes possible indecision about when to sell, out of the equation.

Eve also trades in increments to avoid overreacting. She does follow-up buys on positions that are doing well.

She is currently doing a study of the 1998 market and the characteristics of the leaders at that time. Eve studies past markets to help her identify future market leaders. She examines the technical action that all big leaders have in common. One thing that she has noticed is that many of them have breakaway gap-ups early in their run. These big gap-up moves in price can make investors nervous, but they are often characteristic of true market leaders.

Handling Buyable Gap-Ups

Buyable gap-ups should only be entered in stocks exhibiting strong fundamental strength in an uptrending market. The model stock book of stocks that IBD has researched for over 130 years has many examples of stocks with gap-ups that went on to make big moves in the market, but these companies were also leaders in their industry and had strong earnings and sales along with other key fundamental criteria. A more successful buyable gap-up play occurs in a market leader that has already proven itself but is rocketing higher due to a positive earnings report.

When large institutional money goes into a stock, it is a good indication that they have faith in the company and its products or services and see the likelihood of success in the future.

• KEY POINTS •

- Track stocks that break out right after a follow-through day to determine the health of the rally and to track potential big winners.
- Your best-performing stock should be your largest holding.
- Have a set of written rules near your computer to avoid emotional trading.
- Gap-ups should only be entered in stocks that are exhibiting strong fundamental strength in an uptrending market.
- When evaluating a company, visit a store or buy some of their products.

David Ryan

David's first introduction to the stock market was from his dad, who saw investing as a way to pay for a college education. Since David was pretty young at the time, his dad would talk about companies like Disney so David could relate to them better. When David was 13 years old, he bought his

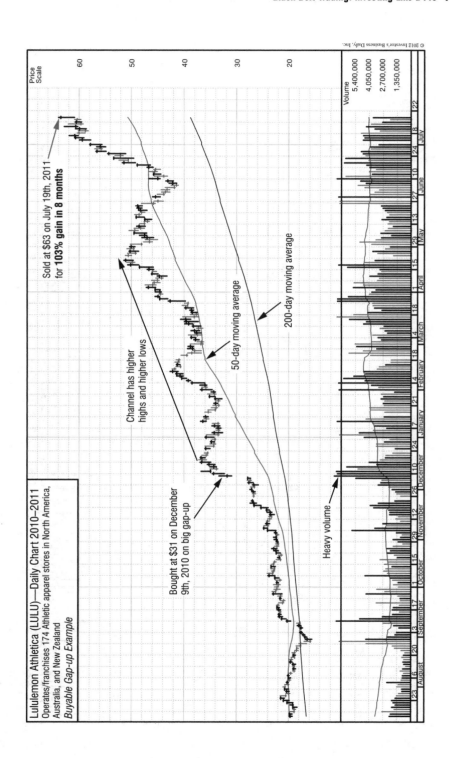

© 2012 Investor's Business Daily, Inc.

Lululemon Athletica (LULU)—Daily Chart 2010–2011
Operates/franchises 174 Athletic apparel stores in North America, Australia, and New Zealand
Buyable Gap-up Example

Sold at $63 on July 19th, 2011 for **103% gain in 8 months**

Channel has higher highs and higher lows

50-day moving average

200-day moving average

Bought at $31 on December 9th, 2010 on big gap-up

Heavy volume

Price Scale

Volume

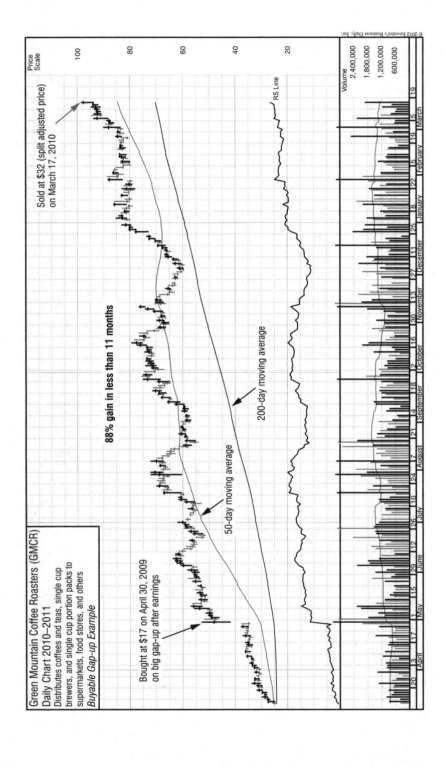

Green Mountain Coffee Roasters (GMCR)
Daily Chart 2010–2011
Distributes coffees and teas, single cup
brewers, and single cup portion packs to
supermarkets, food stores, and others
Buyable Gap-up Example

Bought at $17 on April 30, 2009
on big gap-up after earnings

88% gain in less than 11 months

Sold at $32 (split adjusted price)
on March 17, 2010

50-day moving average

200-day moving average

RS Line

Price
Scale

Volume
2,400,000
1,800,000
1,200,000
600,000

© 2012 Investor's Business Daily, Inc.

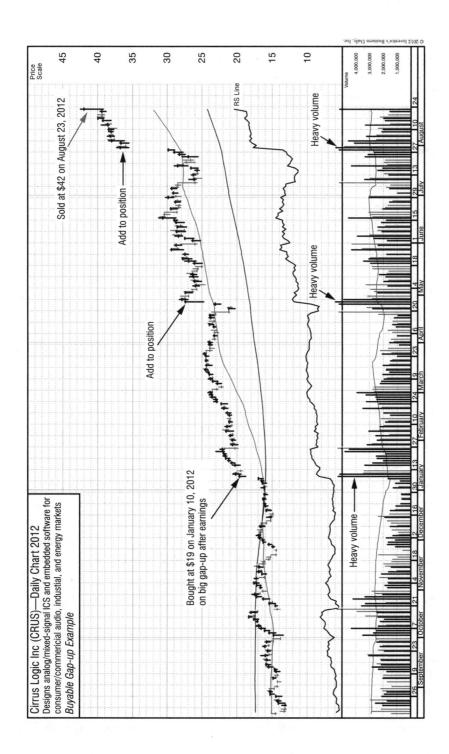

Cirrus Logic Inc (CRUS)—Daily Chart 2012
Designs analog/mixed-signal ICS and embedded software for
consumer/commercial audio, industial, and energy markets
Buyable Gap-up Example

Price Scale

Sold at $42 on August 23, 2012

Add to position

Add to position

RS Line

Bought at $19 on January 10, 2012
on big gap-up after earnings

Heavy volume

Heavy volume

Heavy volume

Volume

© 2012 Investor's Business Daily, Inc.

first stock, 10 shares of Hershey's, the maker of Chunky candy bars. David followed his stock and others in the market, wondering why some stocks would go up and others would go down.

His fascination with the market continued through high school and college. After hearing Bill speak at an investment seminar in Century City, David took a trial of Daily Graphs. When he went down to pick up the chart book each Saturday, Bill O'Neil was often there answering people's questions. David listened to these conversations, riveted.

Once he graduated from UCLA, David showed up at the O'Neil offices and offered to work for free. He met with Kathy Sherman, Bill's executive assistant at the time, who recognized David's energy and enthusiasm for stocks and the market. David left thinking nothing might come of his visit to the O'Neil office, but by the time he got home, there was a message on his phone machine saying that Bill O'Neil wanted to interview him. A few days later, when Bill was interviewing David, he asked him what he wanted to do in five years. David wasn't really sure, but replied, "I know you've been successful. I just want to learn all that I can."

David started in the institutional area of the firm doing research and learning everything about the CAN SLIM Investing strategy. A new bull market began in August 1982, and David started investing, using what he had learned since joining O'Neil + Company®. He says, "I did pretty well for about a year and a half but was making lots of mistakes and gave back most of my gains." David went back and studied his trades and came to the conclusion that he was buying stocks that were too extended. He decided to become extremely disciplined and from then on, "My performance really started to take off."

David rose to national attention by winning the U.S. Investing Championship three times between 1985 and 1990. This competition was sponsored by a former Stanford professor and involved real money in real accounts. Each year, approximately 300 contestants, including portfolio managers, market letter writers, and individual investors competed to see who could achieve the best returns.

David says, "The CAN SLIM principles are all laid out for you, but it's your job to adapt it to your comfort level and make it work. It will require some studying, but to be successful in anything, you have to be willing to put in the time."

From 1982 to 1985, one of David's primary responsibilities was working closely with Bill to advise the firm's 500 institutional clients on individual stock selection. David also managed several investment portfolios for William O'Neil + Company.

David worked with Bill for nearly 17 years, and though he respected Bill enormously and had learned an incredible amount from working with him, he felt it was time to "stretch his wings," so he started his own hedge fund in July 1998.

David feels his longevity as a professional investor stems from the fact that he controls risk as much as possible and doesn't let losses get out of hand, noting that "if it is your own account, you might be able to take more risks, but not when you're dealing with people's retirement money and their family wealth."

He likes investing in retailers because "you can go into a store or restaurant and get a good feel for them." David usually trades around a core position in a stock, so if he owns 20,000 shares, he may cut that down to 10,000 if the stock is basing or the market is pulling back and then "ramp shares back up as the stock begins to take off again."

In recent years, he's had success with stocks like Chipotle Mexican Grill, Apple, and Caterpillar.

Know the Story

The key factor that will help you stick with a winning stock is to make sure you know its underlying story. What is making the company successful? What are the key concepts that will keep it highly profitable? Will the company go from having 250 stores to over 500 in the next few years? Are they producing a product that is in big demand?

David feels that even if someone has another job, it's important to have a trading account of some kind: "Try to put in a half hour of study each day and begin to put the CAN SLIM principles to work. IBD does a great job of highlighting the best stocks in the best groups. All you need are one or two great stocks in a year, and you can achieve some outstanding results."

He says that "CAN SLIM Investing is the fastest way to make money in the stock market, but the key is to have discipline. There are some straightforward rules that you must follow."

David is passionate about the market and investing, "and this has taken me through some difficult, challenging markets."

He also adds that while it's great to make money, there are other things that are more important: "Faith, family, and friends are the most valuable. Keep it all in perspective."

• KEY POINTS •

- Make sure you understand a stock's underlying story. What is making the company successful? What are the key concepts that will keep it highly profitable?

- Try to put in a half hour of study each day and begin to put the CAN SLIM principles to work.

- All you need are one or two great stocks in a year, and you can achieve some outstanding results.

Portfolio Managers: Mike Webster and Charles Harris

*"Fast as the wind, quiet as a forest, aggressive as fire,
and immovable as a mountain."*

—SAMURAI BATTLE BANNER

This saying mirrors the quiet but swift decisions that a professional must make while trading. Mike and Charles have been portfolio managers for O'Neil Data Systems, Inc., for over a decade. They are hard-working and passionate about the market, and both are polite and unassuming despite the tremendous amount of success they have had in their trading accounts, both professionally and personally.

Mike Webster

Mike had been interested in investing since he was very young.

"When I was 24 years old," Mike says, "I read Peter Lynch's *One Up on Wall Street*, which had a profound impact on how I looked at a company's products and services. Lynch was a buy-what-you-know guy, and that just made sense to me, so I was on the lookout for that great next product to give me an edge. Around that time, I took a tour of the Robert Mondavi Winery up in Napa Valley, and I was blown away. I couldn't believe the amount of detail that went into every aspect of the business, from how they avoided diseases that would kill the grape vines down to inventing new nonspill wine bottles. I went home and ordered all of their annual reports and read them cover to cover. Though I was too new to investing to really understand the data, I was absolutely convinced that this was going to be a great stock. The only problem was, I didn't have any money. I was just a couple of years out of college and living paycheck to paycheck. I wanted to buy a round lot of 100 shares but didn't have enough money, so I started saving and scrounging up whatever I could. Meanwhile, the stock didn't wait for me; it ran up from $7 to $14. I realized I was going to miss the stock's move if I didn't act fast, so with all the money I had, $540, I bought my odd lots. As I saved more money, I continued buying more shares, and the stock more than doubled by the time I finally sold. I learned a great deal from that experience. Always be on the lookout for new products; they are what drive a stock's move up."

The Christmas Present That Changed His Life

For Christmas that year, Mike's parents bought him *How to Make Money in Stocks*. "Little did I know this book was going to change my life," After he read Bill's book, he recalls saying to himself, "I've just got to work for this guy."

Mike remembers thinking he had won the lottery after he was hired by William O'Neil + Company to work in the research department. Not long after being hired by the firm, he was in an accident, and his car was totaled. As he sat on the curb waiting for his wife to pick him up, he says, "I felt like I was given a second chance in life and didn't want to waste it. Right then I wrote down my short- to long-term goals. The key goal was to become a portfolio manager for Bill. I looked at that sheet every day, and it kept me highly motivated, working long hours every day."

Soon after that, Bill gave an inspirational speech to the research department. Mike approached Bill afterwards and told him he wanted to be a portfolio manager. Bill said he wasn't really looking for a portfolio manager but said, "Put some of your trades together, and come talk to me."

Mike assembled several past trades and current stock ideas and nervously entered Bill's office. He says, "I've never been so nervous in my whole life. Bill was pretty tough on me." Mike felt "devastated and demoralized" after the meeting but realized that the charts he had given Bill were stretched and not properly sized, so Bill thought a lot of stocks Mike was investing in had charts that were very wide and loose (volatile price movements) when in fact they were not.

A longtime employee asked Mike, "How much time did Bill spend with you?" When Mike responded an hour and a half, she said, "Bill wouldn't have spent that much time unless he saw something promising in you. Hang in there."

Training with the Master and Learning to Live in the Moment

Mike kept plugging away and had more meetings with Bill regarding his trades. Bill saw improvements in how Mike was handling stocks and that he had listened to his feedback. In late December 1999, after reviewing several of Mike's trades that were well executed using the CAN SLIM Investing System, Bill offered Mike a job as a portfolio manager, making Mike's dream come true. The following year, Mike was lucky enough to start working in Bill's office, where he stayed for a few years. He says, "That was such a special learning experience and very motivational. No one works harder and is more positive than Bill. He is a great role model and mentor."

After working with Bill for awhile, Mike realized that Bill lives in the moment as a trader: "One week Bill could dislike a stock and then a couple of weeks later turn around and start buying it. That flexibility has kept him in phase with the market for over 50 years. He doesn't care what he said in the past. When the facts change, he changes with them." He recalls a lesson Bill taught him when reviewing a mistake that he had made. Mike round-tripped (letting a gain fall back to the purchase price) a big position, letting a large gain evaporate. Bill said, "You always need to be flexible, bending like a tree in the wind. Don't freeze up. If a stock starts acting poorly, start selling at least some of it, then reassess and sell more if warranted."

"Bill isn't afraid to make mistakes and doesn't really care what anybody thinks. He doesn't have an ego but has more confidence than anyone I've ever met. If Bill makes a mistake, he'll correct it quickly, but if the stock turns and sets back up, Bill will go back in and buy the stock back, only with slightly more money than the first time around, putting him in the offensive position."

"Bill has the ability to truly capitalize on the market leader. Once he has a profit cushion with a stock, he will sit with it and add at logical points as the stock rises in price. He spreads his purchases over several weeks and months. This great stock-picking skill and patience completely separates him from all other traders."

Always Be Looking for New Ideas

Another thing Mike learned from working with Bill is to always be looking for new ideas. Bill looks at hundreds of charts over the weekend, and so does Mike.

Mike says, "Studying hundreds of charts on a regular basis gives you an edge. You start to notice that stocks have different characteristics, just like people do: some are slow and steady, others are erratic, and there is everything in between. Once you can key into the stock's character, you can know what to expect, when is it acting normal, and, more importantly, when it breaks character. This is a skill that anyone can learn if you study enough charts."

"The only time I said no to Bill as a portfolio manager was when he asked me to teach the IBD advanced workshops," says Mike. "I was absolutely terrified of public speaking." Bill didn't understand Mike's fear but encouraged him by saying, "You know everything about the system backwards and forwards."

Mike continued to struggle with his fear of public speaking but began teaching the advanced workshops with Bill and really saw value in the seminars from the feedback he received from the attendees. Bill always said to everyone who helped out with the workshops, "We are getting as much out of the seminars as other people because of all the tremendous work we put in before we teach. It forces us to really follow the system."

Day-by-Day Stock Chart Simulations Are Extremely Instructive

Mike thinks the workshop animations have helped him the most as a trader: "At the Chart School Seminar that I teach with Charles Harris, we go over animations taking stocks day by day through their move. We stop at various points, letting people know what we would do with the stock. When I'm conflicted with a decision in a real trade, I imagine I'm going over it at a seminar, and it gives me clarity."

For a newer investor, Mike cautions, "Don't try to make a lot of money right off the bat. Making money shouldn't be the primary goal. Learning the system should be, then the money will come. The worst thing that could happen is that by a fluke, you make a lot of money with bad habits in a more forgiving market." He suggests, "At first just trade with 10% of what you were planning on investing. Learn to make mistakes and how to correct them before investing a larger portion of your capital."

Look for Historically Similar Market Periods

The study of bull and bear markets helps illuminate the larger up and down trends that the market goes through and repeats decade after decade. Helping investors understand the overall market trend has been one of Bill O'Neil's goals since before the inception of the newspaper in 1984. Having historical data to help interpret the market's trends over the years is enormously helpful.

"If you enjoy studying the market and past winning stocks, eventually you'll find a perfect precedent for a current time period. In early 2003, I realized that a chart of the Dow from 1929 to 1932 looked just like a chart of the 2000 to 2002 period on the Nasdaq; in fact, they were almost identical. I also found a precedent from the bull market that started in March of 1933, in which the Dow looked just like the Nasdaq in March of 2003. So I used that precedent as a roadmap to trade aggressively during that time frame. That is why Bill has us studying past stocks and markets because nothing ever changes."

Creating Highly Useful Investment Tools

Over the years, Mike has created many products used for the company. His first was Stock Checkup for Investors.com. He also created the IBD Composite Rating because Bill wanted a way for investors to quickly evaluate the overall strength of a stock fundamentally. The Composite Rating combines key characteristics like earnings growth, profit margins, the level of institutional buying over the last 12 weeks, and other fundamental data designed to help investors find the best stocks faster. Stocks are given a numerical rating from 1 to 99, with 99 being the best.

Mike also helped develop the MarketSmith 250 Growth Screen. He admits to being a "screen junkie," so this product was created to save people time with just one comprehensive list of stocks worth researching rather than building countless screens. This list has over 30 different themed screens that are combined into one list that filters for technical and fundamental stock data like price performance, earnings, liquidity, return on equity, and pre-tax margins, among other criteria. Mike says, "Learning how to screen properly takes years, and we wanted to speed up everyone's learning curve. The product was really created to save people time. I use it every week."

Pattern Recognition, another product that Mike helped develop for MarketSmith, uses algorithms to create chart base patterns and to identify buy points. Through a lot of hard work, Mike was able to get the computer to identify and draw the base. If an investor is newer to chart reading, this helps locate the stocks that are consolidating and getting ready to break out. For the more seasoned trader who already knows how to read charts, it's a time saver: "Having the percent from the pivot, depth, and stage of the base is great—it's like using a calculator instead of doing the math by hand."

Market School is a new seminar that Mike teaches with Charles Harris. Mike says, "Charles and I worked with Justin Nielsen to come up with several buy and sell rules based on the market's price and volume action to give us a guideline for how deep to be invested. We knew that a follow-through day would get us in the market. And a lot of distribution days would signal a top. But the problem was the period of time in between a market bottom and a market top. Bill has a great sense for how deep to be invested based on his decades of experience, but we aren't Bill. So with countless hours of back-testing, we came up with a set of rules that work extremely well. Our goal was to be in line with how Bill trades and looks at the market."

A product that Mike didn't work on but that he really likes is Chart Arcade. He said his 10-year-old daughter got him hooked on it. It's a stock market game created by the MarketSmith team, where investors can buy or sell historical charts based on price and volume action. Mike says, "You get immediate feedback whether a stock you bought or sold was the right decision, and this can really speed up your learning curve."

(Investors can practice their skills for free at Chartarcade.com.)

Mike's overall advice is, "Read *How to Make Money in Stocks*, and stick to the CAN SLIM Investing System. Put in a few hours of study each week, and you will be able to have that extra spending money or a larger amount of money to retire on. But if you want to truly change your life, it's like everything else: it takes a lot of time and hard work, but it pays off."

• KEY POINTS •

1. Always have an up-to-date watch list.
   - Create a ready list with stocks that are nearing a buy point.
   - Keep a universe list for stocks that are worth following but are not quite near a buy point.
   - After you purchase a stock, have a sell, hold, and add plan for each stock.
   - Plan your trade, and trade your plan.
2. Watch for a sign of strength.
   - If the indexes are living above the 21-day moving average, the market is strong.

Charles Harris

Charles was a commercial real estate appraiser working toward his MAI designation (Member of Appraisal Institute), but he was very unhappy with the work and wanted to find a new career. He had always been interested in the stock market, so when he saw a posting on the UCLA jobs board for William O'Neil + Company, he decided to apply. Charles got a rejection letter that thanked him for his application but said he wasn't quite right for the job. A few years later, William O'Neil + Company was looking for an MBA to work as an analyst in the research department. Although Charles did not have an MBA, he applied for the position anyway, and this time he prevailed. At the time he was hired, Charles was primarily a value investor and was "dabbling in the market and investing in low P/E stocks without much success. I didn't even know who Bill O'Neil was back then."

Charles' initial plan was to get his foot in the door, spend a year or two getting some valuable work experience in the financial industry, and then move on to a job as a securities analyst. Toward that end, he began pursuing his CFA designation.

His responsibilities in the Research Department gave him access to stock data and detailed reports of individual stocks prepared by securities analysts from all of the major investment firms. Charles figured that with access to these reports, he would be able to pick the very best stocks and make a killing in the market: "When I read these reports that were so well researched and so persuasive, I called my wife and told her, 'We're going to be rich!' Instead, I lost half of my money in about three months. I was very naïve, but it taught me a very important lesson: Don't rely on the opinions of others. Do your own research, and come to your own conclusions."

From September 1995 through the end of 1996, Charles didn't have much overall success with investing, despite trying to learn all that he could about the CAN SLIM Investing System. Although he was able to pick some winning stocks, he had a tendency to hold onto his losers far too long, and as a result he lost money on a net basis.

Assess Your Trading Strengths and Weaknesses

So in December 1996, he sat down and had a serious discussion with himself. He contemplated, "Who am I as a trader? What are my strengths and weaknesses? What are the basic rules that I must follow if I am to be successful?" Charles wrote down a whole set of trading rules based on a post analysis of his actual trades over the prior year, as well as the teachings of some of the great trading legends, including Bill O'Neil, Nicholas Darvas, and Jesse Livermore. This became his "Trading Manifesto," which detailed his personal strategy to take advantage of his inherent strengths and laid out the trading rules that he would be bound to from that day forward. Immediately after that, Charles began to have "big success" in the market, running his personal account up over 1,500% over the next 18 months.

Unfortunately, Charles learned the hard way that great success often results in an inflated ego, and during the brief bear market that took hold from July 1998 through early October 1998, Charles lost three-quarters of his money: "My failure was brought on by my own hubris, and I continued to trade stocks despite the fact that the environment was treacherous, and the odds were against me. I had lost my discipline and self-confidence and almost gave up trading altogether, figuring that my earlier success was just beginner's luck." Having earned his CFA designation several months earlier, he applied for an analyst position at a money management firm.

Up Over 1,000% in 1998

Thankfully, Charles did not receive an offer, because as the market turned in October 1998 to begin the last leg of the great bull market, he went back to the rules that led to his earlier success and reclaimed both his discipline and confidence. In 1999, Charles had a huge year in his personal account and was up over 1,000%. Upon hearing of his success in the market, he remembers Bill saying to him, "Just remember, we all put our pants on one leg at a time." Based on his own successes over the years and having worked with dozens of traders, Bill knew that successful traders often get a "swelled head. Maybe he was trying to warn me not to get too carried away with myself. I wish I would have listened."

Toward the end of 1999, Charles approached senior management and expressed his desire to be a portfolio manager for Bill. A couple of weeks later, after his trading results were reviewed, Bill took Charles to lunch and explained that he didn't need a portfolio manager but was looking for someone to support the current portfolio managers as a research analyst. Bill added, "Maybe in the future, you'll get some money to run."

In January 2000, Bill moved Charles to a cubicle just outside his office and had him research stocks that he and the portfolio managers were interested in. During the first eight months of 2000, Charles was up over 800% in his personal account. After observing his trades, Bill gave Charles money to manage in June 2000, which coincided with the beginning of a brief, yet incredibly strong countertrend rally. After just six weeks of managing money for Bill, Charles' account was up more than 50%. "I was on top of the world," he said. Little did Charles know, that was the beginning of a long, dry period.

"My hubris had once again raised its ugly head. I had become overconfident and loose with the rules. When the market broke badly in September 2000, I ignored the fact that the bear market trend had resumed and kept trading anyway. I had done so well up to that point that my ego was totally out of control. I had lost all my discipline. I was like an addict."

Charles ended up giving back the bulk of his profits in his firm account and lamented that his personal account took a huge hit as well. "There is no substitute for experience, and until you've been in the investing battlefield, it's hard to understand this," he says. "The market was cracking wide open. The Nasdaq dropped over 45% in just four months. I started losing huge amounts of money. The only thing that saved me was my experience from the 1998 bear market, when I had nearly blown up my account. I knew I was out of control, so I just started wiring funds out of my personal account so I couldn't trade. I ended up preserving about two-thirds of my capital. The rest of the money…gone. This was demoralizing and left a big impact on me."

Never Break the Rules

Charles went back to his trading plan and, with a little time and a few "good" trades, recovered his discipline and confidence. He has learned the hard way to "always maintain your discipline and keep your ego in check, because breaking rules in the market will cost you a lot of money." He added, "I've really learned the importance of trading in line with the trend of the market, and to not draw down too much because it's so hard to come back psychologically after you've dug a deep hole. It can take years just to get back to even…what a waste."

When Charles and Mike Webster first became Portfolio Managers for Bill, they worked side by side in his office for two years. Each day they would compare their trading results. "I guess it was an ego thing, a way of measuring yourself. But in truth, comparing my progress with Mike put an enormous amount of pressure on me. Even if I was trading well, I'd feel crummy if he was doing better than me. But if I was beating him, I'd feel just fine, even if I wasn't really trading that well. It made absolutely no sense.

"I learned to go into a cocoon and stay isolated, like the legendary trader Nicolas Darvas, or the 'lone wolf' Jesse Livermore, so that I wouldn't compare my trades or my results to anyone else's. You don't have to be a genius to do well in the market, but you do have to keep your ego under control so you won't break the rules and make careless mistakes." To his credit, Bill isolates all of his Portfolio Managers and doesn't let them know where they stand in performance relative to each other. He knows that doing so would only put additional pressure on them.

Learning from Your Weaknesses and How to Overcome Them

The many years of teaching investing workshops have made Charles realize that every trader has their own inherent strengths and weaknesses: "For some, it's very difficult to cut losses. Other investors may not have the patience or fortitude to hold on for the big move. They satisfy their ego by locking in their profits early and miss out on the big money."

"To overcome weaknesses, Bill has taught me to

1. Admit that you have some shortcomings. Some investors refuse to take responsibility for their own results, and they end up never succeeding.

2. Do a post analysis of your trades; your weaknesses will pop right out.

3. Write down rules to help you overcome your trading flaws."

"In writing down my own rules and strategy, I really defined what style of trading comes most naturally to me. I am more of a swing trader. I am most comfortable taking profits into strength when my analysis of the stock's action tells me that a pullback is in store, and I tend to buy on pullbacks to the major moving averages or other support levels in stocks that have proven that they are market leaders. I am a much better singles hitter than a homerun hitter. That style is consistent with my personality, so I don't fight it. Bill has proven over the years that he is a great homerun hitter, so he may trade a little differently than I do. That's okay. Bill said to me a long time ago, 'If what you're doing is working, don't change it.'"

"Bill has been an inspiration in many ways. For one thing, his work ethic is unparalleled. There is nobody at the firm who works harder than he does. He is very flexible when it comes to the market and individual stocks. He can change his mind on a dime, and yet he has conviction when it's appropriate. One of the things that I admire most is the fact that he has never blown up his account, which is rare among traders. He will never hesitate to cut a loss if his stock starts acting poorly, no matter what he thinks of the company or how much he likes the stock. He is one of the few investors who made a fortune trading his own money. Most of the wealth in the financial field is based on trading other people's money. Bill is proof that making a fortune in the market can be done . . . it's just a matter of stringing together a few big winners and handling them properly. Of course, that's easier said than done."

A Few Big Winners Over a Lifetime Can Make a Fortune

"Bill's genius is that he truly has a knack for finding that special stock in a bull cycle that turns out to be a gigantic winner, and he has the ability to capitalize on it and make the big money. He doesn't always find every great stock; he misses some. I remember him telling me once that 'you can't kiss all the babies.' But you only need a few big ones over your lifetime to make a fortune. Look for the game changing stock, a company that has something really new and unique. Bill devised CAN SLIM to help investors identify these types of stocks.

"I'm up over 40 times my original principal since 2001 in a non-margined personal account. This is during a period when the broad market indexes have been relatively flat on a net basis. To achieve gains like this, you need to trade the windows of opportunity that present themselves and not give it all back in a correction.

"The stock market has changed my entire life. Everything I own and have been able to provide for my family has been the result of trading successfully. Anyone can do it, but you have to really want it and work hard at it. It's not easy, and it doesn't happen overnight. There are no shortcuts. You have to believe in yourself, and you have to believe in your trading strategy. With patience, hard work, and discipline, you will be successful."

• KEY POINTS •

On Market Psychology

- Detach your ego from trading.

- Don't focus on your last trade if you made a mistake.

- Don't aim for perfection.

- The best traders are detached from their results. Focus on the CAN SLIM System.

On Trading

- Don't put too much money in a thinly traded stock average daily volume of 400,000 or less..

- Don't enter a trade that doesn't have a high probability of winning (a stock should be coming out of a proper base pattern on volume that is 40% higher than average).

- You can have a lot of mistakes and still make a lot of money.

- Stay out of bear markets; it's too easy to lose a lot of money trying to fight the overall trend.

Grandmaster: Legendary Investor Bill O'Neil

"Victory is reserved for those who are willing to pay its price."

—SUN TZU

*"The arrow flies straight and far because of the strength
and quality of the bow. The success of the arrow is dependent
on its relationship with the bow. The relationship we share with
our teacher is unlike any other we will have in our lives. It is through
our loyalty and commitment, our attention to even the slightest
instruction coming from the master, that we will see
maximum benefits in our own development."*

—GRANDMASTER HEE IL CHO, 9TH DEGREE BLACK BELT

185

A grandmaster is one who has achieved the highest level. In the investing world, Bill O'Neil is a legendary trader and one of the most successful investors of all time. But what sets him apart from some of history's greatest traders is his dedication to teaching and helping other investors.

William J. O'Neil

The Man

Layers of complexity are often found in highly successful people. Bill is a man who is not easily defined, whose work ethic was developed at an early age. He came from a modest background and always held down part-time jobs. Whether it was delivering the newspaper or working in the produce section of a local grocery store, Bill O'Neil has worked very hard most of his life.

He is also an intensely private man, somewhat reserved and modest, but compelled to help other people, even if this puts him in the limelight. Bill scoffs at the notion that he is anything other than a regular guy and is uncomfortable with too many compliments.

His simplicity, sense of humor, and down to earth attitude can be observed by his choices in watches; he often wears a Mickey Mouse watch when he speaks in front of an audience and needs to keep track of the time. In other somewhat amusing instances when he has forgotten his watch, Bill will borrow other people's watches and lay them on the podium to help him keep track of time. Bill has often inadvertently put several of these watches in his pocket and forgotten about them after he finishes speaking. IBD National Speaker Justin Nielsen works with Bill on special projects and has had to hunt down many "borrowed watches" from Bill and return them to their rightful owners before they go through the wash cycle.

But underneath Bill's unassuming nature is a fiercely driven man. In 1958, Bill started his career as a stock broker at Hayden, Stone & Company after a tour in the U.S. Air Force and college.

In 1960, Bill was accepted to Harvard Business School's first Program for Management Development (PMD).

Determined to succeed, Bill studied the greatest stock traders of all time: Gerald Loeb, Bernard Baruch, Jesse Livermore, and Nicolas Darvas. As a young stock broker, Bill also studied Jack Dreyfus, who, at the time, was outperforming all of the other funds. Jack was a great bridge player and had a sharp mind that Bill admired, so Bill sent away for the Dreyfus prospectuses and began studying all of the stocks that the fund bought. Bill found that they were buying stocks that were reaching new highs, which seemed crazy at first. Bargain hunting was a common myth in the investing world.

Bill also began to realize from his extensive studies that Jack was brilliant at reading charts, and this would forever change the way Bill approached investing.

Bill began an in-depth study to find out what all of the biggest stock market winners had in common before they made their big price moves. He went back to 1950 and realized that the biggest winners all had similar fundamental traits in common. Out of this incredibly detailed research, Bill created the basis of the CAN SLIM Investing System and became the top performing broker in his firm.

At the age of 30 (the youngest at that time to do so), he bought a seat on the New York Stock Exchange and started Century Information Sciences to program and analyze stock data. During that same time, he started William O'Neil + Company, Incorporated which became a successful investment research firm.

In 1972, Daily Graphs was created as a weekly printed book of stock charts.

In 1973, Bill founded O'Neil Data Systems, Inc., to provide a high-speed printing and database publishing facility.

Investor's Business Daily was launched in 1984 (called *Investors Daily* at the time) and became the first national daily newspaper to exclusively focus on stocks, revealing data to individual investors that was, prior to the creation of the paper, available only to professional investors.

In 1998, Daily Graphs Online was launched as a comprehensive equity research tool, providing investors for the first time a chart with all of the key fundamental data on one page, making research much faster.

In 2010, the next generation of Daily Graphs, MarketSmith, was launched. And the evolution continues with Leaderboard services that have the highest screening capabilities so far.

The Legacy

Bill could have chosen to keep all of his market discoveries to himself but instead chose to share this knowledge, knowing it would help countless investors for decades to come, and very likely into perpetuity, since market psychology never changes. This is Bill's philanthropic gift to investors that could never be quantified or ever measured.

His legacy is compounded by another unique and very comprehensive study into the most successful people of all time. It's a database of the common traits of legendary people, from Aristotle to Oprah. From those studies came IBD's *Ten Secrets to Success* which can be found in *IBD* every day.

Investor's Business Daily

When asked why he created IBD, Bill says, "I saw a need among the general public for better information about the financial markets, especially the stock market. Having already spent 30 years in the investment business, I'd read about all there was to read on the market and how it worked, including all the major newspapers that devoted space to the subject."

"As good as some publications were, they all lacked an understanding of what works in the market and what doesn't. With *Investor's Business Daily*, we sought to fill this void and, in doing so, help people get more out of life." The cornerstone of IBD has been the ability to screen for early emerging trends in both the general market and stocks.

Every feature that is in IBD includes things that Bill feels are important for investors to understand. In many ways, IBD is Bill's written trading plan of how to be a successful investor. IBD went online with Investors.com in 2000 and added enhanced research and lists to help investors find great stocks.

Bill has authored numerous books including:

How to Make Money in Stocks (first edition 1988)

24 Essential Lessons for Investment Success (2000)

The Successful Investor (2003)

Business Leaders & Success (2003)

Sports Leaders & Success (2004)

Military and Political Leaders & Success (2005)

How to Make Money in Stocks: The Complete Investing System (expanded sixth edition, 2011)

The Discipline

Bill has always eaten healthfully and worked out regularly. As legendary trader Jesse Livermore said, "A good stock trader is not unlike a well-trained professional athlete who must keep the physical side of their life in perfect form if they want to keep at the top of their mental form."

Bill also has a work ethic that would frankly exhaust most mere mortals. An enormous amount of Bill's success appears to be sheer genius, but he is a man who is willing to outwork almost everyone, and this gives him the edge. Bill has said, "The most successful people are those willing to do what others are not." He also has a laser beam focus of attention. When he was a younger man, this must have been somewhat intimidating.

Whenever I have had discussions with Bill, whether it concerns a business matter or a chart that I might have asked a question about, he has an ability to focus like few people I have ever met. Bill's ability to focus so intensely is part of his investing success. He can study a chart and can zero in on its intricate details in a way that is truly amazing.

The Teacher

When Bill started IBD, he knew that investors needed to be introduced to the concepts and features, and he also knew that if he spoke in front of large groups, that more and more investors across the country could learn an investing system that would help them financially. So for years, Bill would give free workshops and share his market knowledge. It is impossible to track how many people Bill influenced through these free workshops, but the numbers are large, given the quantity of testimonials that have come into IBD over the years. For many people, hearing Bill speak changed their lives forever.

Over the years, Bill has taught at countless IBD Workshops and always stays afterwards to answer questions from attendees until the hotel where the event is held literally turns off the lights in the room. He is always incredibly patient and wants to answer everyone's questions.

It is the same when Bill speaks in front of an IBD Meetup Group. I have had the great privilege of opening many of these Meetup groups in the Southern California area with Bill. He is giving in every situation, staying after the presentation to help answer questions, patiently addressing each investor's concerns until the last question is answered. When the local library or community room where we were holding the Meetup had to close, Bill would graciously continue the conversation and take it outside to the curb, patio, or whatever was available, always wanting the individual investor to find success in the market.

You will never find Bill on the finest golf courses in America, nor sailing on an expensive yacht, but you will find him giving endlessly of his time so that other lives may be transformed by what he has learned from over 50 years in the market.

The kind and sincere part of Bill O'Neil is that he is a great teacher at heart, and he knows that other people can transform their lives because he himself has done so.

Through Bill's generosity, combined with his tireless work ethic, he has influenced thousands of professional and individual investors through his teaching.

Of all the legendary traders, Bernard Baruch, Jesse Livermore, Nicolas Darvas, Gerald Loeb and others, it is my personal opinion that Bill O'Neil's discovery and creation of the CAN SLIM Investing System will be talked about for decades to come, and will have more influence on those that want to learn about the market than any other trader in history.

The Legendary Trader

To become the very best trader you can be, imagine that Bill O'Neil is standing behind you, looking over your shoulder, and ask yourself: Would you execute the trade you're about to make? Would you sell? Why?

Did You Follow the System?

> *"Do or do not. There is no try."*
>
> —YODA, JEDI MASTER, *STAR WARS*

To become the very best trader you can be and achieve the highest returns possible, stick to the time tested CAN SLIM Investing System. These are not Bill's opinions but how the market and leading stocks have actually worked, with research going back to 1880.

If Bill's portfolio managers stray from the CAN SLIM rules, he will call them on it. Imagine he is doing the same for you. Reading IBD daily will help reinforce these investing principles and familiarize you with parts of the paper that identify top CAN SLIM stocks that are performing well in the current market.

Be Flexible

> *"The stiffest tree is most easily cracked, while the bamboo or willow survives by bending with the wind."*
>
> —BRUCE LEE

Bill is never married to an opinion, and this includes the overall market trend as well as leading stocks. He remains flexible, which is one of his greatest strengths as a trader. He is not stubborn and feels no need to be right. Ego is the death of success, and Bill learned this a long time ago watching many investors lose everything because of an inflated ego and the need to be right all the time.

As an example of Bill's flexibility, he was very bearish in 1999 before the last and final run that the market made. But when the market issued a follow-through day in September of 1999, he totally changed his mind and accepted what the trend was telling him.

Bill could also be glowing and excited about a stock but will immediately move on if he's wrong and not give it another thought. He has no need to be right, and makes no apology if he is wrong. Bill simply moves on to what the market is telling him. He truly lives in the moment.

Charts Tell You What Is Really Going On

Bill looks at charts above everything else and is always searching for new ideas. He studies charts and goes through many graphs on the weekend. Bill flips through them until something catches his eye about the pattern. He has a nearly photographic memory of charts going back in history, and this is probably his greatest gift. Bill can see a stock setting up in a pattern that looked the same as another winner from previous decades. This skill can be learned, perhaps not to Bill's level, but it can be achieved by studying previous market winners and recognizing what they looked like prior to making their big price moves. One hundred charts are annotated with chart patterns and descriptions of the overall market trend in the beginning pages of *How to Make Money in Stocks*.

"Every stock is like a person; it has a personality. I study stocks the way I study people. After a while, their reactions to certain circumstances become predictable."

—JESSE LIVERMORE

"Some stocks are steady movers; others have more volatile price swings. Know what you're dealing with."

—WILLIAM J. O'NEIL

What to Look for in a Big Winner

- Is the product something people want or need? Are the earnings and sales increasing? This will show you that there is a desire for the product or service. What is their competitive edge in the market? How unique are the company's products or services? Do they dominate, or are they easily copied? Look for a company that has something that is completely innovative and revolutionary that the masses will want to buy.

- Volume is a measure of supply and demand and can be seen on a chart. Look for spikes in volume that are well above average, showing institutional buying in a stock. This will signal to you that the professional investors are committing serious capital in the company (free charts can be found at Investors.com).

- Institutional money is the only thing that will drive a stock's price higher, so always look for volume, the higher the better.

- Return on equity in many big market leaders will often be 30%, 40%, 50%, or higher. This shows how efficient a company is with its money and is often an indicator of how successful a stock may be if other key fundamental factors are in place, such as double- or triple-digit earnings and sales.

- Increasing quarters of earnings and sales is another indication of strength. (This fundamental data can be found in Stock Checkup at Investors.com.)

- Bill remembers similar base patterns and what they looked like in previous bull markets. Study chart patterns at IBD University for free at Investors.com to learn what the basic chart patterns look like.

- Focus on the very liquid stocks that trade at least one million shares per day, because these are companies the institutional investor can enter. They must establish large positions and cannot put money into thinner traded companies.

When Bill is asked how he always finds the biggest winner in every cycle, he says modestly, "I never thought of it that way, but here's what I look for: After 4 to 6 weeks of a strong new uptrend, you've identified stocks that have the big earnings and sales and are setting up in the proper chart patterns, but you still may not know which one or ones will be the big market winners for that new cycle. Some may look good, but they may not work. You have to cut the ones that aren't performing well that you buy when other stocks in your portfolio are acting strong. It's like weeding a garden: you are pruning to find the very best stocks. If you're keeping your rules and looking for stocks with the strongest earnings and sales with truly innovative products setting up in the right chart patterns, you'll end up with the next Google or Apple.

"I make a lot of mistakes, but if a stock doesn't work out, I sell it, period. If the general market is right and you're buying top quality merchandise, your stocks should be working, particularly in the beginning of a new bull market.

"The biggest winners should make themselves obvious to you. Apple was our best performing stock for the last eight years. We didn't necessarily catch onto it right away because the prior three years to the company taking off, Apple hadn't done tremendously well in terms of earnings. But once the earnings began to go up sharply and we began to understand their out-standing products better, we realized that this was a very unusual and inno-vative company.

"Every new bull market cycle brings in a new industry group. Part of your job as an investor is to uncover what it is leading the market. Look for IPOs that are gaining market share and showing big earnings and sales far above other stocks in the current market. Many of these stocks will show up in the *IBD 50.*"

• KEY POINTS ON MONEY MANAGEMENT •

- Figure out which stocks are the true market leaders and put the most amount of money into them.
- Shift money from your lesser performing stocks into your winners.
- Consider using margin to enhance your performance, but only after you have more experience in the market and only in a healthy bull market.

Opinions

"Markets are never wrong, opinions are."

—JESSE LIVERMORE

"You cannot go by what you think or feel. You must see what is actually happening in the market and with leading stocks."

— WILLIAM J. O'NEIL

Lessons from a Market Legend

- Set goals and always stay positive.
- Many of the market's biggest winners will shake you out. You have to find a way to get back into them once you have identified them to be the leaders in the current bull market cycle.
- Never chase a stock; wait till it offers an alternative entry, such as another base pattern or a pullback to the 10-week line. And make sure that it continues to outperform other stocks in the market in terms of earnings and sales.

The Eternal Optimist

"Choose the positive. You have a choice and are master of your attitude. Optimism is a faith that leads to success."

—BRUCE LEE

"The opportunities are there for anyone willing to put in the work. Each cycle is led by brand new inventions or entrepreneurial companies that are going to change the industries that they are in . . . somebody will always come along with a different and better way of doing things, and every new bull market will have a Google or an Apple.

"If you put into practice the principles from these success stories, don't be surprised if you change your life for the better."

The Method of Our Success

W. Scott O'Neil

Back in the early 1960s, when my father began William O'Neil + Company, the investing landscape was vastly different. Mutual funds were at their early growth stage, whereas today the big funds dominate the market, and anyone can open an online trading account. In the interim, countless investing methodologies have come and gone. For example, the Buy and Hold strategy—a favorite of the bullish 1980s and 1990s that we never believed in—buckled under the two rough bear markets of the past decade. Institutions have fallen, too. Big ones. When Bill started his firm, Merrill Lynch; EF Hutton; Dean Witter; Shearson, Hammill & Co.; Kidder Peabody; and Bache were part of a long list of national brokerage houses. Does anyone remember Bateman Eichler, Goodbody, Hayden Stone, Mitchum Jones, or Bear Stearns? Nearly all are gone or transformed beyond recognition. You don't need that many years under your belt to know how hard it is to keep the lights on in this business; this past decade saw many mergers, while other firms just disappeared.

So how is it that our firm, William O'Neil + Company, has survived for five decades with its portfolio intact and growing? How has our firm not only kept its lights on but expanded to cover global markets, with offices in Los Angeles, New York, Boston, and London? Because, since 1964, our time-tested methodology has guided us profitably in our portfolios and proven applicable to markets around the world.

I want to be clear: we do not think that we are smarter than anyone else in the business. But what we do better than most is *observe* the market's action and react according to a set of well-defined, historically proven rules. Those market rules—based on a half-century of studying the characteristics and behavior of rising and falling individual stocks and stock markets—encompass market directional analysis, stock picking, and portfolio management. For long-term success, you have to be good at all three—and not be satisfied with exceling at only one or two.

Many of our rules sound contrarian to investors who do not use stock charts and thus do not treat the market as the pure supply and demand mechanism that it is. For example, our research shows that many stocks will top while their quarterly earnings are still increasing. Therefore, you can't rely on fundamentals to determine when to sell. You must consult a chart and monitor the technicals, as a stock's breakdown in price usually precedes the breakdown of fundamentals.

Another cornerstone of our method is keeping losses to 7 to 8%. What would have happened if most investors had cut their losses at 7% in 2000–2001, as the market was imploding? Or, even better, if they had used some of our stock-selling rules that would have locked in gains during the first three months of 2000? A few years later, dark clouds were again gathering on the horizon, and I remember closing all of my long positions in November 2007—well ahead of the devastating 2008 break. In fact, all of our portfolio managers saw the mounting institutional selling (distribution) on the major indexes and quickly exited the market. We sat on the sidelines in cash as the S&P 500 fell more than 50%.

Operating in the stock market, for most people, is an exercise in extremes. When it's good—it's great—when it's bad—it's terrible. Our method helps keep us from getting caught up in the extremes that eventually may bring down individual investors and cause even the best institutional investors to stumble. The first step of our method is to determine the overall trend using market directional analysis. This might sound simple to some investors—buy during an uptrend, don't buy during a downtrend—but correctly tracking the trend is the least understood aspect of investing. This became really apparent during the past decade, where a protracted choppy market got the better of most investors. In this kind of environment, uptrends are short and tend to end just as investors reach a comfort level with their positions. But when the charts give clear warning signs, our sell rules guide us to take the correct action when the market direction is starting to change. Sometimes it's not easy to put on the brakes and sell because of what the charts are indicating, but investors who don't act quickly enough usually experience a larger drawdown. Over time, especially in a back-and-forth market, their equity continually gets chipped away in a kind of death by a thousand cuts.

There is also a whole generation of investors out there who didn't find a need for learning to analyze the general market's direction. Some of these investors started trading during the booming 1990s and continued looking at post-2000 market action through a 1990s' lens. Many have given up. Those who started investing *after* March of 2000 actually have an advantage. They know how bad it can get. Knowing what you're up against in the market is essential to being successful long term. Most people don't realize that decades of success in the stock market is the exception, not the rule. They think it requires a strong offense, riding the big winners, fully loaded. Not true. Like a good sports franchise, long-term success requires that you build a dominating defense *and* a great offense.

Our defense is a robust set of sell rules that apply to circumstances in the general market and in individual stocks that often change without notice. Our approach may sound rigid, but historically determined rules, in fact, offer us the flexibility to wade in, build positions, back away, and go to the sidelines when necessary. This flexibility has kept us mainly on the right side of the market—especially at critical times of opportunity or real danger. I'm thinking of 1987, 2000, 2008, and all of the less drastic 20% drops in-between.

Ultimately, capital preservation has been the number one rule this past decade. So many investors slipped backwards because they never made the mental shift from offense to defense. They continually focused on making money—not preserving it. They forgot that not going backward is a much higher priority than trying to squeeze out a few extra percentage points. Remember, cash can be a position no matter how low the interest income.

Other investors have bought into the concept that their money always has to be working for them, even when they're asleep. That sounds good, but isn't always practical in the stock market. The buy and hold strategy comes to mind again here, an approach where you take your hands off the steering wheel and hope it all works out. And when it doesn't (and it *hasn't*), it takes some phenomenal gains to make up losses over time—no matter how low that price was when they started.

Our method also gives us a clear view of the stocks most likely to become the next new leaders. That's because our approach is based on a comprehensive analysis of every big winning stock since the late nineteenth century. Actually, picking the right stocks using our products isn't very hard at all. All of our products are designed to bring the best stocks to the surface in every cycle. That's not to say there's no art to picking stocks, but an investor can quickly narrow the field from thousands to a few dozen. We look for a company that is a leader in its space, with solid short-term and long-term earnings, plus a strong return on equity or high pretax profit margins. Bottom line, if the fundamentals aren't outstanding, we're not interested. Some of the stocks in which we invest may tend to have low brand-awareness. Usually they have gone public within the last 12 years. We tend to shy away from a stock that is too well-known or has become a market darling.

Most important to long-term success in the market is having the discipline to consistently follow a well-thought-out set of portfolio management rules. At William O'Neil + Company, we have time-tested rules that offer guidance on: how to enter positions while minimizing risk, when to be more aggressive, when to lighten up, and when to exit and sidestep bad markets. This last set of rules, which allows us to recognize the signs of a topping stock or a topping general market, is perhaps the most unique and powerful part of our method. Investors with a strong sell discipline are rare. Once a stock is purchased, many emotions will work against selling it—sometimes until it's too late. On top of this, the stock market has an uncanny way of exploiting human beings' character flaws and leveling all egos. When operating in the market, we want to remain balanced and humble, always learning from our mistakes.

The ability of our method to keep pace with the natural lifecycle of leading stocks—to identify them early, own them during a good part of their run, and sell them when the move is likely over (often when a new innovation or breakthrough outmodes them)—is what keeps our approach ever current. The chart patterns stay the same, only the names fade away, with new ones continuously taking their place. That is the nature of the U.S. stock market. Stock market cycles and American business have always been driven by entrepreneurs and their brilliant innovations. Entrepreneurs are the real drivers of capitalism and job creation. As long as entrepreneurs exist and are supported in their pursuit, we should participate in their success for the next 50 years and beyond. Remember, there will be many big opportunities in the future, but you have to do your homework and stay on top of the job to fully capitalize on these opportunities. Never give up.

Chris Gessel

Chris Gessel is executive editor and chief strategy officer for *Investor's Business Daily*. He is keenly focused on content to help investors. I talked with Chris about some of his approaches to investing. I also wanted to share with you a sense of our "behind the scenes" work.

Amy: Chris, over the years what have you found are the most important things for an investor to do in order to succeed?

Chris: Many investors want to make money in the market *all* the time. They find it nearly impossible to step back from the market when it's in a downtrend. Yet, the worst time to be buying stocks is when the general market is in a correction. If investors continue to buy stocks during a downtrend and lose money, they eventually give up and walk away from the market.

    The secret is to stay engaged in *every* market, but especially while it is correcting. Yet many people, even if they aren't losing money, become demoralized and pessimistic. I know the feeling, After weeks, months or sometimes even a year of a declining stock market, it's hard to stay focused and positive. What's fun about watching stocks grind lower day after day?

Over the years I've talked with too many investors who turn away entirely from the market during corrections. The irony is that market corrections are *when the big leaders of the next cycle are shaping up.* These companies are reporting strong earnings and innovations that can't overcome the general market weakness. But they are often the first stocks out of the gate when the market turns back up.

Amy: You don't want to miss those. Many of us have made our biggest gains after staying tuned in during corrections and finding the real leaders.

Chris: Right—and three to six months into a new bull market, those discouraged investors notice that stocks have really taken off. But now they're late to the party and find that most leaders have already broken out and made big gains.

So stay in phase with the market. When the stock market follows through after a correction, you want to be there and take advantage of all the great opportunities that present themselves. Even in a modest rally, you can make a lot of money by following the market rules and staying on top of the current leadership.

Amy: Great advice that a lot of us live by. Once someone understands the rules of the overall market, what is the next biggest challenge for investors?

Chris: Portfolio management is absolutely essential. Once you understand the basics of CAN SLIM stock selection and investing, you need to master very specific buy, hold and sell rules.

Justin Nielsen, David Chung, and I teach the IBD Level 3 Workshop, which focuses on advanced investment strategies. The primary element of the seminar is a trading simulation where investors get to walk through buying and selling scenarios with us from a real market cycle. You learn to spot the right time to invest; find top stocks, and see how wise it is to take many 20 to 25% profits so you're making money along the way. Not every stock will turn into a super winner, but many leading stocks in an uptrend will deliver solid 20% profits. If you get into the habit of selling and locking in those gains you'll see real progress in your portfolio.

Amy: How do you know when you've found a big winner?

Chris: One very important rule to follow is the 8-week holding rule. When a stock breaks out and runs up more than 20% in less than 3 weeks, you need to hold that stock for a full 8 weeks before you make a longer-term decision. The power of the rule is that it helps you sit through short-term shakeouts and go for much larger gains.

The majority of stocks, however, won't trigger that rule; they may go up 25% in 5 or 6 weeks. If you take your profits at that point, you'll have banked real money and then you can reinvest it in a new breakout. And the stock that you just sold in many cases will build another base over the following weeks or months and then give you another opportunity. You're compounding your profits. The reason this works so well is the fact that many growth stocks typically run up 20 to 25% and then consolidate and form another base.

Amy: Where can you find these stocks in IBD?

Chris: *Investor's Business Daily* is loaded with new stock ideas every day. There are two features every investor should monitor all the time. The first is the *IBD 50*, which is published Mondays and Wednesdays. We screen for the best stocks with strong fundamentals and excellent price performance. There's a mini chart with each stock along with a description of its base pattern, and whether it is near a buy point. These quick descriptions are how many investors hone their chart reading skills.

Another great way to find stocks is to review the names at the top of each sector in the Research Tables. These Sector Leaders come from our most demanding screen and are the result of years of research into what makes a top-tier leading stock. Very few stocks can meet all the criteria to become a Sector Leader, so those that make this list should definitely be on everyone's watch list. Analyze their chart patterns and read as many archived stories as you can. Most of the biggest leaders stay on the Sector Leader list during prolonged market uptrends.

Amy: Can a newer investor or someone who is short on time succeed with these features?

Chris: Doing exceptionally well in any field takes some work, but IBD has a lot of resources to make it easier for investors. We have hundreds of Meetup Groups across the country where IBD readers gather each month to share ideas, use our market courses created for these groups, and help each other understand how the stock market works. We also introduced a new service in 2011 called Leaderboard. I think of Leaderboard as real-time education that also does a lot of the legwork for you. In Leaderboard, the market team scours all of IBD's best lists to find stocks that meet most if not all the CAN SLIM criteria. Then we mark up the charts to find the bases, the buy points, when to hold and when to sell.

What is gratifying is that we see people who are brand new to the stock market succeeding, as well as seasoned money managers who take the service for a second opinion of what they are seeing in the market.

I've seen roaring bull markets, punishing bear markets and everything in between since I've been at IBD. But what is amazing is that every time we start a new uptrend, the vast majority of big winners show up in IBD's stock screens and stories. The opportunity is there for everyone to succeed in the stock market.

Matthew Galgani

Matthew Galgani is co-host of *IBD*'s *How to Make Money in Stocks* radio show, editor of the IBD*extra! Newsletter* and host of the Daily Stock Analysis video at Investors.com.

Amy: Matt, while I was writing my book *How to Make Money in Stocks Success Stories*, you were working on a complementary book called *How to Make Money in Stocks: Getting Started*.

Matt: It's inspiring when you read the stories in your book. It got me pumped up. These people literally changed their lives simply by learning how to invest. So I think the next question folks will have is, "How can *I* do that too—and how do I get started?" They may also wonder: "Can I really do this? Do I have the time? Can I learn what these people learned?" That's where my book comes in. Using simple, step-by-step checklists, I walk you through the three basic things you need to know— what to buy, when to buy, and when to sell.

And let's be honest. People come to investing with the *hope* that they'll make lots of money, and the *fear* that they'll lose their shirt. I know I did. But I'll show you how to set realistic expectations that are absolutely achievable, and I'll also give you two simple rules that will make sure you never suffer a big loss. So if you're ready to jump in but are a little nervous (and, by the way, that's completely natural and healthy), the buying and selling checklists in my book will get you started in a safe and sensible way.

Amy: You also worked closely with IBD Chairman and Founder Bill O'Neil on the 13-part IBD *Meetup Investor Education Series*, which is available exclusively to IBD Meetup members. Can you tell us about those lessons?

Matt: In retrospect, I think the *Getting Started* book was inspired by that experience. Our goal was to create easy-to-follow lessons that would walk Meetup members through the must-know concepts of investing. Bottom line is, we wanted to make sure people understood how to both grow and protect their money. So lessons cover all the key things: When to get into and out of the market, what telltale traits to look for in a winning stock, and how to use charts to give you an extra edge by pinpointing the best time to buy and sell.

After I finished each lesson, Bill and I would go through it slide by slide, word by word. Sometimes I felt like I was working with Steve Jobs to design an Apple product—we kept cutting and cutting, until we got the lesson down to its most simple and tightly-focused form.

One thing really hit home as we were doing this: Investing is a skill best learned in stages. You can't dump *everything* on someone all at once and expect them to understand it, let alone use it effectively. So we broke the lessons up into bite-size chunks that people could wrap their heads around. When one stepping stone was in place, then we moved on to the next.

The *Getting Started* book takes a similar approach. Step by step, you'll learn what to look for in a stock before you buy. Then, you'll see how to determine the best time to buy that stock. And then you'll learn a specific selling game plan to decide when to lock in your gains or nip any losses in the bud.

I'm a very hands-on learner. I can't just read—I have to jump in and start doing it. That's just how things sink in for me. So both the IBD

Meetup lessons and the *Getting Started* book reflect that. At the end of every chapter, I have "action steps" that give you specific, easy-to-do tasks that reinforce what you just read. It could be watching a *2-Minute Tip* video on the same subject, or using certain tools to put together a watch list of top-rated stocks. Whatever it is, it gives you that hands-on experience you need to start putting the rules and checklists into action in the real world.

So, Amy, I guess the bottom line is this: Now that folks have been inspired by the remarkable stories in your book, the next step is to start creating their *own* success stories. I realize I'm a little biased here, but I know from my own personal experience that what you learn in *How to Make Money in Stocks: Getting Started* can help anyone create lifelong, financial peace of mind.

IBD Workshops

I sat down with some of IBD's education experts and talked about the workshops that are offered throughout the United States.

Ralph Perrini is a National Speaker for IBD and Vice President of Sales. Jonathan Howard is Vice President of Education and in charge of IBD's paid workshops. Justin Nielsen is a National Speaker and works on special projects with Bill O'Neil. All three travel throughout the U.S. teaching the CAN SLIM Investing System.

Amy: Describe IBD's workshops and why the different levels were created.

Ralph: The biggest impediment that most investors face is a lack of understanding how the market works. That's why we've constructed four core workshops. The Level 1 workshop helps investors new to the CAN SLIM System learn how to interpret the market, buy stocks at the right time and sell to protect profits. It's primarily for investors who are new to CAN SLIM Investing. Our first goal was to dispel a lot of myths about investing such as buy low, sell high, or buying stocks with a low P/E. Our primary theme in the workshop is to help investors buy stocks with great fundamentals coming out of a sound base pattern. We teach investors to buy on strength with a stock that has already proven itself. We help investors learn a fact based system founded on decades of research gleaned from studies of the best performing stocks from the 1880s to the present day.

Justin: The Level 2 workshop which I teach with Scott O'Neil shows investors how to spot market tops and bottoms, how to read charts more accurately and profitably, and screening techniques to identify emerging winners.

Jonathan: The Level 3 workshop was designed to teach investors what to do between the initial buy and the final sell. We teach advanced holding and selling strategies, the intricacies of portfolio management, and the importance of post analysis. Finally, the speakers will put all the pieces together in a unique trading simulation, applying the CAN SLIM System in a real-market environment.

Ralph: And the Masters Program or the Level 4 features Bill O'Neil, IBD's founder, and includes sessions with O'Neil Data Systems portfolio managers. We bring together the best financial minds to provide two days of intense, comprehensive training that can turn attendees into successful investors for the rest of their lives.

Justin: In addition to those workshops, we have three other workshops that are subject-specific such as Chart School, Marketschool, and the Model Stock Summit.

Jonathan: All of the workshops are designed to help investors reach a higher level of investing. However, we realized that some people, due to job commitments or travel considerations, can't attend some of the workshops, so many of these great learning moments are available in the Home Study Courses.

Ralph: We started this series of workshops in 2004 and have been able to help countless investors who have taken the courses.

Amy: Why do you think so many people have had success after attending these workshops?

Justin: The vast majority of the investing public doesn't follow an investing system. They purchase stocks solely based on gut feelings or poor advice and that is where we're unique at IBD because we get into the facts behind why stocks move up and why they eventually falter and turn down. Investors walk away with a clear understanding of what to look for in potential leaders.

Jonathan: Through the years, we've heard horror stories of people losing much of their life savings because they don't have a system that they follow, or they've received poor professional advice. The aim of our workshop series is to give investors a proven system with sound rules that will provide the tools necessary to make money when the market is in an uptrend, and more importantly, protect their capital in a downtrend. We want our investors to leave the workshops feeling confident and prepared to handle whatever the market throws at them.

Ralph: Another impediment to investing are emotions, most people invest from an emotional point of view. When they take a position in a stock and it begins to go down in value, they typically rationalize why it will come back. So at IBD's workshops, we give you some specific rules that will help take the emotions out of it. We've found in our many years of teaching workshops that thousands and thousands of investors now feel much more secure with their finances and with their retirement because we've had a dramatic impact in helping them improve their investing returns.

• KEY THINGS TO REMEMBER •

Market Direction Is Everything

- Invest when the market is in a confirmed uptrend. Most stocks follow the overall market trend so it's important to invest when the market and leading stocks are moving higher.

Preservation of Capital Is the Most Important Part of Investing

- Always sell a stock if it falls 7 to 8% below what you paid for it. Keep your losses small and let your winners run.

Success Is Definitely Attainable If You Stick to the CAN SLIM Investing System

- It's necessary to have a set of rules. If you follow CAN SLIM, gains of 20 to 25% and more are very possible during a bull market. You can and will outperform the major moving averages.

- The successful investors that you've read about in this book achieved their stock market gains by staying true to the CAN SLIM System. Don't add other methodologies or techniques. You will find this lowers your odds of success.

Helpful Information

Understanding the Trend

Secular Bull and Bear Markets

Secular bear markets can last 12 to 18 years in length where the major indexes don't make significant price progress and can suffer sharp overall price drops over portions of the period. They are followed by secular bull markets that can last from 20 to 30 years. Since 1900, the indexes have gained from 200% to 1355% during these secular bull market periods.

Cyclical Bull and Bear Market Cycles

There are cyclical bull and bear market cycles within the overall secular trend. A cyclical bull market lasts on average from 2 to 4 years. A cyclical bear market lasts from 3 to 9 months and in rare cases as much as three years.

IBD has studied the 27 bull and bear market cycles going back to 1880.

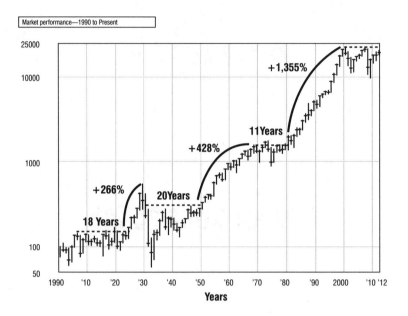

Market performance—1990 to Present

Uptrends and Corrections Within Cyclical Bull and Bear Market Cycles

Within the cyclical bull and bear market cycles there are tradable rallies or uptrends and there are periods of time when the market pulls back and corrects.

• FOLLOW THE TREND •

- Read *The Big Picture* column in IBD daily.
- Watch the *Market Wrap* video at Investors.com/IBDTV.

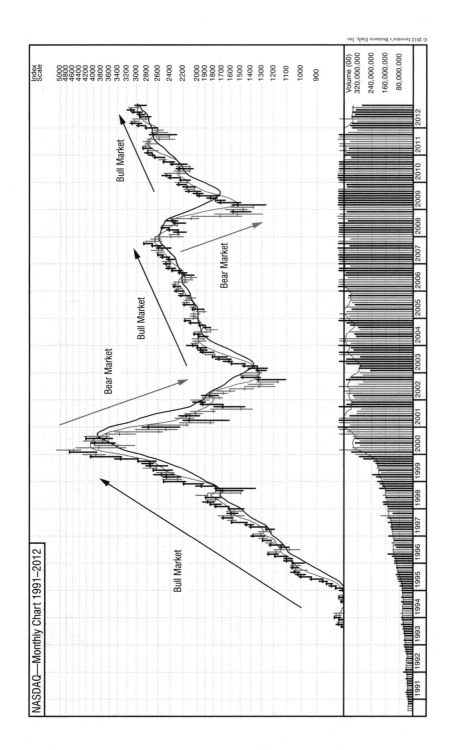

NASDAQ—Monthly Chart 1991–2012

Bull Market

Bear Market

Bull Market

Bear Market

Bull Market

Index Scale

5000
4800
4600
4400
4200
4000
3800
3600
3400
3200
3000
2800
2600
2400
2200
2000
1900
1800
1700
1600
1500
1400
1300
1200
1100
1000

900

Volume (00)
320,000,000
240,000,000
160,000,000
80,000,000

1991 1992 1993 1994 1995 1996 1997 1998 1999 2000 2001 2002 2003 2004 2005 2006 2007 2008 2009 2010 2011 2012

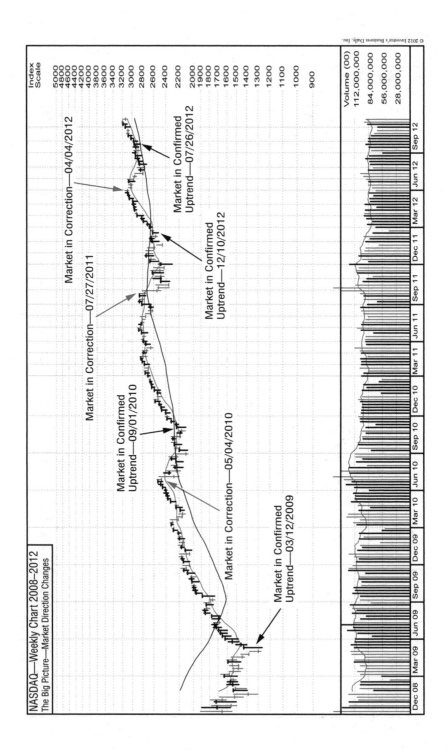

© 2012 Investor's Business Daily, Inc.

NASDAQ—Weekly Chart 2008–2012
The Big Picture—Market Direction Changes

Index Scale
5000
4800
4600
4400
4200
4000
3800
3600
3400
3200
3000
2800
2600
2400
2200
2000
1900
1800
1700
1600
1500
1400
1300
1200
1100
1000
900

Market in Correction—04/04/2012

Market in Confirmed Uptrend—07/26/2012

Market in Correction—07/27/2011

Market in Confirmed Uptrend—12/10/2012

Market in Confirmed Uptrend—09/01/2010

Market in Correction—05/04/2010

Market in Confirmed Uptrend—03/12/2009

Volume (00)
112,000,000
84,000,000
56,000,000
28,000,000

Dec 08 Mar 09 Jun 09 Sep 09 Dec 09 Mar 10 Jun 10 Sep 10 Dec 10 Mar 11 Jun 11 Sep 11 Dec 11 Mar 12 Jun 12 Sep 12

Amy's Suggested 20-Minute Daily Routine

To Determine the Market's Current Trend:

1. Read the *Market Pulse* in the IBD's *Big Picture* column. Is the market in an uptrend or downtrend?

2. Watch the *Market Wrap* Video at Investors.com/IBDTV to learn more about the market's daily action and to stay on top of leading stocks.

To Find Leading Stocks:

1. Follow the stocks in the *IBD 50* (published Monday and Wednesday). Keep a watch list of stocks nearing a potential buy point. (Read the short sentence under each chart to help identify the proper buy point.)

2. Check *Stocks on the Move* at Investors.com for stocks rising on heavy volume, indicating institutional buying.

3. Read *The New America* article to learn about innovative companies with exciting new products or services.

4. Find out more about a stock's fundamentals with *Stock Checkup* at Investors.com.

Amy's 1-Hour Weekend Routine

1. As you're going through *IBD 50*, jot down names of companies that you're not familiar with. Read articles and learn more about what the company does at Investors.com. Articles can be accessed by entering the ticker symbol in the "enter symbol, keyword" section and then clicking on "search site."

2. Watch the *Daily Stock Analysis* videos at Investors.com/IBDTV to learn more about chart reading.

3. Update your watch list:

   - Have a ready list, stocks that are nearing a potential buy point that you have researched and are prepared to buy if they break out on volume that is at least 40% above average.

- Consider entering trade triggers through your brokerage service so a stock could be bought or sold even if you are busy.

- Keep another list of stocks that aren't close to a breakout but that are building a base or consolidating gains, particularly if the stock has already proven itself to be a market leader.

4. Read sections of *How to Make Money in Stocks* for continuing education and to help understand the CAN SLIM Investing System better.

Extended Daily Routine

Add these steps to the daily routine above:

1. Check the mini charts in *Stock Spotlight*. This list materially outperforms the S&P 500, so any new names that appear on the list may be well worth researching further.

2. Learn more about Sector Leaders in the *Research Table Review* and find out how they are performing in the current market. These sector leaders are stocks with the best fundamentals, such as outstanding earnings, sales, and a high ROE (return on equity).

3. Read the *Industry Themes* article to keep up with leading trends among industry groups or to see if there is a shift from one leading industry group to another one.

4. IBD's *New High List* shows stocks that have reached new 52-week highs. IBD research shows that stocks making new highs tend to go higher. The *New High List* Analysis describes more about the companies that are making new highs and have top fundamentals.

5. Read and study the historical charts from William J. O'Neil's article, *How to Find and Own America's Greatest Opportunities* in the Wednesday edition.

For continuing education read articles in *Investor's Corner*.

Extended Weekend Routine

Add these steps to the weekend routine above:

1. Check *Your Weekly Review* (found in the Friday edition) mini charts for stocks approaching a potential buy point. Research more about the company with articles found at Investors.com.

2. Study chart patterns of stocks setting up by using Investors.com charts or by using MarketSmith charts, a premium charting service and IBD sister company.

3. Listen to IBD's *How to Make Money in Stocks* radio show at Investors.com/radioshow.

4. Study the 100 charts that are in the front of *How to Make Money in Stocks* to learn more about base patterns and life cycles of the big market winners.

5. Write in a journal your trades for the week or thoughts about the general market. This will help as you do a year-end post analysis.

CAN SLIM Investing System

C = Current Quarterly Earnings of at Least 25%

Where to find earnings in IBD:

- *Stock Spotlight* charts
- *IBD 50* charts (Monday and Wednesday editions)
- *Big Cap 20* charts (Tuesday)
- *Your Weekly Review* (Friday)

A = Annual Earnings Growth of at Least 25% over the Past 3 to 5 Years

Return on equity (ROE) of at least 17%. Where to find annual earnings in IBD:

- *Stock Spotlight* charts
- *IBD 50* charts (Monday, Wednesday)

- *Big Cap 20* charts (Tuesday)
- *Your Weekly Review* charts (Friday)

N = New Companies with New Products, New Services, New Price Highs

Where to find in IBD:

- *The New America* (daily)
- *IBD 50* (Monday, Wednesday)
- *Internet & Technology* (daily)
- IBD *New High List* (daily)

S = Supply and Demand

Huge increases in volume compared to the daily average = demand. Where to find in IBD:

- Volume % change
- Accumulation/Distribution Rating
- *Stocks On The Move* (print edition, *e*IBD and Investors.com)

L = Leader vs. Laggard

Look for the top stocks both fundamentally and technically in the very best-performing sectors and industry groups. Where to find in IBD:

- IBD *Stock Checkup* (Investors.com)
- *IBD 50*
- *Your Weekly Review*
- *52 Week Highs & Lows*

I = Institutional Sponsorship

The big money. The smart money. Where to find in IBD:

- Accumulation/Distribution Rating
- Volume % change
- *Stocks on the Move* (Investors.com)

M = Market Direction

Is the general market currently in a confirmed uptrend or downtrend? Where to find in IBD:

- *The Big Picture*
- *Market Wrap Video* (IBD TV, Investors.com)

• ACKNOWLEDGMENTS •

I want to express my gratitude to Bill O'Neil for his support; Kathy Sherman for multiple reads and edits on the manuscript; and Christina Wise, Brian Gonzales, Jason D'Amore, Justin Nielsen, and Eric Urquilla, who helped significantly with the chart annotations.

Other individuals who helped with manuscript edits include Mike Scott, Kevin Marder, Tom Ellis, and John Mackel.

I also want to thank Mary Glenn and the fine staff at McGraw-Hill.

7 to 8% sell rule
  adhering to, 34, 112, 143, 148
  "Aloha Mike" and, 41
  Jerry Powell and, 91
  Kevin Marder and, 140
10-week moving average line
  Dave Whitmer and, 64
  as investment indicator, 13–14, 25,
    92, 194
  Kier McDonough and, 146, 148
  living below, 35–36
20 to 25% profit rule
  Barbara James and, 109, 112
  importance of, 34–35, 44
  Jerry Powell and, 91
  K. Basu and, 82
  Kier McDonough and, 148
  Lee Tanner and, 64–66
  Paramjit Chumber and, 84
20% threshold rule, 126–127
*24 Essential Lessons for Investment
  Success* (O'Neil), 124, 188
50-day moving average line
  Ed Hornstein and, 124

Jim Roppel and, 153, 158
  sell rules and, 35, 128
250 Growth Screen, MarketSmith,
  176

Abercrombie & Fitch Co., 48, 50
"Aloha Mike"
  emotional control and, 41, 43
  investing guidelines of, 45–46
  motivating factor for, 2
annual earnings, stock increases
  in, 12
Apple Inc.
  historical charts of, 132, 135
  institutional investors and, 3
  investing in, 51, 54, 100, 105
  as winning stock, 193
Aruba Networks Inc., 85
Auvian, Stuart, investment strategies,
  24–25

bad investment habits
  consequences of, 39, 41
  making money and, 175

Baidu Inc.
Jeff Heimstaedt's investments, 100, 104
Jim Roppel's investments, 157–160
Ken Chin's investments, 51, 53
Baldwin, Townsend
motivations of, 2
reviewing investments, 75, 80
Baruch, Bernard, 33, 119, 186, 190
base(s)
buying early stage, 14, 15, 24
patterns, 12–14, 25
Basu, K., business approach of, 80–83
The Battle for Investment Survival (Loeb), 119
bear markets
in market cycles, 39
positive aspect of, 154
staying away from, 115, 183
studying, 175–176
Bharani, motivations of, 2
The Big Picture column, IBD's
Barbara James following, 108
indicating market direction, 57
Jeannie McGrew following, 101–102
Jerry Powell following, 91
Kent Damon following, 89
Lee Tanner following, 66
Steve Power following, 86
Bishoyi, Prabin, 19–20
Bobach, Eve
avoiding emotional trading, 165–166
early investment years, 163–164
structured approach of, 164–165
The Books of Han Dynasty, 1
breakouts
as investment indicator, 12–13
keeping lists of, 86
looking for, 51, 55
sell rules and, 34
Buckeye Technologies Inc., 87

bull markets
finding winning stocks in, 3, 64, 192, 193
locking in gains in, 69, 72, 112–113
losing stocks and, 138–140
studying, 59, 175–176
business approach of K. Basu, 80–83
Business Leaders & Success (O'Neil), 188
"buy and hold" approach, 3, 91
buy lists, creating, 84, 86
buying stocks, right time for, 12–14, 46

CAN SLIM Investing System. *See also* investing
basis of, 11–12
creation of, 187
distribution days and, 10
importance of following, 190
CBS MarketWatch, 141
Centennial Technologies Inc., 144–145
Century Information Sciences, 187
Chan, Jackie, ix
Chart Arcade, 177
charts, 192
Bill O'Neil's use of, 191, 192
historical, 132–133
investing and, 150, 174–175
for perspective, 165
simulation, studying, 175
Chin, Ken
daily/weekly investing routine, 48, 51, 52–54
motivations of, 2
Chipotle Mexican Grill, 96
Cho Hee Il, 185
Chumber, Paramjit, keeping losses small, 83–84, 85
Cirrus Logic Inc., gap-ups and, 169
climax runs, 153
Cole, Stephen, 24
Composite Rating, IBD's, 176

Confucius, 129
consecutive down days, selling rules
    and, 35
Continental Resources Inc., 74–75, 76
Crocs Inc.
    Jeff Heimstaedt's investments, 100,
        103
    Kier McDonough's investments,
        146, 147
    Lee Tanner's investments, 66, 68
cup-with-handle base pattern, 13, 18,
    61, 64
current quarterly earnings
    as investment indicator, 192
    stock increases in, 12, 24

Dai, Kevin, 31–32
Daily Graphs charting service, IBD's,
    61, 138, 140, 187. *See also*
    MarketSmith, IBD's
Daily Graphs Online, creation of, 187
daily routine
    of Jeff Heimstaedt, 100
    of Steve Power, 86
Daily Stock Analysis video, 26–29
Damon, Kent, 86, 89
D'Amore, Jason
    fear of losing money and, 38
    utilizing IBD radio show, 29–30
Darvas, Nicolas, 59, 61, 119, 186, 190
Dave, Ashish, 25–26
DBC Online, 141
discipline
    Bill O'Neil and, 188–189
    importance of, 151, 170, 171, 180
distribution days, downtrends and, 10,
    131, 142, 177
Dollar Tree Inc., 27–29
double bottom base pattern, 13
downtrends
    causes of, 10
    leading stocks in, 157
    prolonged, 154
    sell rules and, 69, 72, 91

Dreyfus, Jack, 186–187
Dryships Inc., 95

earnings
    as investment indicator, 16, 192, 193
    not buying before, 109–110
    stock increases in, 12, 24
ego, liability of
    for "Aloha Mike," 41, 43
    for Charles Harris, 179–181
    investing and, 31, 183
    for Kevin Marder, 140–141
Ellis, Tom
    focus of, 72, 74–75, 76–79
    historical charts and, 132
EMC Corp., 92–93, 94
emotions
    control of, 41, 43, 113–115
    investing and, 37–41, 42, 44, 165–166

F5 Networks Inc., 109–111
falling in love with stocks, 39. *See also*
    emotions
fashion trends, as investment indicator,
    59, 61, 62–63, 146
fear, investing and, 38
First Solar Inc.
    Gennady Kupershteyn and, 48
    Kier McDonough and, 146,
        148–149
flat base pattern, 13
flexibility
    of Bill O'Neil, 174, 190–191
    investing and, 31
follow-through days
    as investment indicator, 7, 24–25,
        164–165
    waiting for, 46–48, 82–83
Fuqi International, 48, 49

gambling, investing vs., 46–48
gap-ups, stock
    buying, 66, 69, 124–125
    stock strength and, 166, 167–169

Garmin Ltd, 117–119
generosity, of Bill O'Neil, 188–189
Gessel, Chris, 100
Gonzales, Brian
  fear of losing and, 38
  motivations of, 2
  utilizing IBD videos, 26–29
Google groups, 91–93
Google Inc.
  Ed Hornstein and, 124–125
  Mike Scott and, 66, 69, 70
greed, investing and, 38–39
Green Mountain Coffee Roasters
  gap-ups and, 168
  investing in, 61, 64, 65
Guensch, Katrina
  IBD Meetup Groups and, 19
  motivations of, 2
  post analysis and, 129–131

Hansen's Natural (Monster Beverage
  Corp.), 59, 61, 63
Harris, Charles
  early investment years, 178
  investment advice of, 64
  Market School and, 176–177
  personal rules/strategy, 181–182
  strengths/weaknesses of,
  178–181
heavy volume days, selling and, 35,
  109, 124
Heimstaedt, Jeff, investment
  lessons of, 97, 100–101,
  103–105
Herbalife Ltd., 75, 78
Hicks, Mike
  breakthrough of, 117–119
  early investment years, 116–117
  pivotal investment of, 119–122
historical charts, investing and, 132
Holmes, Oliver Wendell, 51
Home Depot Inc., 139–140
Hong Hi Choi, 33
hope, investing and, 37–38

Hornstein, Ed
  early years of, 123–124
  investment strategies of, 126–128
  trial and error investing, 124
  winning stocks and, 124–126
*How I Made $2 Million in the Stock
  Market* (Darvas), 59, 119
How to Make Money in Stocks
  (O'Neil)
  Ashish Dave and, 25
  Ed Hornstein and, 123
  Eve Bobach and, 163
  investment advice in, 34
  Jeff Heimstaedt and, 97
  Jim Roppel and, 151
  K. Basu and, 82
  Kevin Marder and, 138, 141
  Kier McDonough and, 143, 150
  Mike Webster and, 173
  Pat Reardon and, 59
  publication of, 188
  Randall Mauro and, 55
  Tom Ellis and, 132
*How to Recognize Great Performing
  Stocks* (O'Neil), 132

IBD University, 192
Industry Themes, IBD, 31–32
influence, of Bill O'Neil, 190
initial public offerings (IPOs)
  as investment indicator, 193
  profiting from, 66, 69, 70–71
innovative companies
  finding, 160–162
  institutional investors and, 12
  as investment indicator, 100, 101,
  138, 154, 192
institutional investors
  signs of selling by, 35
  volume and, 192
  winning stocks and, 3, 12, 160,
  163, 166
Intel, 40
Internet, investing and, 140–141

Intuitive Surgical Inc., 72, 73
investing
    analysis of indexes/leaders,
        141–143
    back testing and, 131–132
    bad habits and, 39, 41, 42
    base stages and, 14
    business approach to, 80–84
    "buy and hold" approach, 3
    cutting losses in, 33–34, 109–110
    daily/weekly routines for, 48, 51,
        85, 93, 108–109
    determining trends. *See* market
        direction
    emotional control and, 41, 43–44,
        113–115, 165–166
    falling in love with stocks, 39
    fear and, 38
    finding leading stocks, 16, 46, 90,
        91, 160. *See also* winning stocks
    flexibility in, 190–191
    following rules for, 190
    greed and, 38–39
    hope and, 37–38
    inflated ego in, 191
    in innovative products, 160–162
    IPO bases and, 66, 69
    key elements of, 45–46
    maintaining focus, 72, 74–75
    motivations for, 2
    news media and, 61, 64
    post analysis in, 93, 97, 130–131
    reviewing mistakes in, 75, 80, 90,
        93, 97, 126–127
    selling rules for, 34–36, 64, 66,
        83–84
    stock splits and, 158
    stock's key concepts and, 171–172
    studying bull/bear markets,
        175–176
    studying charts and, 132, 150, 152,
        174–175, 191
    success/failure in, 3–4, 124
    time to buy, 12–14, 46

    investment tools, 176–177
    in winning stocks. *See* winning
        stocks
Investor's Business Daily (IBD)
    IBD 50, finding winners with, 16,
        17, 23–26, 82–83
    launching of, 187
    Market Pulse section, 7, 14, 20,
        108
    Market Wrap/Daily Stock Analysis
        videos, 14, 16, 26–29
    Meetup Groups, 18–22
    radio show, 29–30
    reasons for publishing, 188
    research of, 3, 10, 11
Investors.com
    Stock Checkup at, 20, 21, 176, 192
    Stocks on the Move at, 16, 26, 48,
        51, 102, 109
IPOs. *See* initial public offerings
    (IPOs)
Isshin-Ryu karate, 23

James, Barbara
    buying before earnings and,
        109–112
    daily routine of, 108–109
    motivating factors for, 2–3
JDS Uniphase, 39, 41, 42

Kakvand, Jahandar, learning from
        mistakes and, 90
Kloote, Debra
    capitalizing on uptrends, 93, 97
    investments of, 98–99
Kuhn, Greg, 141
Kupershteyn, Gennady
    follow-through days and, 46–48,
        48–50
    greed and, 38–39

Langout, Norm, 20
Leaderboard charts, IBD's, 57, 59, 60,
        109, 150

Leaders and Success column, IBD's, 126
leaders index, 115–116
leadership, winning stocks and, 12
Lee, Bruce, 45, 190, 194
Lefevre, Edwin, 59, 119
legacy, of Bill O'Neil, 187–188
Leplat, Ted, IBD Meetup instructor, 20–22
liquidity, as investment indicator, 126, 160, 163, 192
Livermore, Jesse, 33, 186, 190, 191, 194
Loeb, Gerald, 119, 186, 190
losses, stock market
  accepting, 33–34
  sell rules and, 109–110, 112, 138–140
low debt, as investment indicator, 26
Lululemon Athletica
  gap-ups and, 167
  three-weeks-tight base pattern in, 29–30
Lynch, Peter, 172

Mackel, John
  forming Google groups, 91–93
  investments of, 94–96
Majumdar, Anindo
  locking in gains and, 69, 72, 73
  motivations of, 2
Marder, Kevin
  early investment years, 138
  importance of daily analysis, 141–143
  selling rules and, 138–140
  utilizing Internet technology, 140–141
market corrections
  for determining trends, 6, 7, 10, 27–29
  investment losses and, 124
market direction
  The Big Picture column for, 91, 101
  CAN SLIM trait, 12

importance of, 162
Randall Mauro and, 51, 55–57, 58
routine for determining, 14
watching for changes in, 69, 72
market psychology, 80, 183, 187
Market Pulse section
  for determining trends, 14, 108
  market stages shown in, 7
  Ted Leplat's routine with, 20
Market School, 176–177
Market Wrap video, 14, 16, 26–29
MarketSmith, IBD's
  back testing and, 131
  daily routine using, 108–109
  investment tools for, 176
  launching of, 187
  tracking stocks with, 72, 75, 92, 100–101
Mastercard Inc., 97, 99
Mauro, Randall, 51, 55–57, 58
McDonough, Kier
  daily routine of, 150–151
  early investment years, 143–144
  following shoe trends, 146
  solar craze and, 146, 148–149
  winning stocks and, 144–146
McGrew, Jeannie
  following market trends, 101–102
  motivating factor for, 2
  optimistic attitude of, 37–38
Meetup Development Department, x
Meetup Groups, IBD
  Bill O'Neil speaking at, 189
  participation in, 19–20
  Ted Leplat's routine at, 20–22
Michael Kors Hldgs Ltd., 69, 71
Military and Political Leaders & Success (O'Neil), 188
mistakes, reviewing
  Debra Kloote and, 93, 97
  Ed Hornstein and, 126–127
  Jahandar Kakvand and, 90
  Townsend Baldwin and, 75, 80

money management, investing and,
  46, 192–193
Monster Beverage Corp. (Hansen's
  Natural), 59, 61, 63
Moses, Cedd, 141
motivations, for making investments,
  2
Muhammad Ali, 137
My Own Story (Baruch), 119

Nasdaq chart, for market direction, 6,
  8, 55–57, 176, 180
NetEase, Inc., 61, 62
Netflix Inc.
  base stages and, 14, 15
  investing in, 160–161
New America articles, IBD's, 51, 52,
  66, 119, 150
new companies
  finding, 160–162
  institutional investors and, 6
  as investment indicator, 100, 101,
    138, 154, 192
news media, investing and, 61, 64
Nielsen, Justin, 176, 186

One Up on Wall Street (Lynch), 172
one-day price drop, selling rules and,
  35
O'Neil, Scott, 93
O'Neil, William J.
  accomplishments of (background
    of), 186–187
  on cutting losses, 34
  David Ryan and, 170–171
  discipline of, 188–189
  Eve Bobach and, 163
  flexibility of, 190–191
  on following rules, 190
  investment advice of, 100, 141,
    142, 192–193, 194
  Jim Roppel and, 152
  legacy of, 187–188
  logic of, 90

meeting, ix–x
  Mike Webster and, 173–175
  publications of, 188
  on risk control, 83
  strengths of, 181–182
  study of charts, 191
  as teacher, 189–190
  visionary approach of, 11–12
O'Neil Data Systems, Inc., 187
optimism, importance of, 194

patience, investing and, 90, 151
Pattern Recognition, MarketSmith,
  176
Phillips, Kathleen
  falling in love with stocks, 39, 40
  following Leaderboard, 57, 59, 60
  motivating factor for, 2
pivot points
  breakouts and, 165
  pullbacks and, 36
PMD (Program for Management
  Development), 186
post analysis of trades
  guidelines for, 130–131
  importance of, 93, 97
  for personal strategy, 181–182
Powell, Jerry
  following market trends, 90–91
  motivations of, 2
Power, Steve, trading plan of, 84, 86,
  87–88
price
  consolidation. *See* base(s)
  highs, 55–57, 75, 152, 192
  increase, 35
  spread, 35
Priceline.com Inc., 75, 79
professional investors, limitations
  of, 3
profits
  from bull market, 69, 72
  celebrating, 75, 80
  good routine and, 108–111

profits (*continued*)
    IPOs and, 66, 69
    taking at 20 to 25%. *See* 20 to 25%
        profit rule
Program for Management
        Development (PMD), 186
publications, of Bill O'Neil, 188
pullbacks
    sitting through, 158, 160
    Whole Foods Market and, 55

Qlogic Corp, 113, 114
quarterly earnings
    as investment indicator, 192
    stock increases in, 12, 24

Rackspace Hosting Inc., 57, 60
radio show, IBD, 29–30
Ramamoothi, Bharani, 26
Reardon, Pat, 59, 61, 62–63
Reazor, Tim, x
relative strength (RS) line
    for Baidu Inc., 158, 159
    in Daily Charts, 139–140
Reminiscences of a Stock Operator
        (Lefevre), 59, 119
Research in Motion Ltd., 154, 156
return on equity (ROE)
    finding leading stocks, 16
    as investment indicator, 16, 24,
        26, 192
Roppel, Jim
    Baidu investment, 157–160
    determining trends and, 162
    downtrends/uptrends and, 154, 156
    finding unique products, 160–162
    investment fundamentals and,
        151–152
    mistakes made, 152–153
    pullbacks and, 158, 160
    sell rules and, 153–154
    stock splits and, 158
RS (relative strength) line. *See* relative
        strength (RS) line

Ryan, David
    at IBD seminar, 152
    interviewing, 141
    stock's key concepts and, 166,
        170–172

S&P 500, 155, 158
sales growth, as investment indicator,
        16, 20, 24, 64, 86, 116, 144
Samet, Jerry
    bull market cycle and, 112–113
    leaders index and, 115–116
    learning emotional control,
        113–115
Scott, Mike
    IPO bases and, 66, 69, 70–71
    motivation of, 2
Select Comfort Corp., 74–75, 77
sell rules
    50-day moving average and, 124,
        128, 153
    following, 64, 66, 109–110
    market downtrend and, 10
    overview of, 34–36
    technical analysis and, 138–140
Sherman, Kathy, 170
Shih, Calvin, 2
Shontere, Carole
    IBD Meetup Groups and, 19
    motivating factor for, 2
Sina Corp., 81–82
Solarwinds Inc., 88
Sports Leaders & Success (O'Neil),
        188
Staub, Ted, 25
Stock Checkup, 20, 21, 176, 192
stock market
    analysis of indexes/leaders for,
        141–143
    back testing and, 131–132
    base stages and, 14
    business approach to, 80–84
    in correction, 6, 7, 10
    cutting losses in, 33–34, 109–110

daily/weekly routines for, 48, 51, 108–109

determining trends. *See* market direction

emotional control and, 41, 43–44, 113–115, 165–166

falling in love with stocks, 39

finding leading stocks, 16, 46, 90, 91, 119–122, 160. *See also* winning stocks

flexibility in, 190–191

following rules for, 190

inflated ego and, 191

in innovative products, 160–162

IPO bases and, 66, 69

key elements of, 45–46

maintaining focus, 72, 74–75

paying attention to, 61, 64

post analysis in, 93, 97, 130–131

reviewing/accepting mistakes in, 75, 80, 90, 93, 97, 126–127

selling rules for, 34–36, 64, 66, 83–84

stock's key concepts and, 171–172

studying bull/bear market periods, 175–176

studying charts and, 132, 150, 152, 174–175, 191

success/failure in, 3–4, 124

time to buy, 12–14, 46

understanding trends in, 5–6

uptrends in, 7–9

winning stocks and. *See* winning stocks

written trading plan for, 84, 86

stock splits, 158, 163

Stock Spotlight, IBD's, 72, 74, 150

Stocks on the Move, Investors.com's, 18, 26, 48, 51, 102, 109

stops, updating, 86

The Successful Investor (O'Neil), 124, 188

Sun Tzu, 5, 185

supply and demand, 12

Tanner, Lee

back testing and, 131–132

bad habits and, 39, 41, 42

following sell rules, 64, 66, 67–68

TASER International, 119–122

Taub, Jim, 2

teacher, Bill O'Neil as, 189–190

Tempur Pedic International, Inc., 67

Ten Secrets to Success, IBD's, 187–188

Tennessee Coal & Iron, historical charts of, 132, 134

three-weeks-tight base pattern, 13, 29–30

Timesaver Tables, IBD, 20, 21

Tractor Supply Co., 97, 98

traits, of winning stocks, 11–12

uptrend, market

capitalizing on, 93, 97

determination of, 7–9, 14, 108–109

factors initiating, 7

investing in, 55–57

U.S. Investing Championship, 170

volume, as investment indicator, 192

Walsh, Gay

IBD Meetup Groups and, 19

motivating factor for, 2

watch lists

adding to, 86

back testing and, 131

creating, 84, 177

in finding leading stocks, 24–25

Webster, Mike

creating investment tools, 176–177

early investment years, 172–173

studying bull/bear market periods, 175–176

training with Bill O'Neil, 174–175

weekend routine, for investing
    K. Basu's, 82–83
    Ken Chin's, 48, 51
    Stephen Cole's, 24
    Steve Power's, 84, 86
Whitmer, Dave
    ignoring news media, 61, 64, 65
    new company investments, 101
Whole Foods Market, 55–57, 58
Wilburn, Dennis, 20
William O'Neil + Co., Inc., 171, 173,
    178, 187
winning stocks
    gap-ups and, 165–166, 167–169

    leaders index of, 115–116
    repeating patterns of, 113–115,
        150–151
    returning to, 194
    signs of, 192–193
    staying with, 119–122, 124–126
    studying charts of, 132, 150
    traits of, 11–12
Wisdom to Live By column, IBD,
    51
work ethic, of Bill O'Neil, 188–189
Wyckoff, Richard, 83

Yamada Jirokichi, 37

• ABOUT THE AUTHOR •

Amy Smith is the host of Investor's Business Daily's *Market Wrap* Video at Investors.com and co-host of AM 870 The Answer's *How to Make Money in Stocks* weekly show. She is also IBD Meetup Development Director and IBD Radio and TV Market Commentator.

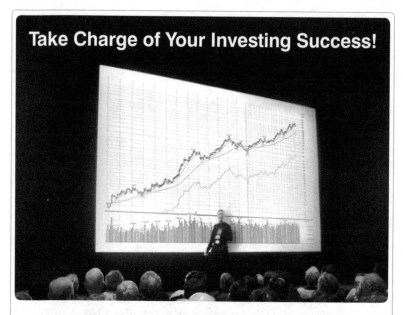

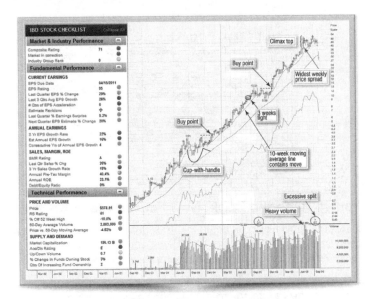

Get 10 Free Issues

You've Read the Book. Now You Can Take Action!

Investor's Business Daily has helped people just like you be more successful for over 28 years. IBD gives you vital data to help you make better investing decisions and improve your results.

IBD helps you zero in on leading stocks in leading industries and shows you how to get the most out of IBD's top-performing Investing Strategy.

Try IBD and get:

- Top Stock Lists
- Proprietary Stock Ratings
- Exclusive Market Analysis
- Industry-leading Investor Education
- And, you'll get access to the powerful investing tools and personalized features on IBD's web site, Investors.com.

Try 10 FREE Issues of IBD, call:

1.800.831.2525
or go to: Investors.com/IBDoffer
to get your free trial

Hours: Mon - Thu: 5:30am - 4:30pm (PT) | Fri: 5:30am - 3:30pm (PT) | Sat: 7:00am - 3:30pm (PT)

INVESTOR'S BUSINESS DAILY   INVESTORS.com